Dear Mat

I bought this book many
years ago after reading
an article about the author.
I guess I was kind of
hoping I might do something
like this someday.

Maybe it will give you
some ideas for your
pack trips.

I would love to go with
you sometime. I can,
however, just live vicariously
through all your great
activities Teaching, Surfing,
Mexico, backpacking,
horse packing

There are some yummy
recipes in here. Have fun
you are in my thoughts
and in my heart
Every day
I love you — Mom

THE
ROCKY MOUNTAIN
COOKBOOK

Introduction

F ood identifies a region as powerfully as landscape. Sometimes the two seem so inextricably bound that a taste of the cuisine becomes a journey to the place. The fantasy of travel awaits at the table.

Over the past several years, Americans have become increasingly fascinated by America. Beguiled by its beauties, we also seem bent on a search for what is simple, honest, and strong. In these circumstances, the growing popularity of American regional cooking seems natural. The cooking reflects the region's character; it becomes a souvenir to take home, an ongoing memory that is a connection with our roots. At the same time, we have become sophisticated enough about the regional cooking of other countries to realize that we, too, have superb culinary traditions of our own.

Besides that, I suspect we've gotten hungry. The aesthetic spareness of the still lifes set before us recently has probably made not a few of us long for a real meal. In the Rocky Mountain West, a full platter is a basic assumption.

While food is one mirror of our history, the Rocky Mountain West is the source of our wildest, wooliest, "rootinest, tootinest" past; birthplace of the American Myth. The frontiersman, the cowboy—that glorious image of the man bigger than life that plays

so great a part in forming the American mind and the American energy—is native to this spectacular, wondrous, and hard country. The cuisine that nurtured him suits him. One might be tempted to call it macho, but it is a macho well tempered by the traditions multifarious immigrants brought to the mountains.

When explorers Meriwether Lewis and William Clark arrived in 1805, the northern Rocky Mountains was a wild country, Indian territory entered by few white men. The region was so unknown that the Rockies were thought to be a single chain, not far from the Pacific. At the time, most people believed that somewhere through those mountains lay the fabled Northwest Passage to the Pacific. President Jefferson, who got the Rockies as part of his Louisiana Purchase, sent Lewis and Clark out to find it.

While exploring the territory to study the life and possibilities it held, the Lewis and Clark expedition lived off the land for two years. According to journals kept by both Lewis and Clark, their food consisted almost entirely of meat, the product of their hunts.

When the expedition returned to civilization with word that the West was full of beaver, the fur companies that were headquartered in the East began their scramble for the mountains' riches. Distant and wild as it was, the Rocky Mountain West would not remain unknown for long. The trappers who headed west in the employ of

Contents

Acknowledgments

I am especially grateful to my son, Nick Maricich, and my daughter, Maria Maricich, for their enthusiasm and encouragement. Nick kept me supplied with game birds and fish and Maria lent me her creative ideas and expertise in the kitchen.

I am indebted to many friends, organizations, and relatives who have been generous with their treasured recipes and all sorts of stories and information about the Rocky Mountain West. I thank Wes Mc-Dorman, Gloria Batis, the members of the Custer County Cowbells, Selene Isham, Hildegard Raeber, Sharon Ikauniks, Audrey Bashaw, Eleanor Burke, Sandy Snyder, Herman and Marian Maricich, Stuart and Carla Dole, Patricia Rowe, Laurie Lynch, my mother-in-law, Odette Chesnel, and my mother, Mildred Rowe.

I am very grateful to Claudine Martin, Tony Smith, Polly Read, and Loy Carrington, all close friends and professional cooks who tested recipes and shared ideas and advice and their own recipes with me. I thank Don and Myrtle Holm for permission to quote from their wonderful book, *The Complete Sourdough Cookbook*.

There were many who were enthusiastic and encouraging and who offered their time or their homes or restaurants for entertaining and for photographs. I can hardly name everyone, but I wish especially to thank Verjemma Wyler, Maggie Yellowtail, Bev Morgan, Sophie Craighead, Bob Jonas of Sun Valley Trekking, and David and Sheila Mills of Rocky Mountain River Tours.

Thanks to Ruth Rudner for her Rocky Mountain style and verve and to Lucy Sisman for her original design work.

This book belongs not only to me, but to Shirley Wohl, my editor, whose patience, attention, and enthusiasm made it possible; and it belongs also to Alexandra Avakian, whose spirited, sensitive photographs have portrayed the reality of life in the Rocky Mountain West that I so much wanted to include; and above all I am grateful to Carol Southern of Clarkson N. Potter for supporting my vision.

For Jean-Pierre

Text copyright © 1989 by Connie Chesnel
Photographs copyright © 1989 by Alexandra Avakian

Published by Clarkson N. Potter, Inc., 201 East 50th
Street, New York, New York 10022

CLARKSON N. POTTER, POTTER, and colophon are
trademarks of Clarkson N. Potter, Inc.

Manufactured in Japan

Library of Congress Cataloging-in-Publication Data

Chesnel, Connie.
    The rocky mountain cookbook / by Connie Chesnel.
    p.   cm.
    Includes index.
    1. Cookery, American—Western style.   2. Cookery—
Rocky Mountains.   I. Title.
TX715.C5246   1988
641.5978—dc19   88-4061
ISBN 0-517-56090-9   CIP

10 9 8 7 6 5 4 3 2 1

First Edition

THE ROCKY MOUNTAIN COOKBOOK

BY CONNIE CHESNEL
TEXT WITH RUTH RUDNER

PHOTOGRAPHS BY ALEXANDRA AVAKIAN
DESIGN BY LUCY SISMAN

Clarkson N. Potter, Inc. / Publishers

the fur companies were young, strong, self-reliant, and adventurous enough to have nothing to lose. Living like the Indians, and often with them, they shared the life of the hunter, eating what the land and their skills provided. As it had for Lewis and Clark, this meant meat. Man's food. Game was plentiful, with elk, deer, buffalo, antelope, bear, and fowl usually available for the shooting. It was a diet that provided energy and sustenance,  whatever it lacked in refinements. Often long on hunger, the mountain men were short enough on patience when it came to food that dinner was as apt to be half-cooked bear as anything else.

Today, meat in any form, wild or domestic, is still the mainstay of the Western diet. Hunting in the region is actually part of a semisubsistence economy, a way of filling the family freezer. The venison a New Yorker may consider a luxury is common food in the mountains. And buffalo, which fed, clothed, and sheltered the Indians for generations, and the early whites as well, can be found on menus in the whole gamut of Rocky Mountain restaurants, from gourmet establishments to hamburger joints.

All but eradicated by the 1880s, buffalo is no longer exactly considered a game animal. Most buffalo meant for the table these days are raised on ranches, although their meat retains the attributes of game, which is far lower in fat and cholesterol than the meat of domestic animals.

Traditionally, most Western men eat few vegetables. When Meriwether Lewis mentions a vegetable in his journal, it is because Sacajawea, the expedition's Indian guide, "busied herself in serching for the wild artichokes which the mice collect and deposit in large hoards. this operation she performed by penetrating the earth with a sharp stick about some small collections of drift wood. her labour soon proved successful, and she procured a good quantity of these roots. the flavor of this root resembles that of the Jerusalem Artichoke, and the stalk of the weed which produces it is also similar."

Many trappers took Indian wives, thereby adding to their diets the wild roots, tubers, berries, and greens traditionally gathered by the women. A wife also meant that there was someone with more patience to do the cooking . . . and chew the hides they used for clothing, besides. But these mountain men were actually assimilated into the tribes, and their more elaborate cuisine had almost no effect on the settlers who came later. Out of fear and disdain, the settlers had little use for any Indian customs. It is really only in recent years that Indian food traditions have entered the white man's diet in the Rockies and elsewhere in the United States.

Things were different at the southern end of the Rockies. The Pueblo Indians had lived for centuries in permanent villages, tending their fields of corn, squash, and beans; hunting rabbit and deer; foraging for wild plums and pine nuts. Then, in the sixteenth century, the *conquistadores* marched north from Mexico looking for gold. Not finding any, they built churches instead, settled in a few places, started farming on a small scale, and founded a few of North America's oldest cities—among them Santa Fe in 1609 and Taos in 1617. Superimposing their own traditions on this stable, agrarian, pre-Columbian Indian culture, they gave it the Church, chiles, and chocolate.

The chile, which grew exceedingly well under irrigation close to the banks of the Rio Arriba—the upper portion of the Rio Grande running from Taos down to Santa Fe—was quickly appropriated by the agricultural Indians.

The Spanish added Indian corn bread and beans to their own diets, and slowly the

cuisines of Indians and Spaniards mingled. By the time the American white man entered New Mexico, after the Mexican War of 1846 when Sante Fe was captured by the United States, the two cultures had for 200 years been adapting one another's foods to their own traditions. Even this was still twenty years before anybody in the north was eating much of anything he couldn't hunt.

Obviously, the immense variations in the foods available and the differences in weather, terrain, and ways of life between the agricultural southern Indians and the hunter-gatherers of the north made culinary differences enormous from the beginning.

The differences were reinforced by the customs the white settlers brought with them to the respective areas. The history and traditions of the southern Rockies were (and are) ages old, while in the north history was more or less invented by a ragtag assortment of trappers as they went along. Yet the Indian-Spanish food of the south—beans, corn, and chiles—could be easily dried to travel and quickly became the staple of the whole chain.

The common denominator of all the sections of the Rockies is not really food, but the region's breathtaking beauty and the fact that these mountains, extending more than a thousand miles in length from Canada to Mexico, are a hard country. Never a place for the timid or the weak, the Rocky Mountain West (except for New Mexico) was the last region of America to be settled by the white man. (The West Coast offered far more ease to American pioneers looking for land, and they simply made their

way across the dreaded Rockies as best they could.)

When the fur market gave out, the next wave of adventurers arrived: prospectors and cattle men lured by the promise of striking it rich one way or another. For these men hardship was inconsequential if the rewards were big enough. But while the mountain men had been entirely self-sufficient, the newcomers required the services offered by towns. Indeed, towns sprang up in every gulch, as entrepreneurs appeared, ready to open shops, saloons, restaurants, and lodgings. Immigrants poured in from everywhere. Welsh, Irish, English, Scandinavians, Italians, Germans, and Croatians came to work the mines. French and Spanish Basques found work herding sheep. Chinese arrived to help build the railroads.

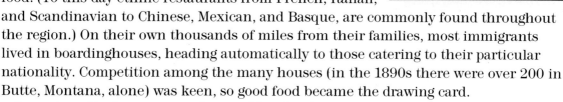

All the immigrants brought their own traditions of food. (To this day ethnic restaurants from French, Italian, and Scandinavian to Chinese, Mexican, and Basque, are commonly found throughout the region.) On their own thousands of miles from their families, most immigrants lived in boardinghouses, heading automatically to those catering to their particular nationality. Competition among the many houses (in the 1890s there were over 200 in Butte, Montana, alone) was keen, so good food became the drawing card.

Some boardinghouses served special holiday fare to lure boarders, but it was still a hearty, country cuisine. Elegance came later, when the presence of the railroad allowed the rich—mining barons and cattle lords, czars of industry, and presidents

and royalty—to travel west in comfort. Eager to experience the fabled Rocky Mountains, these travelers nevertheless held a certain luxury to be a matter of course. Hotels and restaurants catering to them provided it.

The breakfast menu for a 1911 visit by President Taft to the Silver Bow Club in Butte is a fair sample: Grapefruit, Mountain Trout with Tartar Sauce, Potatoes Saratoga, Broiled Squab on Toast, Southern-style Sweet Potatoes, Currant Jelly, Silver Bow Club Rolls, and Coffee.

Even in the Rocky Mountains, nobody eats like that anymore, but those epicurean menus did set a precedent for style. Today's good Rocky Mountain restaurants pamper the sophisticated palate with a cuisine that is more or less continental, although the pampering is in keeping with modern tastes. The simpler food served in small cafes is usually more authentically regional. Good home cooks, with access to game and fish, are able to present the most authentic food of all.

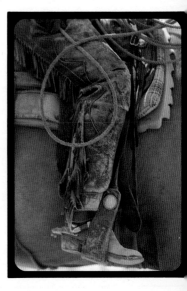

The ski towns, and there are plenty of them, are full of splendid restaurants, many of which are open in summer as well as during ski season. Alex's in Park City, Riverhorse Café in Deer Valley, and the Lodge at Snowbird, all located in Utah's Wasatch Range near Salt Lake City, offer wonderful menus to an international trade. In Ketchum, next to Sun Valley in Idaho, the elegent French-style Evergreen restaurant and the tiny Soupçon, housed in a log cabin, both serve innovative and memorable meals. The Edelweiss, an authentic Austrian *stuberl* in Big Sky, Montana, specializes in authentic Austrian cuisine. But one expects to eat well in ski areas worldwide. Somehow more interesting, or at least more indigenous, are those special places in cities outside the ski areas, as well as off the beaten track.

The Rattlesnake Club in Denver has a wonderful menu that includes such Rocky

Mountain specialties as venison, rabbit, pheasant, and sometimes buffalo. The Cafe Pierpont, located in a handsomely renovated old brick office building in downtown Salt Lake City, serves an updated, sophisticated Mexican menu using mesquite grills and turning out freshly made tortillas. In Boise, Idaho, the Idan-Ha Hotel is a perfect example of the Rocky Mountain style. The hotel is one of many historic buildings throughout the Rockies that have been restored, although both restored and unrestored buildings remain in use, a vital sign of the strong connection between Rocky Mountain residents and their history. Chef Peter Schott, former head chef of the Sun Valley Lodge, presents his extraordinary continental cuisine here. The Boulderado Hotel in Boulder, Colorado, has been faithfully restored to its turn-of-the-century grandeur and has three good restaurants: one Italian, one seafood, and one continental.

Off the beaten track in the Rockies often means more or less in the middle of nowhere. This requires a willingness to deal with mountain distances, where a mile is longer than a mile in other places, roads more winding, the space between one restaurant and the next more empty or more full, depending on one's point of view of wild country. Some restaurants are so far from anything else that some sort of sleeping accommodations, often quite charming, are attached. These restaurants are frequently connected to the history of the region.

For example, the Miner's Delight Inn, near Lander, Wyoming, was a nineteenth-century miners' boardinghouse, a fact belied now by the elegance of both the restaurant and the food. The building was refurbished by transplanted New Yorkers Georgina Newman and her late husband Paul, both of whom learned to cook in

Park City, Vail, and Aspen before opening their own, unique establishment. Whatever the day's menu, the food here is superb.

Brannons' Wilderness Lodge, near Cody, Wyoming, is a special little Italian restaurant where Dave and Nancy Brannon prepare enormous feasts of many courses, using herbs from their own greenhouse and building into their menu little pauses for a walk around the grounds or a stroll along the nearby stream.

In a converted stable in Espanola, New Mexico, about twenty-four miles north of Santa Fe, El Paragua serves some of the best New Mexican food in the region. This is a family-run establishment that makes many authentic dishes "from scratch," roasting fresh peppers, for example, for the chiles rellenos.

One could travel the length of the Rockies sampling such gems, although for dinner in many of them a traveler must make reservations well in advance. Part of the delight of such a journey is that, en route, one may come upon some of those other simpler, less heralded, usually more regional establishments. A cafe along a road where there is nothing else for miles—no town, no gas station, no restaurant—may well be worth a stop. Whatever the food turns out to be (and it is often quite good), you are bound to find a few local characters who will, at once, involve you in the place and provide you with a real sense of the region. In these cafes you truly enter the Rocky Mountain West. Besides that, they may well serve the best homemade pie you ever tasted.

The menus and recipes that follow allow you to bring the best of Rocky Mountain cuisine to your table. Some of the recipes are traditional; others are adaptations of traditional dishes that are in keeping with today's taste for healthful eating, or incorporate certain foods, spices, and condiments that not so long ago did not exist in the region; and some are original creations based on local recipes and foods used in new ways.

Eating outdoors is very popular in the Rocky Mountains. It would be odd if it were not, for this region of spectacular beauty and clear, crisp, dry air has an atmosphere that makes even the simplest meal an event. But the menus included for outdoor meals can all be cooked and served indoors and still be every bit as special. Rocky

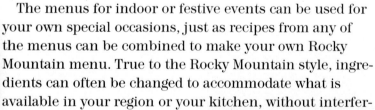

Mountain cuisine is nothing if not adaptable.

The menus for indoor or festive events can be used for your own special occasions, just as recipes from any of the menus can be combined to make your own Rocky Mountain menu. True to the Rocky Mountain style, ingredients can often be changed to accommodate what is available in your region or your kitchen, without interfering with the basic character of the dish or the menu.

Here, then, is a genuine melting-pot cuisine—hearty, healthy, satisfying, and full of flavor in all its diversity. Quite simply, Rocky Mountain cooking makes you feel good.

Mountain Menus

HIGH COUNTRY BARBECUE

The quintessential Western party, a barbecue can take on almost any form, as long as some kind of meat is roasted or grilled outdoors, over some kind of fire. In the Rocky Mountains, any meal cooked outside includes the view as much as the food: snow-capped peaks, broad valleys, the alpenglow of a mountain sunset, the nearness of star-studded skies.

The menu that follows is based on a private barbecue held at the Idaho Rocky Mountain Ranch in the Sawtooth Valley. Tables were set up on the ranch veranda overlooking the spectacular Sawtooth Mountains. Hosted by several people who had all once been involved in dude ranching, the festive occasion combined barbecue tradition with a touch of sophisticated elegance in the choice of such dishes as Idaho Potato Skins with Red Caviar and Smoked Trout with Caper Sauce. The guests, appropriately dressed in Western clothes, contributed as much to the atmosphere of the rugged, wondrous West as did the food and setting.

For the original barbecue, a whole lamb was roasted on a spit over an open fire by Basque cooks, the West's recognized experts with lamb. For this menu I've substituted Barbecued Buffalo Roast, since they

MENU for 12

Anchovy Cocktail Turnovers

Sliced Tomato Salad with Basil Dressing

Idaho Potato Skins with Red Caviar

Smoked Trout with Caper Sauce

Black Beans Mexican Style

Barbecued Buffalo Roast

Basque Sheepherder Bread

Wild Huckleberry Pie

Jewel's Chocolate Zucchini Cake
(page 180)

Wine • Beer • Coffee

Above: *Spit-roasting the buffalo meat. A young apprentice observes the Idaho technique.*

Right: *Smoked trout with caper sauce is served from an attractive earthenware platter.*

are easy enough to prepare for any backyard barbecue.

The important factor here is the fire. Traditionally, almost any wood fire will do, but in fact, the fire over which meats are cooked greatly influences how the meats taste, as well as how the air smells. Flavor-bearing hardwoods—mesquite, hickory, and applewood—are all available these days wherever charcoal briquets are sold and are often used in combination with briquets. I prefer cooking over the coals of an all-wood fire. To be avoided at all costs are clinically treated briquets, or lighter fluid to start the fire, since both can impart an unpleasant taste to the food. Matches, paper, dry twigs, and kindling get a proper fire going quickly.

Barbecue tradition also ordains a sweet-sour sauce, based on ketchup, and usually smokey, for the meat. The hottest and best sauce of its kind is on page 167. Texans are quick to take credit for it, but the taste for hot red barbecue sauce spread like wildfire over the West with such spontaneous combustion that no claims for the original have much chance.

The Idaho landscape, viewed from the deck of Sophie Craighead's log home in Sun Valley. The sculpture is by local artist Red Kegan.
. . . .

Updates on the tradition are the marinades made of exotic spices like coriander, ginger, anise, juniper, and cardamom in place of, or along with, the old standbys of parsley, thyme, and bay leaf, and a wide variety of oils, vinegars, wines, beers, and honeys.

Throughout the Rocky Mountains there are restaurants, dude ranches, and inns specializing in barbecues, but making your own is wonderfully satisfying.
. . . .

ANCHOVY COCKTAIL TURNOVERS

    3 ounces cream cheese, softened
 ½ cup (1 stick) unsalted butter
    1 cup presifted all-purpose flour
    1 (2-ounce) can anchovies, drained and
        chopped
 ¼ cup minced fresh parsley
    1 egg beaten with 2 tablespoons milk

Place the cream cheese, butter, and flour in the bowl of a food processor. Turn the machine on and off several times just until the ingredients are well blended. Roll the dough out on a floured board, about ¼ inch thick. Cut into 2-inch rounds using the rim of a glass or a biscuit cutter.

Preheat the oven to 450° F.

Spread the rounds with the anchovies, and sprinkle with parsley. Fold in half, pinching the edges together. Prick the tops with a fork and brush with the egg yolk (see Note). Place on ungreased cookie sheets and bake for 5 minutes, or until nicely browned.

Makes 1 dozen

Note: Turnovers can be made ahead to this point and refrigerated or frozen until ready to serve. If frozen, do not thaw before baking; bake for 10 minutes.

SLICED TOMATO SALAD WITH BASIL DRESSING

- 5 large tomatoes, thinly sliced
- 1 teaspoon balsamic vinegar
- 1 teaspoon red wine vinegar
  Pinch of sugar
- 2 teaspoons minced fresh basil
- 1 teaspoon minced fresh mint
- ¼ cup minced fresh parsley
- 1 teaspoon salt
- ¼ teaspoon freshly ground black pepper
- 1 garlic clove, minced
- ½ cup vegetable oil
  Mint sprigs, for garnish

Arrange overlapping tomato slices in a shallow casserole or on a deep platter.

Combine the vinegars, sugar, basil, half the parsley, salt, pepper, and garlic in a small bowl. Slowly add the oil while stirring constantly with a fork or whisk. Pour over the tomatoes, sprinkle with the remaining parsley, and garnish with mint.

Serves 12

IDAHO POTATO SKINS WITH RED CAVIAR

POTATOES
- 6 medium Idaho baking potaotes
- 4 tablespoons (½ stick) unsalted butter, melted
  Seasoned salt
  Freshly ground black pepper
- 2 tablespoons red lumpfish caviar, for garnish

FILLING
- 1 cup cream cheese, softened
- 1 tablespoon minced fresh chives
  Dash of Worcestershire sauce

Preheat the oven to 425° F.

Scrub the potatoes, dry, and prick with a fork. Bake for 50 to 60 minutes, or until soft. Cool slightly, then cut into wedge-shape quarters. Scrape out all but a thin layer of the pulp and reserve for another use.

Place the shells skin side down on an ungreased baking sheet. Brush the insides with melted butter and sprinkle with seasoned salt and pepper to taste. Return to the oven and bake for 10 minutes, or until crisp.

Mix the cream cheese, chives, and Worcestershire sauce. Fill the skins with the mixture and top each with a dab of caviar. Serve immediately.

Serves 12

Showing off our handmade native jewelry.

The youngest guest tries the huckleberry pie.

Above: The buffet table ready for guests.

Far left and center left: Men first at the buffet table! Meanwhile, dessert—wild huckleberry pie—is cooling on the woodpile.

Left: Serious attention is given to the food by Jan Cox and her children, a local family.

9

SMOKED TROUT WITH CAPER SAUCE

In some towns in the Rockies, there are private smokehouses where you can have your own catch of trout smoked for a nominal charge. Smoked trout are also available at many markets throughout the country, but if you want to smoke the fish yourself, here's a simple way to do it. If possible, use fresh-caught trout that were immediately cleaned and refrigerated; otherwise, buy the freshest trout you can find. The light caper sauce complements the rich, smoky flavor of the fish.

12 fresh-caught trout (6 to 8 ounces each)
¼ cup light brown sugar, tightly packed
1 cup rock salt
½ teaspoon coarsely ground black pepper
   Lemon slices, cut in half

CAPER SAUCE
2 tablespoons fresh lemon juice
½ cup olive oil
2 tablespoons drained capers
¼ teaspoon salt
   Freshly ground black pepper

Put the trout in a glass or pottery dish in 2 or more layers, sprinkling each layer evenly with brown sugar, rock salt, and pepper. Cover with plastic wrap and place a dish on top as a weight. Refrigerate for 2 to 3 hours.

Preheat a smoker (see Note).

Rinse the trout under cold running water and let dry at room temperature about 1 hour, or until the skin looks glazed.

Place trout in smoker for 5 to 6 hours, following manufacturer's instructions. When done, refrigerate until ready to use.

Before serving, bring the trout to room temperature. Prepare sauce by combining ingredients in a small bowl and whisking until well blended.

Arrange trout on a platter, spoon caper sauce over, and garnish with half slices of lemon and parsley.

Serves 12

Note: I use a Little Chief Home Smoker, which has racks and a small electric burner at the bottom so you can replenish the smoldering wood chips as needed.

....

BLACK BEANS MEXICAN STYLE

Here is my favorite bean dish, which I greatly prefer over the refried beans—even those prepared from scratch—that are always included on Mexican menus. I find this recipe to be less work and much more rewarding to the taste buds. It is a perfect dish to serve with barbecued meats.

BEANS
4 cups dried black beans
1 large onion, stuck with 12 cloves
2 medium carrots
2 celery stalks with leaves
1 tablespoon coarsely ground black peppercorns
4 bay leaves
6 tablespoons vegetable oil
3 medium onions, chopped
2 medium green bell peppers, seeded, pith removed, and finely chopped
1 medium red bell pepper, seeded, pith removed, and finely chopped
2 large garlic cloves, minced
½ teaspoon dried oregano
3 teaspoons salt
½ teaspoon chili powder
½ teaspoon ground cumin
2 or 3 grindings black pepper

TOPPING
1 cup sour cream
6 scallions, chopped, including 2 to 3 inches of green part
   Tabasco

Soak the beans overnight in cold water to cover.

Drain and pick through the beans, then put in a large pot with cold water to cover by 1 inch. Add the onion, carrots, celery, peppercorns, and 1 bay leaf. Bring to a boil over medium-high heat, skimming off any foam on top. Turn the heat down to maintain a good steady simmer and cook, covered, for about 1½ to 2 hours, or until the beans are tender. At the end of the cooking time there should be about 1 cup of liquid left in the pot. If not, add 1 cup water. Remove and discard the vegetables.

Meanwhile, heat the oil in a large frying pan. Add the chopped onions and peppers and sauté gently for 10 minutes, or until they are soft, but not brown. Add the garlic and cook 1 minute. Add the sautéed mixture to the beans with the rest of the spices and the remaining bay leaves. Taste for seasoning. Cook for another 10 minutes over low heat to blend the flavors.

Serve with sour cream, chopped scallions, and Tabasco, if desired. The beans keep well and reheat beautifully.

Serves 12

Note: You can add cooked and drained chorizo sausage for a heartier dish.

. . . .

BARBECUED BUFFALO ROAST

SAGE MARINADE
½ cup olive oil
½ cup dry red wine
2 tablespoons chopped fresh sage
1 tablespoon chopped fresh mint
½ small onion, chopped
¼ teaspoon salt
 Few grindings of black pepper

1 buffalo roast (6 to 8 pounds) (see page 187 for buffalo meat sources)

BARBECUE SAUCE
2 tablespoons vegetable oil
½ medium onion, chopped
1 cup beer
1 cup chili sauce or ketchup
1 tablespoon Worcestershire sauce
2 tablespoons balsamic or cider vinegar
¼ cup dark brown sugar, tightly packed
¼ teaspoon dried oregano
1 teaspoon dry mustard
 Pinch of ground cloves
 Pinch of cayenne (ground red) pepper

 Sprigs of fresh sage and mint, for garnish

Combine the marinade ingredients in a small bowl and whisk with a fork. Put the roast in a large, deep bowl, pour the marinade over, and cover with plastic wrap.

Refrigerate for 3 to 4 hours.

To make the sauce, heat the oil in a medium, heavy-bottom pot. Add the onion and sauté at low heat for 10 minutes, or until soft. Remove from the heat and add the beer. Add the chili sauce, Worcestershire sauce, and vinegar, mixing with a fork or whisk until well blended. Simmer, uncovered, for 10 minutes. Add the seasonings, using more cayenne or brown sugar, if desired.

Drain the roast, discarding the marinade, and bring to room temperature. Meanwhile, prepare a charcoal or hardwood fire. Let the coals burn somewhat less time than you would if cooking beef. The coals should be only partly covered with white ash before you put the roast on since buffalo cooks best at a temperature lower than for beef.

Slather the roast with the barbecue sauce, and skewer it. Place about 12 inches above the fire. Cook for about 12 minutes per pound for rare, basting with the sauce every 5 minutes. Test for doneness with the point of a knife. The meat should remain quite pink in the center. If cooked past this point the meat will toughen.

Put the roast on a carving board. Let rest for 20 minutes, then cut on the diagonal into ½-inch-thick slices. Arrange the slices on a warmed platter and garnish with sage and mint. Warm the remaining barbecue sauce and spoon some over the meat. Serve extra sauce on the side.

Serves 12

. . . .

BASQUE SHEEPHERDER BREAD

This recipe is made with yeast rather than sourdough starter, but is baked in the traditional way. The addition of cracked wheat is an innovation. In the early days, before serving the bread, a sheepherder would slash the sign of the cross on top of the loaf, then serve the first piece to his invaluable dog.

      3 cups very hot tap water
    ½ cup (1 stick) butter
    ¼ cup honey
    2½ teaspoons salt
      2 packages active dry yeast
      9 cups bread or all-purpose flour
    ¼ cup bulgur (cracked wheat), soaked in warm water to cover for 2 or 3 hours (optional)

Combine the hot water, butter, honey, and salt in a mixing bowl. Stir until the butter melts, then let the mixture cool down to lukewarm (110°–115° F). Stir in the yeast, cover, and set in a warm place for about 15 minutes, until bubbly.

Add 5 cups of the flour and beat with a

Fresh-from-the-garden tomatoes, especially inviting on a bright pottery platter.

. . . .

heavy-duty mixer, using a dough hook, or by hand using a wooden spoon, to form a thick batter. Mix in the bulgur, if using, along with enough of the remaining flour to form a stiff dough.

Turn the dough out onto a floured board and knead for about 10 minutes, until smooth. Add a little flour to the board if necessary to prevent the dough from sticking. Turn the dough into a greased bowl, cover loosely with a cloth, and let rise in a warm place for about 1½ hours, until doubled.

Punch down the dough, turn it out onto a floured board, and form it into a smooth ball with your hands.

Cut a circle of foil large enough to cover the bottom of a 12-inch Dutch oven. Grease the sides of the Dutch oven and the underside of the lid with some salad oil.

Place the ball of dough in the pot smooth side up and cover with the lid. Let rise in a warm place for about 1 hour, or until the dough starts to push against the lid.

Preheat the oven to 375° F.

Bake the bread, covered with the lid, for 12 minutes. Remove the lid and bake for another 30 to 35 minutes, or until the loaf is golden brown and sounds hollow when tapped. Turn out onto a rack to cool.

Makes 1 very large loaf

. . . .

WILD HUCKLEBERRY PIE

I must include this recipe for my father's favorite pie. When I was a child, the promise of real huckleberry pie was part of the pleasure of visiting my aunt's ranch in the Payette Lakes region of Idaho, where my father grew up.

Huckleberries are plentiful in the Rocky Mountains, where they grow wild, but if they are not available in your part of the country, you can use blueberries with good results. For an authentic American pie, make the crust by hand. It will definitely be lighter and flakier than a crust made in a food processor. You will need two pies for this menu. You can double the filling recipe but make the crust twice. If you double the recipe the crust won't be as tender.

OLD-FASHIONED FLAKY CRUST
  2 cups presifted all-purpose flour
  ¼ teaspoon salt
  ⅔ cup solid vegetable shortening
  6 to 8 tablespoons ice water

FILLING
  ¾ cup sugar
  2½ tablespoons all-purpose flour
    Pinch of salt
  4 cups fresh huckleberries, washed and drained

To make the crust, sift the flour again into a medium bowl and add the salt. Cut in the shortening with a pastry blender or 2 knives until the mixture is in pea-size chunks. Add the water 2 tablespoons at a time, tossing the mixture lightly with your hands after each addition until the chunks cling together.

Form the dough into 2 balls, one slightly larger than the other. Wrap each in wax paper and refrigerate until thoroughly chilled.

Roll out the larger portion of dough to a round big enough to line a 9-inch pie pan. Roll out the other portion to a 10-inch round, and place on wax paper. Refrigerate both crusts.

Preheat the oven to 350° F.

Combine the sugar, flour, and salt; stir in the huckleberries, and pour into the pie shell. Cover with the pastry round and crimp the bottom and top edges of the pastry together. Prick the top with a fork to allow steam to escape. Bake for 30 minutes, or until browned. Cool at room temperature for at least 15 minutes before serving.

Makes 1 9-inch pie to serve 6

. . . .

The zucchini cake, baked in the Western tradition in a square pan, decorated with flowers and vines.

At the trailhead a double view of the Sawtooth Mountains is only a hint of the beautiful scenery to come on our seven-mile hike.

HIKING PICNIC TO CRAMER LAKE

One of the loveliest mountain picnics I have prepared was for a *National Geographic* crew photographing Idaho's Sawtooth Mountains. Six of us carried backpacks filled with exotic and wonderful foods, carefully packed to withstand the jostling of the hike up the long, dusty seven-mile trail to Cramer Lake. Hiking is the only way to get there.

We carried the Almond Soup and coffee in preheated thermoses; the Galantine of Chicken in a well-secured plastic bag further protected by foil wrapping; the Brown Rice Salad and Lemon Chutney in plastic containers, the lids well sealed with duct tape. We chose pita bread, bought at a local market, because it takes up little space and travels well. The cheese went into a plastic bag. The tart, which had been cooked in a metal pie pan, was covered with another pie pan, taped together, then placed on top in one of the backpacks, so it would remain level.

When we finally arrived at the end of our trail we gratefully (and hungrily) settled into an alpine meadow at the uppermost lake. Melting snow, on its way to the icy blue depths of the lake, watered the lush meadow grass and its carpet of wild flowers. Our end of the lake was protected by an immense rock formation 2,000 feet high, the rock reflecting gold afternoon sun onto our picnic site. A large flat rock was handy to serve as a table for our final preparations. Setting the dishes out on a batik cloth on the grass, we ate luxuriously in the immense comfort that nature provided.

The Cramer Lake menu can be easily prepared for your own very special picnic.

```
┌─────────────────────────────────────┐
│  M E N U  for 6                      │
│  ..................................  │
│  Almond Soup                         │
│                                      │
│  Galantine of Chicken with          │
│  Lemon Chutney                       │
│                                      │
│  Brown Rice Salad                    │
│                                      │
│  Assorted Cheeses                    │
│                                      │
│  Pita Bread                          │
│                                      │
│  Rhubarb-Ginger Tart                 │
│                                      │
│  Basque Mocha Coffee                 │
│  Mineral Water  •  White Wine        │
└─────────────────────────────────────┘
```

ALMOND SOUP

> 3 cups homemade chicken stock, or 1 (10¾-ounce) can rich concentrated broth with enough water added to make 3 cups
> 2 tablespoons (¼ stick) butter
> 1 tablespoon finely ground millet or flour
> 1 garlic clove, crushed in a garlic press
> Pinch of ground cloves
> Pinch of ground mace
> 1 cup finely chopped blanched almonds (see Note)
> 2 pinches of dried thyme
> 1 teaspoon paprika
> ¼ teaspoon ground cumin
> Pinch of cayenne (ground red) pepper
> 2 tablespoons dry sherry
> 1½ cups plain yogurt

Heat the stock in a 2-quart saucepan. Melt the butter in a small frying pan, add the millet or flour, mix well, and stir into the stock. In a small bowl, combine the garlic with the remaining dry ingredients, except the cayenne. Stir into the broth, then simmer for 10 to 15 minutes. Just before serving, stir the cayenne and sherry into the yogurt, then add to the soup.

Serves 6

Note: The almonds can be chopped by hand or ground in a blender or food processor. (Be careful not to grind them to a paste; they must remain dry.)

GALANTINE OF CHICKEN WITH LEMON CHUTNEY

CHICKEN
   1 large roasting chicken (about 4 to 5
      pounds)
      Salt
      Freshly ground black pepper
   2 to 3 tablespoons butter, melted with 1
      garlic clove, crushed
   ¼ cup dry white wine
   1 tablespoon heavy cream
      Lemon Chutney (recipe follows)

STUFFING
   2 tablespoons (¼ stick) butter
   1 shallot, finely chopped
   1 chicken liver, soaked in 2 tablespoons
      brandy
   1 pound ground pork
   4 ounces prosciutto, chopped
   ¼ teaspoon *quatre épices* (nutmeg, ginger,
      cloves, white pepper)
      Pinch of dried thyme
   1 whole chicken breast (8 ounces), boned
      and cut into small pieces
   1 cup heavy cream
   1 tablespoon pine nuts

To bone the chicken, put it breast side down on a cutting board. With a sharp knife, cut through the skin down the length of the backbone. Starting at the center, scrape the flesh from one side of the backbone. Repeat on the other side. Try not to tear the skin.

Cut off the wing tips, but leave the bones in the wings. To remove the bones from the legs, sever the large leg joint with a knife or shears and continue scraping the flesh from the bone until you can pull out the leg and thigh bones. Repeat with the other leg. Turn the carcass over and scrape the flesh from the breastbone. Set aside. Make the stuffing.

Melt the butter in a small frying pan. Add the shallot and sauté over low heat for 5 minutes, until soft. Add the chicken liver and brandy and cook gently for 5 minutes, just until liver is lightly browned. Transfer the mixture to the bowl of a food processor. Add the pork, prosciutto, spices, thyme, and chicken breast. Turn the machine on and off several times until ingredients are finely ground. Add the cream and pine nuts and turn the machine on and off quickly once or twice.

Fill the carcass, including the legs, with the stuffing. Sew up the back with a poultry needle, shaping the chicken with your hands to resemble a whole bird.

Preheat the oven to 350° F.

Put the chicken in a shallow roasting pan, breast side up. Sprinkle with salt and pepper, and cook for 1½ hours, or until the juices run clear when the bird is pricked. Combine the melted butter and white wine. Baste the chicken every 30 minutes with the mixture, and the last 10 minutes brush with the cream. If the bird is not nicely browned at this point, turn the oven up to 450° and roast for about 10 minutes more. Let the bird cool to room temperature, then refrigerate. Wrap it in a leakproof plastic bag if you're going to take it to a picnic. Serve with Lemon Chutney.

Serves 6

. . . .

Lemon Chutney

   2 large or 3 small lemons, cut into
      quarters and seeded
   1 tablespoon salt
   2 large garlic cloves, sliced
   1 teaspoon ground cumin
      Pinch of cayenne (ground red) pepper
   ½ tablespoon peeled, minced fresh ginger
 1½ tablespoons yellow mustard seeds
   1 cup distilled white vinegar
   1 cup sugar
   ½ cup golden raisins

Put the lemons in a small glass or pottery bowl, sprinkle with the salt, and refrigerate for 3 days, turning once or more a day. On the third day, add the garlic, spices, and vinegar. Refrigerate for 24 hours.

Transfer the lemons to the bowl of a food processor, and add ½ cup of the marinating liquid. Turn the machine on and off several times until the mixture is in uniform pea-size pieces.

Combine the lemon mixture, sugar, raisins, and the remaining marinating liquid in a heavy 2-quart saucepan. Bring to a boil. Reduce the heat, and simmer for 10 to 20 minutes, stirring occasionally until the liquid is reduced and the mixture has thickened to the consistency of marmalade. Taste for seasoning.

The chutney will keep indefinitely in the refrigerator. For long-term storage, process in Hot-Water Bath, see page 170.

Makes 2 cups

. . . .

BROWN RICE SALAD

3 cups cooked short-grain brown rice
½ cup raisins
½ cup cooked peas
1 medium zucchini, finely chopped
2 medium carrots, finely chopped
1 medium red onion, finely chopped
¼ cup finely minced fresh parsley
¼ cup finely minced fresh mint
1 tablespoon fresh lemon juice
¼ cup olive oil
½ teaspoon salt
½ cup toasted slivered almonds

Combine the first 8 ingredients in a medium mixing bowl. Mix the lemon juice, oil, and salt; pour over the rice, tossing lightly to coat. Before serving, sprinkle with the almonds.

Serves 6

. . . .

RHUBARB-GINGER TART

SUGAR CRUST
1 cup (2 sticks) unsalted butter, chilled
½ cup sugar
2 cups pastry or presifted all-purpose flour
2 eggs, lightly beaten

FILLING
5¼ cups diced fresh rhubarb
1 cup sugar
3 tablespoons minced fresh ginger
2 tablespoons (¼ stick) butter, in small pieces
1 tablespoon sugar mixed with ⅛ teaspoon ground cinnamon

TOPPING
Sweetened whipped cream flavored with vanilla extract and ground ginger

To make the crust, cut the butter into chunks and place in the bowl of a food processor with the sugar and flour. Turn the machine on and off quickly a few times until the mixture resembles coarse meal. With the machine on, slowly add the eggs and process only until the dough pulls away from the sides of the bowl—don't overmix. Roll the dough into a ball, wrap in plastic, and refrigerate.

When the dough is thoroughly chilled, cut the ball in half and roll out a bottom crust large enough to line a 9- or 10-inch tart pan. (As you press the dough against the pan, make sure that the sides of the pastry shell are thick enough to stand when the tart is unmolded.) Make a lattice top crust with the rest of the dough by interweaving ½-inch-wide strips on a piece of foil.

Preheat the oven to 375° F.

Toss the first 3 filling ingredients together, and pour into the tart shell. Dot with the butter and dust with the sugar-cinnamon mixture.

Invert the lattice crust over the tart, and secure the ends to the sides of the shell with a little water.

Bake for about 40 minutes, or until lightly browned. Serve with whipped cream.

Serves 6

. . . .

BASQUE MOCHA COFFEE

2 ounces sweet baking chocolate
3 cups evaporated milk
Pinch of salt
Pinch of ground cinnamon
4 cups hot fresh-brewed coffee
Vanilla extract

Melt the chocolate over low heat in a heavy medium saucepan. In another pan, heat the milk just to boiling; add the salt and cinnamon, and whisk into the chocolate. Mix in the coffee and a few drops of vanilla. Serve immediately.

Serves 6

. . . .

Buffalo grazing on the banks of the Madison, a scene recalling the Old West.

A place of wonders, Yellowstone National Park with 2 million acres set aside by Congress in 1872 as a "pleasuring ground for the . . . enjoyment of the people," attracts thousands yearly.

My favorite time for Yellowstone is September, when the weather is gorgeous and the crowds few. At this time of year you can actually get somewhere near the sights! We drove into the park early one crisp day, giving ourselves time enough to have a full morning of sightseeing before settling down to a welcome picnic on the banks of the Madison River in the early afternoon. In the course of a few hours, elk, bison, and a moose wandered along. We caught a glimpse of an eagle. A flock of Canada geese flew overhead. An osprey came to fish. This late in the season the flowers are gone (you have to go in July for wildflowers), but more than compensation are the beginnings of autumn, brilliantly apparent in the understory turning gold and red; in the scurrying of ground squirrels to prepare their winter nests; in the elemental and wild sound of the first elk bugling.

For our picnic, I prepared the meatloaf and baked the cookies the day before. The pickled eggs were on hand in my larder, made in advance for just such an occasion. Some of the food was packed in a cooler to keep it fresh on the drive to Yellowstone, while a picnic basket held pretty paper

M E N U for 6
Pickled Eggs
Company Meatloaf with Cantaloupe Chutney
Bread 'n' Butter Pickles
Horseradish Mustard
Hard Rolls with Butter
Claudine's Trek Bars
Fruit Juices   **Mineral Water** • **Coffee**

LUNCH BY THE MADISON RIVER IN YELLOWSTONE PARK

plates, napkins, and cups and cutlery along with those foods, like the cookies, which required no refrigeration.

We bought rolls, wine, and soft drinks, and filled the thermos with hot coffee at one of the Hamilton Stores scattered throughout the park. These concessions, a park institution since the nineteenth century, sell food, groceries, outdoor clothing and gear, books, cards, and maps and souvenirs, so whatever has been left out of the picnic basket—and more—can be picked up en route to the lunch site.

Yellowstone Park was a spectacular place for our picnic, but your own favorite spot can be just as special.

. . . .

PICKLED EGGS

Plan to include beets in your diet the day you make pickled eggs, or save the liquid from canned or cooked beets made for a previous meal.

    ½ teaspoon salt
    1 cup beet cooking liquid
    ⅛ teaspoon black pepper
    ¼ teaspoon ground mace
    ½ teaspoon ground cloves
    1 cup distilled white vinegar
    6 hard-cooked eggs, peeled and chilled

Combine all the ingredients except the eggs in a medium bowl. Place the eggs in a large glass or earthenware container, pour the mixture over, and cover tightly.

Refrigerate for several days before serving, stirring at least once a day with a wooden (never metal) spoon.

Serves 6

. . . .

COMPANY MEATLOAF WITH CANTALOUPE CHUTNEY

This recipe was given to me by my friend Claire Trevor Bren with the comment, "This may look complicated, but the result is well worth the effort." It's delicious either hot or cold.

    1½ pounds boneless lean beef
    ½ pound boneless lean veal
    ½ pound boneless lean pork
    3 eggs
    ½ cup heavy cream
    1½ tablespoons finely chopped scallion
    1½ tablespoons finely chopped celery leaves
    1½ tablespoons finely chopped fresh chives
    2 teaspoons dried thyme
    2 teaspoons salt
    ½ teaspoon black pepper
    1 cup bread crumbs
    2 tablespoons (¼ stick) butter
    2 medium onions, finely chopped
    6 chicken livers, parboiled for 2 minutes
      and then finely chopped
    4 to 5 dashes browning and seasoning
      sauce, such as Bovril or Maggi
    3 slices bacon
    2 tablespoons prepared mustard
    1 cup beef stock
      Cantaloupe Chutney (recipe follows)

Have your butcher grind the beef, veal, and pork together, or if they have been ground separately, mix them thoroughly with your hands.

In a large bowl, combine the eggs, cream, scallion, celery leaves, chives, thyme, salt, and pepper. Beat lightly with a fork. Add ½ cup of the bread crumbs and mix in well. Let the mixture stand at room temperature for 30 minutes.

Meanwhile, melt the butter in a medium skillet and gently sauté the onions for 10 minutes, until soft. Do not burn. Add the onions, chicken livers, browning and seasoning sauce, remaining bread crumbs, and ground meat to the egg mixture, combining everything lightly but thoroughly with a fork. Form the mixture into an oblong loaf. Place it on a dish, lay the bacon strips over the top, and refrigerate for 30 minutes, or until firm.

Preheat the oven to 400° F.

Place the meatloaf in a shallow baking pan, spread the mustard thinly over the top and sides, and bake for 1½ hours, basting with the beef stock every 15 minutes.

Serve with Cantaloupe Chutney or mustard.

Serves 6 to 8

. . . .

Cantaloupe Chutney

Make this unusual, piquant condiment when cantaloupes are in season. It is also wonderful with roast chicken, duck, game birds, or lamb.

- 1 quart cider vinegar
- 1 pound light brown sugar
- 3 cardamom seeds, cracked
- 1 teaspoon anise seeds
- 1 teaspoon yellow mustard seeds
- 1 (3-to-4-inch) cinnamon stick, broken in pieces
- 3 teaspoons salt
- ¼ teaspoon cayenne (ground red) pepper
  Pinch of ground mace
- 1 teaspoon ground coriander
- 3 large garlic cloves, minced
- ½ pound fresh hot green chiles (serrano or jalapeño), seeded and thinly sliced
- 1 pound golden raisins
- ½ pound dried apricots
- 1 cup finely chopped preserved ginger
- 1 slightly underripe firm cantaloupe (2 to 3 pounds)

Combine the vinegar and brown sugar in a large, heavy-bottom pot. Place the cardamom, anise, and mustard seeds in a cheesecloth bag, tie closed, and add to the pot. Stir in the cinnamon, salt, cayenne, mace, coriander, and garlic. Bring to a boil, lower the heat, and simmer gently for 15 minutes. Add the chiles, raisins, apricots, and ginger, then continue to simmer gently for 30 minutes more.

Peel and seed the cantaloupe, and cut into 1-inch-long strips. Add to the cooked mixture and simmer for 45 minutes to 1 hour, stirring often to prevent sticking; add a little water if the mixture is too dry.

Remove the spice bag and cinnamon pieces, then ladle the chutney into half-pint sterilized jars and process (see directions on page 170). Keeps up to one year in a cool, dark place. Refrigerate after opening. You can also store unsealed in the refrigerator for several weeks.

Makes 6 half-pints

CLAUDINE'S TREK BARS

These high-energy bars help to sustain skiers on the trail but they're also good to take to a picnic.

CRUST
- 1 cup (2 sticks) unsalted butter
- 1½ cups light brown sugar, tightly packed
- 1 cup rolled oats
- 1 cup whole wheat pastry flour
- 1 cup presifted all-purpose flour
- ½ cup wheat germ
- 4 teaspoons grated fresh orange peel, or 1 teaspoon orange extract

TOPPING
- 4 eggs, beaten
- 1 cup coarsely chopped almonds
- 1 cup coarsely chopped brazil nuts
- ½ cup coarsely chopped dried figs
- ½ cup coarsely chopped dried apricots
- ½ cup unsweetened coconut, in ½-inch strips (see Note)

Preheat the oven to 350° F.

For the crust, cream the butter and 1 cup of the brown sugar in a medium bowl until the mixture is light and smooth. Stir in the remaining ingredients and blend well. Press the mixture into a 9 x 13 x 2-inch pan, pushing it up the sides about ½ inch.

Mix the topping ingredients and the remaining brown sugar in a small bowl. Spread evenly over the crust with the back of a spoon.

Bake for 30 to 40 minutes, but watch after 25 minutes and remove as soon as the topping has set and is slightly browned. If not baked long enough, the bars will crumble when cut; if overbaked, they will be too hard. Cut into any size bars you prefer; I like them large—about 2¼ x 4¼ inches.

Makes 12 to 24 bars, depending on size.

Note: If coconut strips are unavailable, use grated coconut, but the larger pieces make a chewier bar.

TAILGATE PICNIC AT A POLO MATCH

Rodeos and horse shows are part of the Rocky Mountain tradition, but horse people are becoming increasingly fascinated by polo, a relatively new sport here. On summer Sunday afternoons, matches are hosted by the Sun Valley Polo Club on their grounds near the Big Wood River. During breaks in a match, the parking area becomes a huge and festive picnic ground, as spectators set out coolers and hampers on the tailgates of their four-wheel drives. I like to use baskets, which add a certain rustic appeal to the tailgate of my own vehicle. Usually, I add a little jug of some wildflowers I've picked nearby.

For anyone in the environs of Sun Valley, easy fixings are to be had at Miner's Pasty Shop in Hailey, Idaho. Good picnic fare, pasties are meat pies that were introduced to the region in the late 1800s by immigrants who came from the British Isles to work the Rocky Mountain mines. Pasties were made fresh daily for the workers' lunch buckets. The recipe in the following menu is a good one. Warm pasties should be wrapped in foil and put in an insulated bag to travel. They look especially appetizing when served from a basket lined with a pretty napkin.

I carry the slaw, packed in a plastic container, in a small cooler, then transfer it to a wooden bowl to serve. The pears might be presented on a platter lined with green leaves, fig or grape if available, or some you might find near your picnic site. If the cake is transported in a cake carrier, you need only remove the top to serve it.

This picnic would also look and taste every bit as good set out in a meadow or on a beach or under the trees in the park.

MENU for 6

Miner's Pasties

Vegetable Slaw

Fresh Pears Stuffed with Blue Cheese

Glazed Oatmeal Cake

Mineral Water • **White Wine**
Coffee

Ponies have the freedom of a wide-open field at the lower end of the Woodriver Valley in Idaho. The ground is patterned with impressions of their horseshoes.

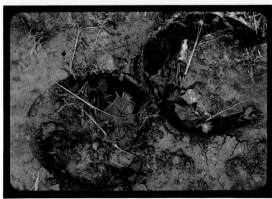

MINER'S PASTIES

During the latter part of the nineteenth century, many Welsh, Irish, and Cornish immigrants came to the Rocky Mountains to work the mines. The Cornish men, known as "Cousin Jacks," were soon followed by their wives, known as "Cousin Jennies," who brought with them their recipes for Cornish pasties. The Irish and Welsh had similar versions. These tasty little pies, affectionately referred to as "letters from 'ome," were made for the men's daily lunchboxes.

This recipe is authentic except for the crust; I've replaced part of the shortening with butter so as to adapt the recipe for mixing in a food processor. However, if you prefer making pastry by hand, use all shortening (1¼ cups) and you will have the original pasties.

CRUST
- ¾ cup (1½ sticks) unsalted butter, chilled and cut into ½-inch cubes
- ½ cup solid vegetable shortening or lard, chilled
- 3 cups presifted all-purpose flour
- ½ teaspoon salt
- 5 to 6 tablespoons ice water
- Milk

FILLING
- 3 small potatoes (red preferred), peeled and thinly sliced

- 1 medium onion, thinly sliced
- 1½ pounds boneless beef sirloin, skirt, or flank steak, cut into thick strips about 2 inches long
- Salt and pepper
- 3 tablespoons butter

To make the crust, put the cubes of butter and the shortening by teaspoonfuls into the bowl of a food processor, and add the flour and salt. Turn the machine on and off a few times until the mixture forms pea-size chunks. With the machine on, add the ice water 1 tablespoon at a time up to 6 tablespoons and process just until the mixture begins to form a ball. Wrap and chill the dough for at least 30 minutes.

Preheat the oven to 400° F.

Divide the chilled dough into 6 equal parts. Roll each part out into a ⅛ inch thick, 4 x 6-inch oblong. Layer equal portions of potatoes, onions, and meat strips in the center of each oblong, add salt and pepper to taste, and dot with butter. Bring up the sides of the dough, moisten the edges with a little water, and crimp them together across the top to make a seam the length of the dough. Poke a small steam hole in the center.

Bake for 15 minutes, then turn the oven down to 325° F. and bake for 1 hour. Brush with a little milk during baking. Serve the pasties warm from the oven or let cool and wrap for later use. They are good either hot or cold.

Serves 6

. . . .

VEGETABLE SLAW

If you're taking this on a picnic, toss the cream with the slaw just before you pack it in a container.

DRESSING
- 1 teaspoon caraway seeds
- 1 teaspoon honey
- ½ teaspoon salt
- Pinch of white pepper
- 2 tablespoons lemon juice
- ½ cup peanut oil
- ¼ cup heavy cream

SALAD
    ½ medium head green cabbage, shredded
    1 medium green bell pepper, seeded and
      cut into matchstick julienne
    1 medium red bell pepper, seeded and cut
      into matchstick julienne
    2 medium carrots, cut into matchstick
      julienne

Combine all the dressing ingredients except the cream in a small bowl. Mix well with a fork. Arrange the vegetables in a large shallow bowl and toss with the dressing. Refrigerate for several hours or overnight. Retoss with the cream before serving.

Serves 6

. . . .

FRESH PEARS STUFFED WITH BLUE CHEESE

    3 ripe pears, Bartlett, Anjou, or your
      preference
    ½ lemon
    ¼ pound blue cheese, Roquefort, or
      Gorgonzola

Wash the pears and cut in half. Cut out the core and some of the flesh to form a hollow in the middle. Rub surface with half a lemon. Pack the hollow with the cheese, mounding it a little and smoothing it with the back of a spoon. Wrap each half in plastic and chill. Bring to room temperature before serving.

Serves 6

. . . .

GLAZED OATMEAL CAKE

Anything made with oats is popular in the Rocky Mountain West. Here is a simple but very good cake.

CAKE
    1 cup boiling water
    1 cup rolled oats
    4 tablespoons (½ stick) butter, softened
    2 cups light brown sugar, tightly packed
    2 eggs
    1 cup pastry or presifted all-purpose flour
    1 teaspoon ground cinnamon
    1 teaspoon ground cloves
    1 teaspoon baking soda
    ½ cup raisins
    1 cup chopped walnuts

GLAZE
    ½ cup buttermilk
    ½ cup honey
    1 teaspoon baking soda
    ⅛ teaspoon salt

Butter and flour a round heat-proof dish, such as a charlotte mold, casserole, or soufflé dish, that is 6 to 7 inches in diameter and 4 to 5 inches deep, or about 2 quarts.

Preheat the oven to 350° F.

Pour the boiling water over the oats and set aside for about 15 minutes, until cooled.

Cream the butter and brown sugar in a large mixing bowl. Beat in the eggs one at a time. Blend in the flour, spices, and baking soda. Stir in the oatmeal, then fold in the raisins and nuts.

Pour the batter into the baking dish and bake for 45 to 50 minutes, or until a cake tester comes out clean. Let the cake cool for 10 minutes, then remove from the dish and place on a rack set over another pan.

Make the glaze. In a small saucepan, combine the buttermilk and honey and stir over low heat just until warm; do not let it boil. Remove from the heat and stir in the baking soda and salt. Immediately pour the warm glaze over the cake.

Serves 6 to 8

. . . .

ORIENTAL BARBECUE

. . . .

C hinese food has been a part of Rocky
Mountain cuisine ever since the
Chinese arrived in the nineteenth
century to help build the railroads. Noodle
parlors and Chinese catering companies
sprang up everywhere, establishing a popular taste for oriental foods and condiments.

The preparation of Chinese food requires
fewer utensils than any other cuisine. The
only real essential is a wok. Some early immigrants brought woks with them, but in
fact, both woks and steamers could be im-
provised. By the early 1900s, a thriving
Chinese commerce existed in San Francisco whereby goods from China could be
purchased or sent by mail to the Rockies.
Today the region's supermarkets usually
have well-stocked oriental sections, and
specialty oriental food shops exist in most
cities throughout the country.

Oriental ingredients have become so incorporated into the Rocky Mountain cuisine that almost every restaurant offers a
teriyaki dish. While some oriental restaurants do exist here, cooks in other sorts of
restaurants often use oriental ingredients
out of a delight in exotic tastes rather than
any penchant for authenticity.

The following menu is a good example of

M E N U for 8

. . . .

Chinese Cabbage Salad

Barbecued Lamb Ribs Teriyaki

**Steamed New Potatoes with
Mint**

Eggplant with Pine Nuts

Popovers

Ginger Cream with Dates

**Mineral Water • Beer
Coffee or Tea**

Rocky Mountain eclecticism, offering pop-overs and potatoes in place of rice with dishes featuring oriental tastes.

....

CHINESE CABBAGE SALAD

3 cups finely chopped Chinese cabbage
1 medium cucumber, peeled, cut in half lengthwise, seeded, and sliced ¼ inch thick
1 small purple onion, thinly sliced
1 cup snow peas, stemmed and stringed
1 small green bell pepper, seeded and very thinly sliced lengthwise
1 small red bell pepper, seeded and very thinly sliced lengthwise
½ cup fresh coriander (cilantro)
1 cup Oriental Dressing (recipe follows)

Soak all the vegetables in ice water for 1 hour. Drain, then spin or towel dry. Add coriander and toss with Oriental Dressing.

Serves 8

....

Oriental Dressing

¼ cup rice vinegar
1 garlic clove, minced
1 teaspoon soy sauce
1 teaspoon sugar
¼ teaspoon white pepper
½ cup peanut oil

Put all ingredients except oil in a small bowl and stir with a whisk or fork. Slowly add the oil, stirring constantly until well mixed.

Makes ½ cup

....

BARBECUED LAMB RIBS TERIYAKI

This recipe is a specialty of Pat LeFavour, who has been in the restaurant business in Colorado and Idaho.

SWEET-AND-SOUR SAUCE
1½ cups hoisin sauce (see Note)
1½ cups orange marmalade
3 tablespoons finely chopped fresh ginger
1½ teaspoons black bean sauce with chili (see Note)
¼ cup mushroom soy sauce (see Note)

6 pounds lamb ribs

Mix all the ingredients for the sauce in a heavy-bottom saucepan, and cook at a low simmer for 30 to 40 minutes. Stir often with a wooden spoon so that the marmalade doesn't burn. This makes 3 cups of sauce, but the recipe can be easily increased, if necessary.

Place the ribs in a single layer in a shallow glass baking pan and pour over 2 cups of the sauce. Refrigerate the remaining sauce. Cover the pan with plastic wrap and marinate the ribs for several hours or overnight in the refrigerator.

One hour before you plan to serve, build a charcoal fire. When the coals are white (in about 30 minutes), grill the ribs for 30 to 40 minutes, turning them every 10 minutes and basting with the marinade. Use the remaining sauce if you run short.

In the last 10 minutes of cooking, add some dried fruitwood chips—first soaked in water for about 30 minutes—to the fire.

The ribs will be dark brown and lightly glazed when done. Remove to a warm serving platter. Heat and spoon over any left-over sauce.

Serves 6 to 8

Note: Sauces are available bottled or canned in Chinese food sections of some supermarkets and in oriental specialty stores.

....

STEAMED NEW POTATOES WITH MINT

16 to 24 new potatoes (about 2 pounds), unpeeled (if medium, 2 to 3 inches in diameter, use 16 cut in half; if smaller, use 24 whole)
4 tablespoons (½ stick) butter
¼ teaspoon salt
¼ teaspoon white pepper
¼ cup finely chopped fresh mint

Put the potatoes in a vegetable steamer, cover, and steam for about 15 to 20 minutes, or until tender.

Melt the butter in a large saucepan. Add the potatoes, salt, white pepper, and mint; mix lightly until the potatoes are well coated with the butter. Serve immediately.

Serves 8

. . . .

EGGPLANT WITH PINE NUTS

2½ **pounds eggplant, peeled and diced**
  Salt
  6 **ounces Canadian bacon, cut into ½-inch**
    cubes
½ **cup vegetable oil**
  1 **ounce fresh mushrooms, diced**
  1 **cup pine nuts (see Note)**
  5 **tablespoons soy sauce**
¼ **cup sweet vermouth**
  1 **tablespoon sugar**
  2 **tablespoons chopped fresh coriander**
    (cilantro)

Thirty minutes before cooking, put the eggplant in a large strainer, salt it, and let rest to release any water. Rinse off the salt and pat thoroughly dry.

Sauté the bacon in a small frying pan until crisp; drain on paper toweling. Heat the oil to sizzling in a large, heavy frying pan. Sauté the eggplant, stirring to brown all sides, for 5 to 10 minutes. Add the bacon, mushrooms, ⅔ cup pine nuts, soy sauce, vermouth, and sugar, then continue to sauté for 10 minutes, or until the mushrooms are browned. To serve, pour into a warmed bowl and garnish with remaining pine nuts and the coriander.

Serves 8

Note: Substitute chopped walnuts if pine nuts are not available.

. . . .

POPOVERS

These are good served hot from the oven with butter and jam.

  1 **cup presifted all-purpose flour**
½ **teaspoon salt**
  3 **eggs, lightly beaten**
  1 **cup milk**
  2 **tablespoons (¼ stick) butter, melted**

Preheat the oven to 450° F.

Combine the ingredients in a medium mixing bowl, and blend thoroughly.

Heat a buttered cast-iron popover pan or medium muffin tin in the oven. When the pan is very hot, fill each cup one-third full with the batter. Bake for 20 minutes, reduce the heat to 350° F., and bake for about 10 to 20 minutes longer, or until the popovers are puffed and brown. Immediately remove from pans to a wire rack. Do not open the oven door during the first 30 minutes of baking or the popovers may fall.

Makes 8 to 10

. . . .

GINGER CREAM WITH DATES

  4 **teaspoons unflavored gelatin**
¼ **cup cold water**
1½ **cups heavy cream**
½ **cup sugar**
2¼ **cups plain yogurt**
½ **teaspoon ground ginger**
  1 **teaspoon vanilla extract**
  1 **tablespoon minced candied ginger**
  4 **pitted dates, halved or chopped (see Note)**

Dissolve the gelatin in cold water.

Place the cream and sugar in a small saucepan and stir over low heat for about 5 minutes, until the sugar dissolves. Off the heat, add the gelatin, mixing well to make sure it is completely dissolved. Cool for 5 to 10 minutes.

Whisk in the yogurt, then the ground ginger, vanilla, and candied ginger. Pour into a 1½-quart glass bowl. Chill for a minimum of 2 hours.

Before serving, arrange the dates on top in a decorative pattern.

Serves 6 to 8

Note: If you prefer, top with Mandarin orange sections instead of dates.

. . . .

MENU for 4
....
Grapefruit-Avocado Compote

Barbecued Trout with Herbs

Sheepherder Potatoes

Baking Powder Biscuits with Strawberry Jam

Gooseberry Fool

**Cowboy Coffee • Tea
Hot Chocolate**

BREAKFAST RIDE COOKOUT IN THE GRAND TETONS

. . . .

Approaching the breakfast site after an exhilarating ride in the crisp morning air, hungry guests are greeted by the aroma of Sheepherder Potatoes and Cowboy Coffee, kept warm at the edge of the fire. A wrangler and guests enjoy the early morning light.

Few things equal the pure beauty of an early morning trail ride. The dew still lies on the grass; the day beckons with all the crispness of a mountain dawn. Saddling up the horses (or for that matter, getting on a mountain bike) to ride out into the foothills of the magnificent Tetons is an experience to be treasured. It's also one that makes you hungry.

For this menu, you can prepare the compote, biscuits, and dessert ahead of time at home, then pack them carefully with the other foods to carry to a breakfast site chosen in advance and accessible by car or four-wheel drive as well as by trail. The cook, obviously, doesn't get to go on the ride, but does get to eat!

The first order of business is to get a crackling fire going about an hour in advance of the riders' arrival. While the fire is blazing, water can be boiled for coffee. An enamel coffeepot is traditional for making cowboy coffee. The pot can then be kept warm by the side of the fire.

Once the water is on, there is time to tend to the table, which I like to cover with a pretty oilcloth and lay with rustic place settings. (If you choose a site without a picnic table, a folding table and chairs can easily be carried in your vehicle.) By the time you've set the table, the fire will probably have burned down to a good cooking flame.

The Sheepherder Potatoes should be put on to cook about 30 minutes before the trout. The biscuits, made early on the same morning and wrapped in foil, will stay warm if placed near the fire. The Grapefruit-Avocado Compote and the Gooseberry Fool can be kept on ice in a cooler until serving time. Just before serving (when you hear the horses approaching on the trail), you can, as I like to do, transfer the compote to a wooden bowl and the Gooseberry Fool to a pottery dish or bowl.

Everything will be ready when the guests arrive to be greeted by the marvelous aroma of fresh-brewed coffee and inviting victuals.

This cookout took place at the Triangle X Ranch at the base of the Grand Tetons, just north of Jackson Hole, Wyoming.

. . . .

Fresh-caught rainbow trout, cleaned and ready for the fire.

GRAPEFRUIT-AVOCADO COMPOTE

> 2 small ripe avocados, peeled and sliced lengthwise
> 1 medium pink grapefruit, peeled and sliced from top to bottom in ¼-inch sections
> 2 tablespoons fresh lime juice
> ¼ cup dry white wine
> 1 tablespoon honey
> ½ teaspoon salt
> ¼ cup chopped fresh mint

Put the avocado and grapefruit slices in a medium bowl. Put the lime juice, wine, honey, salt, and mint in a separate bowl, and stir with a fork until blended. Pour over the fruit and mix lightly. Chill until ready to serve.

Serves 4
. . . .

BARBECUED TROUT WITH HERBS

This recipe is cooked on an outdoor grill. Make sure you use enough coals so that a single layer covers the same space as will the trout when laid side by side.

> 2 tablespoons (¼ stick) unsalted butter
> ¼ cup dry white wine
> 4 whole trout (½ to 1 pound each), cleaned
> Salt and pepper
> 4 sprigs of fresh thyme
> Several fresh basil leaves
> Several sprigs of fresh tarragon
> 1 shallot, coarsely chopped, or 4 scallions, chopped

Melt the butter in a small saucepan, stir in the wine, and brush the mixture all over the outside of the trout and in the cavities. Sprinkle with salt and pepper to taste. Fill the cavities with the thyme, basil, and tarragon, then add the shallot. Refrigerate while you prepare the coals; or if you're taking to a cookout site, lay the fish in a plastic container, seal securely, and carry in a cooler bag.

To prepare the fire, pile the charcoal in a mound. Light the coals and let them burn until most of them are covered with white ash, about 30 minutes, then spread the coals in a single layer.

Fit the trout into a wire fish-grilling basket large enough to hold them securely in 1 layer. Grill over hot white coals about 6 minutes, just until the skin is crisp and the flesh has turned white. Test for doneness by inserting the point of a sharp knife into the thickest part near the backbone.

Serves 4

. . . .

SHEEPHERDER POTATOES

3 tablespoons butter
1 tablespoon olive oil
3 to 4 medium potatoes (2 pounds), scrubbed and sliced ¼ to ½ inch thick, then slices cut in half (if potatoes are small, quarter instead of slicing)
1 large onion, diced (about 1½ cups)
1 garlic clove, mashed
 Salt
 Freshly ground black pepper
½ teaspoon paprika
¼ teaspoon minced fresh rosemary, or ⅛ teaspoon dried
3 chorizo sausages (optional, see Note)
¼ cup finely chopped fresh parsley
 Cayenne (ground red) pepper

Heat the butter and oil in a large, heavy skillet until sizzling. Over low heat, fry the potatoes and onions slowly for 30 minutes, until lightly browned on all sides, turning several times with a spatula or spoon. Stir in the garlic, salt and pepper to taste, paprika, rosemary, and chorizo, if using, and continue cooking for a few minutes. Remove the garlic and sprinkle with parsley and cayenne.

Serves 4 to 6

Note: If using chorizo, boil it whole for 20 minutes, then cut into slices.

. . . .

BAKING POWDER BISCUITS WITH STRAWBERRY JAM

These biscuits are the old-fashioned flaky kind that are irresistible.

Hungry riders stand by, forks in hand, impatiently waiting for the trout to grill.

. . . .

1 cup presifted all-purpose flour
1 cup whole wheat pastry flour
3 teaspoons baking powder
½ teaspoon salt
½ cup (1 stick) butter, diced
2 eggs, lightly beaten
½ cup mik
 Strawberry Jam (recipe follows)

Preheat the oven to 450° F.

Mix the dry ingredients in a medium mixing bowl. Cut in the butter with a pastry blender or 2 knives until the mixture is in pea-size pieces. Beat the eggs and milk together in a small bowl. Make a well in the center of the dry ingredients and pour in the egg mixture. Stir with a fork, gradually incorporating the flour until mixture is thoroughly moistened.

Knead the dough briefly to bring it together, and then roll out on a floured board to a ½-inch thickness. Fold in thirds and roll out again. Repeat twice more. Cut 2-inch rounds with a pastry cutter or a jelly glass. Place them 1 inch apart on an ungreased cookie sheet and bake for 8 to 10 minutes, or until golden brown. Serve warm with butter and homemade Strawberry Jam.

Makes 16 biscuits

. . . .

Riding gear for a chilly Wyoming morning includes several layers of clothing, warm gloves, leather chaps, and a fancy belt buckle.

Left and right: *A slicker and a dashing hat also provide protection from the early morning damp.*

Breakfast is ready, with a steaming pot of coffee on the side. Diners fill their plates straight from the fire before sitting down at the table.

Wetting down the cooking fire before breaking camp.

Strawberry Jam

This jam is made with whole berries, so choose uniformly small or medium fruit at their peak of ripeness but still firm. Do not increase the recipe; the sugar will not be properly absorbed.

    3 cups sugar
    3 cups strawberries, hulled
    1 tablespoon lemon juice

Mound the sugar in the center of a 2- or 3-quart heavy-bottom pot. Pour in the berries around the sugar. Bring to a simmer over medium heat, then cook without stirring for 25 minutes. Do not mix or stir at any time. The sugar will be absorbed, and the berries remain whole and unbruised. In the last 2 minutes of cooking, add the lemon juice, without stirring. Pour the mixture into a glass bowl, cover, and let cool for 6 to 8 hours at room temperature.

If you want to use the jam within a few days, you can simply refrigerate it in tightly lidded jars. For long-term storage, process in a hot-water bath, see page 170.

Makes 3 half-pints

GOOSEBERRY FOOL

Gooseberries grow well in the mountains and are popular with everyone. Here is my version of an old English recipe. Substitute canned gooseberries, if necessary.

    4 cups fresh gooseberries
    1½ cups sugar
    ¼ cup water
       Grated rind of 1 orange
    1½ cups heavy cream, whipped
       Freshly grated nutmeg

If using fresh berries, remove the stems and tails from the gooseberries and rinse in cold water. Place in a large, heavy-bottom saucepan with the sugar and water and cook over low heat for 30 minutes, until the berries are reduced to a pulp. Stir in the orange rind. Purée the mixture in a food mill or put through a sieve.

Refrigerate. Just before serving, fold in the whipped cream, spoon into serving dishes, and sprinkle with nutmeg.

For a picnic or cookout, put the whipped cream and gooseberries in separate jars and carry in an insulated bag. Take the nutmeg in a spice jar.

Serves 4 to 6

. . . .

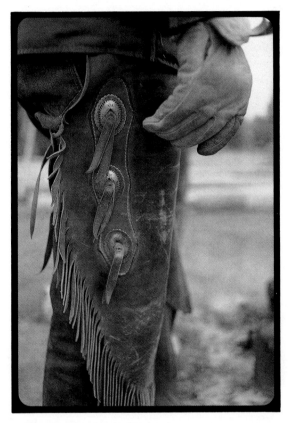

A wrangler's fancy chaps, fringed and adorned with silver, are as handsome as they are rugged and practical.

. . . .

COWBOY COFFEE

Put 12 cups of freshly drawn cold water on to boil in a 4-quart enamel pot (do not use a pot other than an enamel one).

Break up 1 or 2 eggshells in a small bowl, add 1 tablespoon of cold water, and stir. When the water boils, add 1 measure of your favorite brand of regular-grind coffee for each cup of water, plus 1 measure for the pot. Add the eggshells, stirring to keep the pot from boiling over. Adjust the heat to let the coffee boil softly for 5 minutes. Turn off the heat, and let the coffee stand for 5 minutes before serving.

This coffee can stand all day and be reheated without tasting stale. If you run low, add more water and coffee, and gently boil for 2 minutes.

Makes 12 cups

Note: You can make this coffee without the addition of the eggshells if you don't have any on hand, in which case, to settle the coffee grounds, add ¼ cup cold water at the end of the boiling time, and reheat gently.

Maneuvering the middle fork of the Salmon River takes skill and stamina, especially when you hit such rough waters as the Ruby Rapids.

40

DUTCH-OVEN DINNER FOR A WHITE-WATER TRIP

. . . .

The wild rivers of the Rocky Mountains lure hundreds of people down them in rafts, and, wherever there is water to run, white-water outfitters offer their services. The river guides, knowing intimately every rip and riffle, command their oar-powered rafts through exhilarating waters and on into the calm stretches where some secret nook offers landing space. Whether the trip lasts a week or a day, a meal on the river is a high point. Most marvelous of all is to happpen upon a river guide who is also a good cook.

With all the ingredients for their meals carefully packed in large, insulated coolers and waterproof bags, the guides put in at a predetermined campsite at the end of each day on the river. While guests have free time to hike or fish or idle, the guides, all of whom have been trained in outdoor cooking, get a fire going in a predug pit and prepare the food. Once the fire has turned

A cold-cut lunch to hold us until dinner.

to coals, a Dutch oven can be set into it, then covered with more coals and earth and left to cook. The bread is made in advance of the trip and usually wrapped in foil and reheated in the coals. When it's finally ready, dinner is served around the campfire to rafters whose appetites have been well whetted by a day spent so thoroughly outdoors.

Sheila Mills's book, *Rocky Mountain Kettle Cuisine,* offers a collection of Dutch-oven recipes. The menu that follows is one of her meals, served on Rocky Mountain River Tours through the magnificent primitive country of the middle fork of the Salmon River. The menu can be easily prepared and packed for your own river trip.

Getting out of river clothes is no small feat, often requiring a strong helping hand.

ONION SOUP

3 tablespoons butter
1 tablespoon vegetable oil
4 medium onions, thinly sliced
3 tablespoons all-purpose flour
8 cups beef bouillon
1 bay leaf
½ cup dry white wine
½ teaspoon salt
  Several grindings of black pepper
8 slices French bread (cut 1-inch thick), toasted
¼ pound Gruyère cheese, grated

Heat the butter and oil in a Dutch oven. Add the onions and cook over low heat for 30 minutes, stirring often, until they are a deep golden color. Sprinkle the flour over the onions, stir, and cook for an additional 3 or 4 minutes. Off the heat, stir in the bouillon, bay leaf, wine, salt, and pepper. Place over low heat, and simmer for 30 minutes. Discard the bay leaf.

To serve, put a slice of bread in each bowl, ladle the soup over, and sprinkle with the cheese. If you have access to a broiler, run each bowl under the broiler until the cheese melts. Otherwise, serve the soup very hot to melt the cheese.

Serves 8

GARDEN SALAD

1 head leaf lettuce, leaves torn into bite-size pieces
2 medium tomatoes, cut into large dice
1 medium red onion, sliced
1 small head cauliflower, broken into small florets
1 medium green bell pepper, seeded and thinly sliced lengthwise
½ cup pitted green olives, or pimiento-stuffed
½ cup Tarragon Vinaigrette (recipe follows)

Toss all the ingredients in a large bowl with the vinaigrette.

Serves 8

Tarragon Vinaigrette

2 **tablespoons red wine vinegar, or half
  balsamic vinegar and half red wine
  vinegar**
1 **tablespoon minced fresh tarragon**
1 **tablespoon minced fresh parsley**
1 **garlic clove, minced**
½ **teaspoon salt**
  Several grindings of black pepper
1 **tablespoon Dijon mustard**
1 **cup olive oil**

Put all the ingredients except the olive oil
in a small bowl. Stir with a fork or tablespoon until well blended. Gradually add
the oil, drop by drop, continuing to stir
slowly until the dressing is thick and
creamy. Extra dressing will keep well for
several days.

Makes 1 generous cup

. . . .

*Thalweg strudel cooking in Dutch ovens. The
tantalizing aroma of this crab and scallop
dish whets everyone's appetite for Sheila Mills's
famous kettle cuisine.*

*Ruby Rapids rhubarb will be baked to perfection
by the time the main course is finished.*

cream cheese, scallops, mushrooms, scallions, and coriander.

For each serving of strudel, place 1 sheet of phyllo dough on a smooth surface and brush with the melted butter; lay another sheet over the first and brush with butter. Place a generous ½ cup of the filling about 2 inches from the bottom edge of the prepared phyllo, spreading the mixture with the back of a spoon to within 2 inches of the top and sides. Roll up the phyllo sheet about one-third of the way, fold in the sides, and continue to roll the length of the dough.

Place the rolls seam side down in one layer in a Dutch oven or baking pan and brush with the egg white. Cover the Dutch

THALWEG STRUDEL WITH DIJON SAUCE

Sheila Mills names many of the dishes she creates for Rocky Mountain River Tours after certain river conditions. "Thalweg" refers to the swiftest, deepest current of a river. You can make this dish either outdoors or at home in the oven.

    12 ounces fresh crabmeat, or 2 (6-ounce)
       cans
     8 ounces cream cheese, softened
     1 pound fresh bay scallops
     1 pound fresh mushrooms, sliced
     5 scallions, chopped
     1 teaspoon ground coriander
    16 sheets phyllo dough
     1 cup (2 sticks) butter, melted
     1 egg white, lightly beaten
     2 bunches or 16 to 24 medium spears fresh
       asparagus
     2 cups heavy cream
     2 tablespoons Dijon mustard

If using a Dutch oven outdoors, about 30 minutes before cooking create a baking oven by digging a hole about 1 foot deep and 1 foot wide and lighting enough charcoal to form a bed for the pot and to cover it. The coals should be partially covered with gray ash before putting the pot on.

Pick out any cartilage from the crabmeat and drain off any liquid. Put the crabmeat in a large mixing bowl and blend in the oven and put on the bed of hot charcoal. Cover oven entirely with hot briquets, and cook for 20 minutes (or bake uncovered in a preheated, 350° F. oven for 30 minutes, or until golden brown).

While the strudel is baking, steam the asparagus until tender but still firm, about 5 minutes.

Make the sauce by blending the cream and mustard in a small, heavy saucepan and simmering for 20 to 30 minutes over lowest heat, stirring occasionally.

Place the baked strudel on individual serving dishes, garnish with 2 or 3 asparagus spears, and top with Dijon Sauce.

Serves 8

....

RUBY RAPIDS RHUBARB

There is a stretch of fast-moving water on the main Salmon River called the Ruby Rapids. After an exhilarating day on the river, everyone looks forward to dinner, topped off with a special dessert like this one.

If using a Dutch oven outdoors, 30 to 40 minutes before baking, light enough charcoal to make a bed for the pot and to cover it. The fire will be ready when most of the coals are covered with gray ash.

CRUST
 1 cup presifted all-purpose flour
 ⅓ cup confectioners' sugar
 ⅓ cup butter or margarine

FILLING
 3 eggs, beaten well
1½ cups granulated sugar
 ½ cup all-purpose flour
 ¾ teaspoon salt
 3 generous cups finely chopped rhubarb

 1 cup heavy cream

Put the crust ingredients in a medium bowl and mix with a fork until grainy. Press into the bottom of a preheated Dutch oven or into a conventional 9-inch deep-dish pie pan.

Combine the filling ingredients in a medium bowl and stir well. Spread on top of the crust. Put the lid on the Dutch oven, cover over with coals, and bake for 15 minutes, being careful not to burn the bottom (or bake uncovered in a preheated 350° F. oven for 30 minutes). Let stand for 15 minutes before serving. Serve warm with cream.

Serves 8

....

Above left: *Thalweg strudel, enhanced by a spray of wildflowers scattered on the rough board table.*

Left: *Ruby Rapids rhubarb, bubbling and crusty, is served right from the pots.*

M E N U for 10

. . . .

Almond Snack

Hot Spicy Golden Punch

Crudités with Roasted Garlic
Dip

Sardine Puffs

Cream of Spinach Soup

Braised Veal in Tomato Sauce

Finnish Peasant Bread

Baked Boulder Peak

White Wine • Coffee

Above: *At the end of a long forest walk, the yurt is a welcome sight perched among the trees at the edge of a large meadow. We relax before unpacking provisions.*

Above right: *Before long we have a roaring fire going inside for Claudine's cooking needs—and to provide warmth for the chilly evening ahead.*

DINING IN A YURT

. . . .

The yurt, a large, round canvas tent with a wood plank floor and a sky-light in the center of the ceiling is the Asian equivalent of the tepee. Some no-madic Mongolian tribes still use the yurt, and it is supremely functional as a shelter in any cold region. In the Rockies, where it is a practical structure for setting up hut systems that can easily be dismantled come spring, the yurt has been enthusiasti-cally adopted by skiers and mountaineers in all seasons. Some are used for overnight stays; others serve as dining rooms for hik-ers or skiers.

On the clear December night of my first trip to a yurt, the temperature was ten de-

grees below zero. Luckily, the yurt was only a short thirty-minute ski in from the highway. It was lovely to come from that crisp night air into the yurt's cozy atmosphere and even lovelier to be welcomed by my hosts with a cup of hot punch. The yurt was a romantic place, lit by Coleman lanterns and heated by a wood stove going full blast, and warm enough that I could strip down to a cotton turtleneck.

The yurt shown here, which is owned and operated by Sun Valley Trekking, is perched at the edge of a high meadow with the Sawtooth Mountains as a backdrop.

Tables and benches inside comfortably seat up to fifteen people for dinner, all of whom must be willing to make the hour-long trek either on foot or, in winter, on cross-country skis through country that is beautiful at any time of the year.

Food is hauled in early on the day of a scheduled dinner by hikers using backpacks or by a skier pulling a sled, then cooked while guests are served hors d'oeuvres.

We went for dinner in the spring, when the wildflowers are just beginning to bloom and wildlife is active. A black bear, we learned, had visited the yurt the day before our arrival.

Claudine Martin, chef for Sun Valley Trekking, tended to the meal while the rest

of us explored the outdoor hot tub and the meadow or sat back and basked in the warmth and light and wonderful aromas that pervaded the yurt. Claudine's French touch made this unique Rocky Mountain dinner even more special.

. . . .

ALMOND SNACK

1½ cups whole blanched almonds
  1 tablespoon olive oil
  ½ teaspoon salt
    Pinch of cayenne
1½ cups golden raisins

Preheat the oven to 300° F.

Spread the almonds out in one layer on a baking sheet. Bake for 30 to 40 minutes, or until lightly toasted, shaking the pan occasionally to redistribute the nuts. Remove the pan from the oven and sprinkle the nuts with olive oil, salt, and cayenne, shaking the pan to distribute the oil and spices. Mix in the raisins. Let cool and store in a plastic bag.

Serves 10
. . . .

HOT SPICY GOLDEN PUNCH

  1 (4-inch) cinnamon stick
  ½ teaspoon whole allspice
  ¼ teaspoon whole cloves
2½ quarts unsweetened apple juice
1½ cups fresh orange juice
  ¼ cup light brown sugar, tightly packed
  ¼ teaspoon ground cardamom
  ¼ teaspoon grated nutmeg

Put the cinnamon stick, allspice, and cloves in a small square of double thickness cheesecloth and tie it to make a bag. Add it with the remaining ingredients to a 3- to 4-quart pot and bring to a boil. Turn down the heat and simmer for 15 minutes. Ladle the hot punch into individual cups.

Serves 10
. . . .

Lit by Coleman lanterns, the yurt glows like a great beacon in the mountains, beckoning hikers arriving after sundown.

CRUDITÉS WITH ROASTED GARLIC DIP

Choose the most interesting fresh vegetables available for your crudités tray. For this menu I selected the following:

- 1 medium zucchini, sliced on the diagonal
- 2 medium yellow crook-neck squash, sliced on the diagonal ½ inch thick
- 1 small head cauliflower, broken into florets
- 1 pint yellow pear tomatoes
- ½ pound green beans, steamed until crisp-tender, and blanched in cold water
- 1 medium red bell pepper, cut into strips
- 1 bunch red kale to line platter
- 1 small acorn squash hollowed out for garlic dip (cut off bottom to make it flat)
  Roasted Garlic Dip (recipe follows)

Arrange the vegetables on a platter or in a basket. Serve with the dip spooned into the squash.

Serves 10

Roasted Garlic Dip

- 12 large garlic cloves
- 3 tablespoons peanut oil
- 8 ounces cream cheese, softened
- ¼ cup sour cream
- 2 teaspoons Worcestershire sauce
- ½ teaspoon Dijon mustard
- 2 tablespoons chopped fresh parsley
- 1 teaspoon crumbled dried rosemary
- 3 tablespoons coarsely chopped blanched almonds
- 2 tablespoons minced shallots
- ¼ teaspoon freshly ground black pepper
- ½ teaspoon ground cardamom
- ⅓ cup heavy cream

Preheat the oven to 300° F. Place the garlic in a small roasting pan coated with the peanut oil. Roast for 40 minutes, then let cool for 20 minutes.

Put the garlic and oil in a blender, pulse several times, then add the cream cheese, sour cream, Worcestershire sauce, and mustard. Process until smooth, then transfer to a small bowl. Stir in the parsley, rosemary, almonds, shallots, pepper, and cardamom. Beat the cream until firm but not stiff. Fold into the mixture and refrigerate for 1 hour before serving.

Makes 2 cups

Above: *Preparations are done on a rustic table, using tools that are part of the yurt's efficient camp kitchen.*

Right: *Catching the last rays of the sun, trekkers enjoy the day to the fullest.*

52

Braising the veal atop a wood stove requires a hot fire and the cook's careful attention.

Claudine ices one of her famous cakes. The fondant process is too complicated for most home cooks, but she's an expert even in a yurt!

Above: *Relaxing with a glass of wine before dinner.*

Left: *Guests help themselves to crudités and other appetizers.*

53

SARDINE PUFFS

These luscious little puffs are very good appetizers for a special meal.

SARDINE BUTTER
4⅜-ounce can boneless, skinless sardines, drained
4 tablespoons (½ stick) unsalted butter, softened
2 tablespoons capers, drained
2 scallions, chopped
2 tablespoons lemon juice
1 tablespoon Dijon mustard
Ground black pepper to taste

CREAM PUFFS
1 cup water
⅛ teaspoon salt
8 tablespoons (1 stick) unsalted butter
1 cup all-purpose flour
3 large, or 4 medium, eggs

24 capers, drained

The yurt's skylight offers a view of the evening sky.

First, make the Sardine Butter. Using a food processor, process all ingredients together until smooth. Keep at room temperature if using right away; otherwise, the mixture can be refrigerated for 1 or 2 days. It also freezes well.

To make the puffs, put the water and salt in a small heavy saucepan. Cut the butter into small pieces and add to the water. Set the pan over low heat, and stir the mixture with a wooden spoon until it comes to a rolling boil. Add the flour all at once. Remove pan from heat, and stir the mixture vigorously until it comes away from the sides of the pan. Transfer the dough to a mixing bowl. Add the eggs one at a time, beating thoroughly after each addition. The dough should be very soft and shiny. If the dough seems too stiff, beat an additional egg in a small bowl, and add small portions of it to the dough while beating thoroughly, until the desired consistency is reached. Reserve leftover egg. Chill the dough for at least 30 minutes.

Preheat the oven to 400° F. Put the dough in a pastry bag. Pipe little balls, about ½ inch high, onto a buttered baking sheet. With a wet finger or dampened corner of a dish towel, lightly tap any pointed tips to round them off. Lightly brush the tops of the dough balls with the leftover egg. Do not let any of the egg touch the baking sheet, or the puff will not rise to its maximum.

Bake for 10 minutes at 400° F., then reduce heat to 325° F. and bake for 10 to 15 minutes longer. Remove the pan from the oven and slit each puff on one side, cutting halfway around the puff to release the steam. Bake for 5 minutes longer. The puffs should be browned to a light golden color and have a crisp shell.

Fill the puffs by first removing some of the soft, doughy insides with your finger. Using a pastry bag, pipe the sardine butter into each puff. Then pipe a tiny bit of the butter on the tops and garnish each puff with a caper.

Makes 24 puffs; serves 12

A carving platter doubles as a serving tray for the sardine puffs.

CREAM OF SPINACH SOUP

This soup will warm your toes, an important consideration if you happen to be dining in a tent in winter.

9 cups chicken stock, homemade or canned
3 tablespoons all-purpose flour
    Pinch of cayenne (ground red) pepper
    Pinch of ground mace
4 tablespoons (½ stick) butter
1½ pounds fresh spinach, washed and stems removed
1½ cups diced carrots
1½ cups chopped broccoli
1½ cups chopped cauliflower
1½ cups chopped fresh coriander (cilantro) leaves
1½ cups heavy cream
    Juice of ½ lemon
    Salt and pepper

Bring the stock to a boil in a 3-quart saucepan. Mix the flour with the cayenne and mace in a small bowl. Melt the butter in a large heavy-bottom pot, add the flour mixture, and cook over low heat for a few minutes. Add the boiling stock, stirring constantly. Then add the spinach a handful at a time, and cook for 3 minutes. Let cool for about 10 minutes, then purée in batches in a blender. Return the purée to the pot.

Steam each of the vegetables separately until fork-tender but still firm. Stir into the spinach broth, then add the coriander, cream, lemon juice, and salt and pepper to taste. Reheat to serve. Do not boil.

Serves 10

BRAISED VEAL IN TOMATO SAUCE

6 pounds lean veal stew meat, cut into 2-inch cubes
    Salt and pepper
¾ cup olive oil
8 cloves garlic, coarsely chopped
2 (3-inch) cinnamon sticks
4 whole cloves
2 bay leaves
2 cups dry white wine
6 tablespoons apple cider or white vinegar
4 cups onion, finely chopped (about 4 large onions)
4 cups peeled, seeded, chopped tomatoes (about 4 medium tomatoes)
1 teaspoon sugar
¼ teaspoon dried thyme
¼ cup minced parsley
¼ teaspoon hot paprika or cayenne pepper
2 pounds uncooked elbow macaroni
1 cup (2 sticks) unsalted butter, melted
1 cup grated Parmesan or Romano cheese

Wipe the veal cubes with dampened paper towels, and sprinkle the cubes with salt and pepper to taste. Heat 3 tablespoons olive oil in a large skillet and sauté the veal, a few pieces at a time, until lightly browned on all sides. Transfer the browned meat to a large heavy pot. Repeat until all pieces have been browned, adding up to 3 additional tablespoons of the olive oil, if necessary. Add the garlic, cinnamon sticks,

*Candles and lamplight cast
a cheerful glow at dinner.
Finnish peasant bread looks
right at home on the rustic table.*

cloves, and bay leaves. Cook, covered, for 2 minutes over medium heat, shaking the pot. Add the wine and vinegar. Increase heat to high and cook until the liquid boils. Reduce the heat, place a piece of foil on top of the pot, and cover tightly with a lid. Simmer for 30 minutes.

Meanwhile, wipe the skillet clean, heat 6 tablespoons of olive oil, add the onion, and cook over low heat, until soft (5 to 7 minutes). Stir in the tomatoes, salt to taste, sugar, thyme, parsley, and paprika or cayenne. Cook over low heat for 20 minutes, stirring constantly.

After the veal has cooked for 30 minutes, uncover the pot and pour in the tomato sauce. Replace the foil and lid and cook over low heat for 30 minutes more.

Meanwhile, bring a large pot of salted water to a boil and cook the macaroni according to package instructions, until tender. When veal is ready, transfer it to a serving dish, and cover with foil to keep warm. Remove the cinnamon sticks from the sauce and let sauce stand for 4 to 5 minutes, until the oil rises to the surface. Spoon off the oil. When pasta is done, drain and return to the pot and toss with the butter and ½ cup cheese. To serve, top each serving of pasta with veal and sauce, and garnish with a sprinkling of the remaining cheese.

Serves 12

FINNISH PEASANT BREAD

  1 tablespoon yeast
½ cup warm water
  2 cups buttermilk, at room temperature
  1 teaspoon salt
1½ cups whole rye flour
1½ cups whole wheat flour
¼ cup wheat germ plus 2 tablespoons
1½ to 2 cups bread or unbleached all-purpose
    flour

In the bowl of an electric mixer, dissolve the yeast in warm water (110° F.) and let rest for 10 minutes until bubbly. Add the buttermilk, salt, whole rye and whole wheat flours, and ¼ cup wheat germ and mix with whip attachment just until blended. Change to dough hook and mix, adding flour a little at a time until smooth, about 6 minutes.

Turn the dough out onto a floured board and knead for about 5 minutes, or until elastic.

Cover loosely with a towel and let rest for 30 minutes.

Divide the dough into 2 equal parts, and form each into a 6-inch round. Lightly brush each round with water and sprinkle with the remaining wheat germ, pressing it on lightly with your fingers.

Transfer to a greased baking sheet and let rise for 1 hour, until double in size.

Preheat the oven to 400° F.

With a razor blade, cut a crisscross pattern into the top of each loaf. Bake for 30 minutes until nicely brown and the bread sounds hollow when tapped on the bottom.

Let cool completely on racks. Wrap the loaves in clean dish towels or in paper—not plastic—bags.

Makes 2 medium loaves

BAKED BOULDER PEAK

The Boulder yurt is located under Boulder Peak, thus the name of this original dessert —a delectable concoction of cake, chocolate mousse, and meringue. This recipe is simpler for the home cook to make than the fondant covered cake featured at our yard dinner.

FROZEN CHOCOLATE MOUSSE
  8 ounces semisweet chocolate
¼ cup strong black coffee
¾ cup blanched almonds
  1 cup (2 sticks) butter, at room
    temperature
 10 tablespoons sugar
  3 eggs, separated
    Salt
  1 cup heavy cream, whipped

GENOISE MERINGUE

   2 tablespoons (¼ stick) butter
   3 eggs, at room temperature
   ½ cup extrafine sugar
   ½ teaspoon vanilla extract
   1 cup sifted cake flour

   3 egg whites
   ¼ cup sugar
   ¼ cup pine nuts

First make the mousse. Melt the chocolate
with the coffee in the top of a double
boiler. Let cool.

Finely grind the almonds in a coffee or
nut grinder or in a blender. (Be careful not
to overgrind the nuts to a paste.) Set aside.

Cream the butter, add the sugar, and
beat until light and fluffy. Beat in the egg
yolks one at a time. Stir in the ground almonds and the cooled chocolate.

In a clean bowl with a clean beater, beat
the egg whites with a pinch of salt until
stiff but still moist. Using a rubber spatula,
fold the whites into the chocolate mixture.
Fold in the whipped cream.

Line a 9-inch round-bottom bowl with
pieces of foil large enough to hang over the
edge by several inches. Pour in the mousse.
Lay a piece of wax paper on the surface and
fold the overhanging foil over. Freeze for
several hours. (This mousse can also be
made ahead and frozen for as long as 2
months.)

Preheat the oven to 350° F.

To make the cake, first warm a medium
mixing bowl by rinsing it with hot water or
putting it in the oven for a few minutes.
Butter a 9-inch round cake pan, line it with
wax paper, and butter the paper. Set aside.

Melt the butter in a small saucepan and
cool to lukewarm. Put the eggs, sugar, and
vanilla in the warmed bowl and beat with
an electric mixer on high speed until stiff
peaks form. Do not underbeat. Add the
flour in 6 parts, sifting it over the egg mixture and folding it in gently with a rubber
spatula after each addition. Add the melted
butter 1 teaspoon at a time, folding it in
gently but completely. Turn the batter into
the prepared pan and bake for 35 to 40
minutes in the lower third of the oven.

*Good friends share a hearty meal, cozy and warm
in the yurt as night falls on the mountains.*

When done, the cake will bounce back
when gently touched in the center.

To assemble the dessert, put the cake on
a 10-inch pizza pan and place the frozen
mousse on top, rounded side up.

Beat the egg whites until soft peaks begin
to form. Continuing to beat, add the sugar
½ teaspoon at a time until the whites are
stiff and glossy. Spread the meringue over
the mousse and the sides of the cake, making sure the sides are well covered. Form
peak patterns in the meringue by lifting
the meringue with the spatula as you
spread. Sprinkle the pine nuts on the top
and sides.

For an outdoor dinner or in a yurt, the
meringue can be browned in a very hot
wood-fired oven. At home you can place
the cake under the broiler, and broil for
approximately 3 minutes, until the meringue is lightly browned. Cut into wedges
and serve immediately.

Serves 10

MORMON SUNDAY SUPPER

Bountiful, Utah, sitting at the foot of the Wasatch Mountains just north of Salt Lake City, lives up to its name. Each fall I like to travel to Brigham City, just north of Bountiful, to buy fresh fruits and vegetables from the long rows of pro-

duce stands piled high with apples, pears, apricots, peaches, berries, and plums from the orchards that seem to stretch forever. Tomatoes, onions, greens, peas, beans, and corn overflow their bins. At some stands there are homemade jams, preserves, and relishes as well. There is, indeed, a sense of plenty.

Mormon pioneers began cultivating the land as soon as they arrived in the 1840s. Unlike most mid-nineteenth-century pioneers in the Rocky Mountains, they had come not to prospect for the earth's mineral riches but to build a homeland.

Providing themselves with an abundance of healthful foods is not only traditional, it is a part of Mormon religious practice. Grinding wheat at home, baking bread, and canning are as much a part of daily life today as they ever were. The Mormon Church Ladies' Society advises on food preparation, asking each family to store a year's supply of food in their home in case of a natural disaster or other emergency.

When invited to a potluck gathering, a Mormon woman brings twice the amount of food needed to feed her own family. Since families are large, this will prove a prodigious amount. Each family arrives bearing a feast packed in baskets, hampers, and covered dishes. The whole event provides a chance for everyone to sample the specialties of their friends and neighbors.

The following menu, which might be served as a Sunday supper in a Mormon home, would work as well for your own Sunday dinner or as a bountiful spread for a gathering of friends.

MENU for 8

Dilled Beets and Cucumbers

Wilted Lettuce Salad

Tomatoes Stuffed with Fresh Corn

Eggplant Fritters

Blanche's Spicy Pot Roast

Margy's Oatmeal Bread (page 115)

The Original Strawberry Shortcake

Lemon Loaf Cake (page 179)

Mineral Water • Herb Tea

DILLED BEETS AND CUCUMBERS

6 cups water
1 tablespoon distilled white vinegar
1 teaspoon salt
5 medium beets, stemmed and root ends cut off
1 large cucumber
½ cup vegetable oil
2 tablespoons white wine vinegar

1 teaspoon dry mustard
½ teaspoon salt
1¼ teaspoons dried dill
⅛ teaspoon sugar
2 hard-cooked eggs, finely chopped

Place the water, distilled vinegar, and salt in a large saucepan. Heat to boiling and add the beets. When the water returns to a boil, reduce heat to medium, cover, and simmer the beets for about 35 minutes, until tender. Drain, plunge into cold water to cover, then slip off the skins.

Thinly slice the beets. Peel and thinly slice the cucumber. Arrange in overlapping rows on a serving platter.

Place the oil, wine vinegar, mustard, salt, dill, and sugar in a jar with a tight-fitting lid. Shake well, then pour over the vegetables, cover, and refrigerate for 1 to 2 hours. Just before serving, garnish with the chopped eggs.

Serves 8

WILTED LETTUCE SALAD

This is a recipe I learned from my grandmother. It is good made with only very fresh, young, tender leaves—preferably fresh-picked.

    2 medium heads loose-leaf garden lettuce,
       or commercially grown red lettuce
    ¼ pound lean bacon, thinly sliced
    3 tablespoons peanut oil
    2 tablespoons red wine vinegar
       Salt and freshly ground black pepper
    1 egg, scrambled dry (optional)

Wash and dry the lettuce leaves, tear into medium-size pieces, and place in a serving bowl.

Fry the bacon gently for 10 minutes, until lightly browned and crisp. Leave about 3 tablespoons of bacon fat in the pan. Drain the bacon on paper towels, crumble, and reserve.

Add the peanut oil to the bacon fat and heat to sizzling. Quickly whisk in the vinegar and salt and pepper to taste, then pour over the lettuce. Add the bacon and egg, and toss quickly. Serve immediately.

Serves 6 to 8

TOMATOES STUFFED WITH FRESH CORN

This colorful dish is an interesting combination of tastes and textures.

    8 firm ripe tomatoes
       Salt
    ½ cup (1 stick) butter
    ¼ cup onion, chopped
    ¼ cup chopped green bell pepper
    1 tablespoon drained chopped pimiento
    1 cup grated Parmesan cheese
       Kernels cut from 8 medium ears of
       cooked corn (about 6 cups)
       Black pepper

Preheat the oven to 350° F.

Peel and core the tomatoes, remove the pulp, and salt the cavities well. Invert onto a paper towel to drain.

Melt the butter in a skillet, add the onion and pepper and sauté for 10 minutes, until tender. Stir in the pimiento, cheese, and corn, then salt and pepper to taste. Let the mixture cool for a few minutes before stuffing the tomatoes.

Add just enough water to a baking dish to cover the bottom, add the tomatoes, and bake for 30 minutes, or until tops are browned.

Serves 8

EGGPLANT FRITTERS

- 1 large eggplant (about 2 pounds), peeled and cubed
- 1 teaspoon distilled white vinegar
- 1 egg, lightly beaten
- 3 tablespoons all-purpose flour
- ½ teaspoon baking powder
  Pinch of salt and freshly ground black pepper
  Oil or solid vegetable shortening for frying

Cook the eggplant in lightly salted water to cover for 20 minutes, or until just fork-tender. Stir in the vinegar, then drain immediately. (The vinegar keeps the eggplant from discoloring.)

Mash the eggplant in a mixing bowl. Beat in the egg, flour, baking powder, and salt and pepper to taste. Drop by tablespoonfuls into hot fat (about 380° F). Deep-fry, turning once, for about 2 to 3 minutes, or until golden brown. Drain on paper towels. Serve immediately. These may also be fried as pancakes on a hot, well-buttered griddle.

Serves 8

BLANCHE'S SPICY POT ROAST

My friend Blanche Rosenthal gave me this recipe when I was a young wife and was puzzled as to what to cook for dinner.

- 1 blade pot roast (about 4 pounds), or other pot roast cuts can be substituted
- ¼ cup all-purpose flour
  Salt and pepper
- 2 tablespoons vegetable oil
- 1 large onion, sliced
- 1½ cups fresh or canned tomato purée
- 1 cup water
- 2 teaspoons sugar
- 1 teaspoon ground ginger
- ¼ scant cup soy sauce

Preheat the oven to 300° F.

Dredge the beef in flour seasoned with salt and pepper to taste, coating well on all sides. Shake off the excess flour.

Heat the oil in a deep, heavy skillet. Add the beef and brown over high heat for 10 minutes, turning once. Remove to a roasting pan with a lid and spread the onion slices on top.

In a small bowl, mix the remaining ingredients, sprinkle with ¼ teaspoon black pepper, and pour over the beef. Cover and roast for 3 hours, or until tender. Use any sauce left in the pan to serve with meat.

Serves 8

THE ORIGINAL STRAWBERRY SHORTCAKE

Strawberry shortcake is a traditional dessert in the Rocky Mountain West. Shortcake should be true to its name. Here's a recipe for the real thing.

- ½ cup (1 stick) unsalted butter, melted
- 1 egg, lightly beaten
- 1½ cups heavy cream, 1 cup whipped
- 2 cups presifted all-purpose flour
- 2 tablespoons sugar, plus additional for berries if desired
- ½ teaspoon salt
- 4 teaspoons baking powder
- 3 pints fresh strawberries, hulled

Preheat the oven to 450° F. Butter an 8-inch square cake pan.

Place the butter, egg, and ½ cup heavy cream in a medium mixing bowl and stir until well blended. Combine the flour, sugar, salt, and baking powder in a bowl. Add to the egg mixture and mix well. Pour into the cake pan. Bake for about 10 to 15 minutes, or until the top is browned and a cake tester comes out clean.

Meanwhile, slice and partially crush the strawberries, reserving 6 or 8 perfect ones for a garnish. If you wish, the sliced berries can be sweetened with a little sugar.

To serve, cut the cake into squares while still warm, spoon a heaping portion of sliced berries on each, and top with a large dollop of whipped cream. Garnish with the whole (halved, if large) strawberries.

Serves 8 or more

COUNTRY INN
BREAKFAST

More and more wonderful Victorian houses of the Rockies are being refurbished and turned into country inns. Offering bed, breakfast, and a welcome respite from motels, the buildings are usually of real historical and architectural interest. Providing customers with the sense of being a guest in a grand home, these inns, even those located in towns, have a country feeling and often a country garden as well, like the lovely one of wisteria, poppies, and briar roses at the Briar Rose, an elegantly refurbished Victorian brick house in Boulder, Colorado.

The Voss Inn in Bozeman, Montana, serves eggs with salsa, fresh fruits sautéed in butter, and the house special—freshly baked sticky buns. El Paradero in Santa Fe, New Mexico, treats guests to *huevos rancheros* and blue corn muffins, while the Hearthstone Inn in Colorado Springs, Colorado, is known for its freshly baked breads and baked eggs, as well as for its view of Pikes Peak.

The delicious and varied breakfasts these inns serve share equal billing with their unique architectural style. Few things seem more wonderful than waking up in a warm, nostalgic atmosphere to the fragrance of a home-cooked breakfast. Provid-

---

M E N U for 8

Huevos Rancheros with Salsa Picante

Homemade Hot Sausage Patties

Orange-Honey Muffins

Buttermilk Biscuits

Buckwheat Honey

Orange Marmalade

Rhubarb Jam

Fruit Juice • Coffee • Tea

The veranda of the Hearthstone Inn in Colorado Springs. The Inn provides a gracious atmosphere for overnight guests and for those who come just for one of the wonderful breakfasts.

ing your own home with the same kind of atmosphere is equally satisfying.

The menu that follows is a typical country breakfast in the Rocky Mountain West. The nice thing about cooking this special breakfast is that you can get the maximum effect without having to spend hours in the kitchen. For instance, if you use a food processor for the Orange-Honey Muffins or the Buttermilk Biscuits, the preparation takes only a few minutes, and the baking gets done while you tend to the eggs.

HUEVOS RANCHEROS WITH SALSA PICANTE

I use salsa in my version of *huevos rancheros*; the fresh taste of the uncooked sauce is a wonderful complement to the eggs. Cook the eggs in two batches—or more, if you don't have a skillet large enough to hold eight eggs in a single layer.

16 eggs
    Salsa Picante (recipe follows)
    Fresh coriander (cilantro)

Cook eggs sunny side up, transferring them to a warm platter as they are cooked. Spoon the salsa around and over the eggs, but do not cover the yolks. Garnish with coriander. Serve immediately with more salsa on the side.

Serves 8

Salsa Picante

    4 small hot chiles (serrano or jalapeño), seeded and finely sliced
    4 small mild chiles (poblano, banana, or Anaheim), seeded and finely sliced
    4 ripe medium tomatoes, seeded and chopped
    4 scallions, minced
    ½ cup minced fresh parsley
    ½ cup minced fresh coriander (cilantro)
        Juice of 1 lime
        Pinch of sugar
        Salt and white pepper

Do not make the salsa in a food processor or it will have no character. Everything must be chopped by hand.

Use rubber gloves to seed and slice the hot chiles. Toss all the ingredients in a medium mixing bowl and blend well. Pour into a glass jar, cover, and refrigerate if not using the same day. Bring to room temperature before serving.

Makes 4 cups

HOMEMADE HOT SAUSAGE PATTIES

Homemade sausage involves very little work to make and is far superior in taste to ready-made breakfast sausage.

    1½ pounds fatback or salt pork, cut into ½-inch cubes
    3 pounds lean boneless pork shoulder, coarsely ground
    2 tablespoons salt
    ½ teaspoon freshly ground black pepper
    1 teaspoon crumbled dried sage
    ½ teaspoon dried red pepper flakes

If using salt pork, boil it for 10 minutes, drain, and rinse. Grind the fatback or salt pork in a food processor until it is a paste. Add the rest of the ingredients and process briefly, just until everything is well blended. Shape mixture into 3-inch patties. Wrap them separately and freeze or use immediately.

Makes approximately 14 to 16 patties

Note: For mild sausage, eliminate the sage and red pepper flakes, and add 1 teaspoon of a mixture of ground cinnamon, nutmeg, and cloves, or 1 teaspoon of *quatre épices* (a French mixture of seasonings for sausage meats available at gourmet shops).

ORANGE-HONEY MUFFINS

Many of the recipes I have tried for orange muffins haven't tasted orangy enough. This one uses the entire orange and is wonderfully flavorful. I like to serve the muffins warm from the oven with orange marmalade or with buckwheat honey, available at most health food stores.

- **1 orange, with deep color and thin rind**
- **½ cup plain yogurt**
- **4 tablespoons (½ stick) unsalted butter, softened**
- **1 egg**
- **½ cup honey**
- **1½ cups presifted all-purpose flour**
- **1 teaspoon baking powder**
- **1 teaspoon baking soda**
- **½ teaspoon salt**
- **½ cup golden raisins**

Preheat the oven to 400° F. Butter and lightly flour a 12-cup muffin tin.

Peel the orange rind in thin strips with a vegetable peeler, and remove the pith if it is very thick. Cut the flesh into bite-size pieces. Place the peel in the bowl of a food processor, and using the metal blade, chop by turning the machine on and off a few times. Add the orange pieces, yogurt, butter, egg, and honey. Mix well until blended.

Combine the dry ingredients and raisins in a large bowl. Add the orange mixture and stir just until blended; do not overmix. Spoon into the muffin tin, filling the cups almost to the top to make large, high-topped muffins. Bake for about 20 minutes, or until nicely browned.

Makes 12 large muffins

BUTTERMILK BISCUITS

My grandmother used to make these biscuits and serve them with gravy for breakfast. Light and flaky, they taste even better with berry jams or honey. They should be served hot from the oven.

- **1 teaspoon baking soda**
- **1 cup buttermilk**
- **4 tablespoons (½ stick) unsalted butter, chilled**
- **2 cups presifted all-purpose flour**
- **1 teaspoon salt**
- **2 teaspoons baking powder**

Preheat the oven to 425° F.

Dissolve the baking soda in the butter-milk in a medium mixing bowl. Cut the butter into small dice and put it in a food processor with the flour, salt, and baking powder. Turn the machine on and off quickly several times, just until the mixture has the texture of coarse meal. Add to the buttermilk, mixing with a fork until the dough can be formed into a ball.

Turn out the dough onto a floured board and roll to a ½-inch thickness. Cut into 1½-inch rounds with a cookie cutter or a glass. Place about 2 inches apart on an ungreased cookie sheet. Bake for 12 to 15 minutes, or until nicely browned.

Makes 24 biscuits

RHUBARB JAM

- **4 cups sliced rhubarb, about ½ inch thick (about 2 pounds)**
- **4 cups sugar**
- **½ cup chopped dried apricots**

Mix the rhubarb and sugar in a medium glass or pottery bowl, cover loosely with a cloth, and let stand for 12 hours.

Pour the rhubarb mixture into a heavy 3-quart saucepan, add the apricots, and boil until thick, about 30 minutes.

Spoon mixture immediately into hot jars and process in a Hot-Water Bath (see page 170). The jam will keep indefinitely in a cool, dark place. You can also store it unsealed in the refrigerator for about 2 weeks.

Make 3 half-pints

A young Basque musician, after playing a full day of music for dance competitions, might join friends and family for dinner at a favorite Basque restaurant.

BASQUE RESTAURANT FAMILY-STYLE DINNER

....

Many Basque restaurants still serve family-style meals. Their atmosphere varies from country club to boardinghouse to nightclub, but the food is always uniquely Basque and reasonably priced. Proud of their cuisine, early-day Basque boardinghouses in the Rockies vied for business by preparing the best food possible. Dishes reserved for holidays in the old country were often served for everyday meals. If they couldn't be near the families left behind, at least the immigrant Basques could eat well.

Some of the original establishments have been renovated and still operate as boardinghouses, hotels, and restaurants. My favorites are those with the atmosphere of a social hall, with the restaurant functioning as a gathering spot for locals, dinner guests, and tourists. The focal point of these restaurants is the bar, often an ornately carved antique, where the traditional Picon Punch, a Basque apéritif, is served.

Diners, sitting together at long tables, are brought serving platters generously piled with food. There is usually a choice of main dishes, such as beefsteak, roast lamb, or chicken, and as soon as you order, the side dishes begin appearing. A terrine of homemade soup may be followed by pasta, or a stew made with oxtails, tongue, tripe, or pigs' feet, and a green salad. Next comes the main dish, accompanied by French fries and a vegetable. The hearty red jug wine and French bread on the table are constantly replenished. Desserts are very simple—a choice of flan or ice cream.

The authentic Basque-American recipes in the following menu have been collected from both restaurants and friends. (I have not included a recipe for the steak and French fries. Cook them by your preferred method.)

....

RELISH DISH

Raw celery and carrot sticks, radishes, and pickles and olives are what we in the West call a relish dish. This used to be part of every Sunday and holiday dinner table. Arrange the vegetables in contrasting color groupings in a shallow relish dish lined with spinach leaves or parsley. Leave a bit of stem on each radish and a few leaves on the celery sticks.

....

WINTER VEGETABLE SOUP

This is a wonderfully hearty soup, especially satisfying in cold weather.

> 2 tablespoons (¼ stick) butter
> 2 medium leeks, washed well and chopped
> 5 garlic cloves, minced
> 8 cups homemade or canned beef stock
> 3 medium potatoes, peeled and diced
> 1 to 1½ pounds bananas, or hubbard squash, peeled and diced

---

M E N U for 8
....
Relish Dish
Winter Vegetable Soup
Oxtail Stew
Basque Green Salad
Steak
French Fries
Sourdough French Bread
Caramel Custard Flan
Red Wine • Coffee

4 medium carrots, scrubbed and finely
    chopped
½ teaspoon ground cloves
½ teaspoon ground thyme
    Pinch of freshly grated nutmeg
½ cup minced fresh parsley

Melt the butter in a large, heavy-bottom pot. Add the leeks and cook for 30 minutes, until soft. Add the garlic and cook for a few minutes more. Pour in the stock and bring to a boil. Stir in the remaining ingredients and simmer over low heat for about 30 minutes, until the vegetables are tender.

Serves 8

. . . .

OXTAIL STEW

    6 pounds oxtail pieces
    2 tablespoons all-purpose flour
½ teaspoon salt
    Freshly ground black pepper
    3 tablespoons vegetable oil
    2 medium onions, chopped
    2 garlic cloves, minced
    1 (8-ounce) can tomato sauce
    2 bay leaves
    1 (2-inch) branch fresh thyme, or ⅛
        teaspoon dried
    2 tablespoons minced fresh parsley
2½ cups hearty red wine
    1 quart water
    3 medium carrots, cut into thick slices
    1 medium green bell pepper, seeded, pith
        removed, and coarsely chopped

Dredge the oxtails in a mixture of flour, salt, and pepper. Heat the oil in a heavy-bottom pot. Quickly brown the oxtails over high heat, turning them with a fork to brown on all sides. Add the onions and garlic, and continue cooking over low heat for about 15 minutes, until the onions are soft.

Add the tomato sauce, bay leaves, thyme, parsley, wine, and water. Cook at a slow simmer for 3 hours or more, until the oxtails are tender. Add the carrots and green pepper the last 30 minutes of cooking. Before serving, remove bay leaves, taste for seasoning.

Serves 8

. . . .

BASQUE GREEN SALAD

This is a simple lettuce salad, tossed with a delicious garlic-flavored mayonnaise dressing. Many Basque restaurants often make the salad the traditional way, with iceberg lettuce, which I think was the only kind of lettuce available in the early days. You can also use romaine, endive, or chicory—or any combination of greens. Don't use a delicate butter or red lettuce, because the dressing will make the leaves too limp.

½ cup garlic oil (see Note)
    1 tablespoon plus 1 teaspoon white wine
        vinegar
        Salt and freshly ground pepper
    1 hard-cooked egg, chopped
    1 cup mayonnaise, homemade or
        commercial
    1 garlic clove
    2 large heads lettuce or other greens,
        washed and thoroughly dried, then
        chilled

Put the garlic oil, vinegar, and salt and pepper to taste in a small bowl and stir with a fork or whisk. Mix the egg and mayonnaise in a separate bowl with a fork.

Tear the greens into bite-size pieces and place in a salad bowl rubbed with garlic. Add the oil and vinegar mixture and 2 full tablespoons of the mayonnaise mixture. Toss well. Serve immediately. (Leftover mayonnaise can be saved in the refrigerator for another use.)

Serves 8 to 10

Note: To make the garlic oil, soak 2 peeled garlic cloves in 3 cups vegetable or peanut oil for several days.

. . . .

SOURDOUGH FRENCH BREAD

Increase your starter by adding 1 cup water and 1 cup flour. Measure out 1 cup to make the sponge, and return the rest to the refrigerator.

SPONGE

    4 cups bread or all-purpose flour
1½ cups lukewarm water (85° F.)
    1 cup sourdough starter (page 131)

BATTER

    1 teaspoon yeast
    ¼ cup lukewarm water (80° F.)
    2 teaspoons sugar or honey
    2 cups bread or all-purpose flour
    1 teaspoon salt

Combine the 1 cup starter, flour, and water in a large pottery or glass bowl, cover with a cloth, and let ferment overnight in a warm place. The next morning measure out 1 cup of starter mixture, put it in a jar or crock for future use, cover, and return to the refrigerator.

The next morning, transfer the sponge to the bowl of an electric mixer. Mix the yeast into the warm water in a small bowl, set aside for 5 to 10 minutes, until it bubbles. Add the yeast, sugar or honey, and 1 cup flour to the sponge, and mix on low speed until it is incorporated. Continue to beat, adding more flour little by little—up to 1 cup, until the dough is smooth and elastic, beating for a total of 6 minutes.

Turn the dough out onto a floured board and knead a few minutes. Put the dough into a large bowl, cover, and let rise in a warm place until doubled in size.

Turn out onto a floured board and punch down. Cut the dough in half and form each piece into a ball. Roll each ball into an oval loaf about 16 inches long. Place the loaves on a greased or cornmeal-layered baking pan. Cover the loaves with a cloth and let rise until doubled in size, 1 to 2 hours, depending on altitude and strength of starter.

Preheat oven to 400° F. and put a small ovenproof dish of hot water in the bottom. Bake the loaves for 45 to 50 minutes, until nicely browned and hollow sounding when tapped on the bottom. Cool on a rack. Store in paper—not plastic—bags or wrap in a cloth towel.

Makes 2 large loaves

. . . .

CARAMEL CUSTARD FLAN

KESACUMAU

Here is a simple recipe for a classic Basque dessert that has been Americanized by the use of evaporated milk. It makes the smoothest, most perfect flan!

1½ cups sugar
    3 egg whites
    8 egg yolks
    2 (12-ounce) cans evaporated milk
    2 teaspoons vanilla extract

Preheat the oven to 350° F.

Place ¾ cup of the sugar in a heavy skillet and stir constantly over medium heat for 7 to 10 minutes, until it has melted and turned golden brown. Remove from the heat and immediately pour into a 5-cup ring mold. Set aside.

Whisk the egg whites and yolks in a mixing bowl until thoroughly blended. Add the evaporated milk and the rest of the sugar, and mix well. Stir in the vanilla. Pour the mixture through a strainer into the caramel-coated mold. Place the mold in a larger pan filled with enough hot water to come halfway up the mold. Bake for about 1 hour, or until a knife inserted in the center comes out clean.

Let the custard cool for about 10 minutes at room temperature, then unmold onto a serving platter while still warm, or the caramel will stick. Chill before serving.

Serves 8 to 10

. . . .

NEW MEXICO–STYLE SUPPER

New Mexican food, a meshing of Pueblo, Spanish, and Anglo culinary traditions usually referred to simply as "Mexican" throughout the Rockies, is as popular in the region as it is in much of the rest of the country. The intertwining of Native American and Spanish cuisines was a long, slow process, developing over the course of more than two hundred years. They were anglicized more quickly. In recent decades the cuisine and culture of both the Spanish and the Native Americans have gained so appreciative a following they've become downright fashionable.

Good Mexican restaurants in the Rockies offer the whole gamut of New Mexico's culinary styles and heritage, while pure forms of Spanish and Native American cuisines remain alive in private homes, usually those on the reservations.

Traditional foods, like the chiles in the Rice and Chile Casserole, have been used in New Mexican cooking for hundreds of years. Some other foods like posole, a staple in supermarkets throughout New Mexico, are harder to find out of the region, except in markets well stocked with Mexican foods, where posole is also available frozen.

The menu that follows includes a number of dishes that are New Mexican in flavor and style. The Capirotada is an interesting twist on bread pudding, while Chocolate Meringues with Pine Nuts reflect the Mexican penchant for chocolate—and make a perfect, satisfying end to this cozy fireside supper.

POSOLE

Posole is a well-known Spanish-American dish that New Mexicans often serve for festive occasions. It is sometimes difficult to find the dried white corn or the refrigerated hominy widely used in New Mexico, so this recipe is made with canned hominy, with equally good results.

> 3 quarts water
> 1 pork shoulder roast (about 3 pounds)
> 1 medium onion, chopped
> 2 teaspoons dried mint
> 1½ teaspoons dried oregano
> 4 to 6 large dried mild red chiles
>   Salt
> 3 (29-ounce) cans white hominy, drained

Put the water and meat in a large kettle. Add the onion, mint, and oregano. Seed the chiles, break them into 1-inch pieces, and add to the pot. Add salt to taste. Cover and simmer for 2½ to 3 hours, or until the meat is tender.

Shred the meat, discarding any gristle or bone, and return the meat to the pot along with the hominy. Cover and simmer for 30 minutes.

Serves 6

Note: If using dried hominy, place 2½ cups corn kernels in 5 quarts of water, add the onion and spices, and simmer, covered, for 3¼ to 4 hours. Add the meat, cover, and simmer for 2½ to 3 hours more. Shred the meat, discarding any gristle or bones, and return it to the pot. Reheat to serve.

M E N U for 6

Posole

Green Bean Soufflé

Rice and Chile Casserole

Fruit Salad with Brandy Dressing

Karen's Cheddar Corn Bread

Capirotada

Chocolate Meringues with Pine Nuts

Beer • Coffee

GREEN BEAN SOUFFLÉ

2 pounds green beans, stringed and tips
    removed
2 tablespoons vegetable or peanut oil
1 medium onion, finely chopped
1 garlic clove, minced
3 ripe medium tomatoes, peeled, seeded,
    and chopped; or 3 whole canned tomatoes,
    drained and chopped
    Several sprigs of fresh basil, minced; or
    ½ teaspoon dried
½ cup grated Monterey Jack cheese
    Salt and pepper
2 eggs, separated
¼ cup bread crumbs
2 tablespoons (¼ stick) butter, in pieces

Preheat the oven to 375° F.

Put the beans in a large pot, add water to cover by 2 inches, and boil for 15 to 20 minutes, until tender. Drain, cool, and chop.

Heat the oil in a large, deep skillet and sauté the onion and garlic for about 5 minutes, until the onion is soft and transparent. Add the beans, tomatoes, basil, cheese, and salt and pepper to taste.

Put the egg whites in a small bowl and beat until stiff. Beat the yolks briefly in a separate bowl, and fold in the whites.

Butter a 3-quart casserole and sprinkle the bottom and sides with half the bread crumbs. Pour in one-third of the batter, then half the bean mixture. Repeat layers, ending with the egg batter. Sprinkle the remaining bread crumbs on top. Dot with the butter. Bake for 30 minutes until browned.

Serves 6 to 8

. . . .

RICE AND CHILE CASSEROLE

1 (7-ounce) can whole green chiles, drained
8 ounces Monterey Jack cheese, thinly
    sliced
4 cups cooked short-grain brown rice
2 cups sour cream
2 tablespoons minced fresh chives; or
    scallions with some of the green part
½ teaspoon paprika
    Salt and pepper
2 tablespoons (¼ stick) butter, in pieces

Preheat the oven to 350° F.

Slit each chile lengthwise down one side and stuff with 2 to 3 cheese slices.

Spread one-third of the rice in a buttered 3-quart casserole. Spread 1 cup of the sour cream over. Lay the chiles on top. Spread with one-third more of the rice, then another cup of sour cream. Top with remaining rice and any cheese slices not used in the chiles. Sprinkle with paprika, add salt and pepper to taste, and dot with the butter. Bake for 20 to 30 minutes, or until heated through.

Serves 6 to 8

. . . .

FRUIT SALAD WITH BRANDY DRESSING

1 small pineapple, peeled, cored, and cut
    into 1-inch chunks
1 large banana, sliced
1 large grapefruit, peeled, sliced, and
    slices cut into quarters
1 large orange, peeled, sliced, and slices
    cut into quarters
1 green apple, unpeeled, cored and sliced
1 red apple, unpeeled, cored and sliced
1 pound seedless green grapes
½ cup pecan halves
2 tablespoons brandy
½ cup fresh orange juice
3 cardamom seeds, crushed
    Sprigs of fresh mint, for garnish

Toss the fruits in a large bowl. Add the pecans, brandy, orange juice, and cardamom seeds, then toss again. Garnish with mint.

Serves 6 to 8

. . . .

KAREN'S CHEDDAR CORN BREAD

The recipe for this hearty bread comes from my friend, Karen Fisher. Serve it warm from the oven with homemade soup for a filling supper on a chilly fall evening.

¼ cup vegetable oil
½ cup onion, finely minced
3 tablespoons minced fresh parsley

1 cup yellow cornmeal
1 cup presifted all-purpose flour
2 teaspoons baking powder
½ teaspoon salt
½ teaspoon dried thyme
1 egg
1 cup buttermilk
1 cup grated sharp cheddar cheese

Preheat the oven to 375° F.

Heat the oil in a frying pan and sauté the onion for 10 minutes, on low heat, stirring occasionally until soft. Add the parsley.

Mix the dry ingredients in a large bowl. In a small bowl, beat the egg with the buttermilk, and stir into the dry ingredients. Stir in the onion, cheese, and parsley. Pour into a lightly buttered 8- or 9-inch square pan and bake for 25 to 30 minutes, or until the bread is lightly browned and has drawn away from the sides of the pan.

Serves 6

. . . .

CAPIROTADA
Mexican Bread Pudding

2 cups water
1 cup light brown sugar
1 (3-inch) cinnamon stick
1 whole clove
6 slices white bread (about 6 cups cubed)
3 bananas, sliced
1 cup raisins
1½ cups chopped blanched almonds
½ pound Monterery Jack cheese, cubed

Preheat the oven to 350° F. Generously butter a shallow 2-quart casserole.

Combine the water, brown sugar, cinnamon stick, and clove in a small saucepan, and boil for a few minutes until syrupy. Remove the cinnamon and clove.

Trim the crusts from the bread, then toast and cube each slice. Place in casserole. Cover with the bananas and sprinkle on the raisins, almonds, and cheese. Pour the syrup over the top a little at a time; wait until each addition of syrup is absorbed by the bread before pouring more so that it doesn't all sink to the bottom.

Bake for about 30 minutes, or until browned on top. Serve hot or warm.

Serves 6 to 8

. . . .

CHOCOLATE MERINGUES WITH PINE NUTS

1 cup (6-ounce package) semisweet chocolate chips
2 egg whites, at room temperature
Salt
1 cup plus ½ teaspoon sugar
1 teaspoon vanilla extract
½ teaspoon distilled white vinegar
¾ cup pine nuts

Preheat the oven to 350° F. Butter a cookie sheet, and line it with parchment paper.

Melt the chocolate chips in a small pan in the oven and set aside to cool.

With a rotary beater or an electric mixer, beat the egg whites with a pinch of salt until foamy. Add the sugar gradually, ¼ teaspoon at a time, while continuing to beat until stiff peaks form. Stir in the vanilla and vinegar just until thoroughly mixed. Fold in the chocolate and nuts.

Drop the batter by teaspoonfuls 2 inches apart on the cookie sheet. Bake for 10 minutes. The cookies will still feel soft to the touch, but they can be easily removed from the sheet with a spatula. Place on wax paper to cool. The cookies will become firmer as they cool.

Makes 2 dozen

. . . .

MARIA'S MOUNTAIN WEDDING

My daughter's wedding was a perfect garden event on a warm and sunny August afternoon. Wild and garden flowers bloomed everywhere in profusion. On all sides there were clear mountain views. The reception buffet, set under a white canopy in an aspen grove, was spread on tables covered with

---

M E N U for 30 or more

Alaskan King Salmon with Sorrel Sauce

Brie en Brioche

Rounds of Huntsman's Cheddar

Green and Red Goat Cheese Torte

Fresh Fruit Trays

Rabbit Pâté

Freshwater Bass Ceviche with Herbed Toast Rounds

Ham and Rice Pâté

Beef Tenderloin with Béarnaise Sauce

Baguettes

Miniature Croissants

Watermelon Baskets

Poppyseed Wedding Cake

White Wine Punch
Mineral Water • Champagne
Coffee

76

It was a beautiful day for a wedding, clear and warm, with the Sawtooth peaks of Idaho providing a dramatic backdrop. The bride and groom had the first dance to start off the celebration.

flower prints. Flower-print umbrellas sheltered the champagne and cake.

Outdoor weddings, whatever the setting and no matter how lavish or simple, are undeniably romantic and festive. Guests always seem freer, more relaxed. There is a sense of informality at even the most formal affair. It is as if all of nature joined in the ceremony, giving both its blessing and its beauty.

For Maria's wedding, we selected a classic wedding menu that was suited to the mountains. Catered by my staff, we got our croissants and French breads fresh from a local bakery. The season's fresh fruit was presented on three tiers of clear glass dishes. Our arrangements consisted of fresh rosy apricots, seeded and halved; purple prunes and red and green plums, seeded and halved; fresh pineapple sticks; and green grapes and papaya slices. At the top of each tier we placed a whole fresh pineapple.

The recipes given here are adapted to the home kitchen to serve around 30 or more people, but you can easily increase the quantities to serve more. Maria's wedding reception was for 180.

. . . .

ALASKAN KING SALMON WITH SORREL SAUCE

A whole Alaskan king salmon makes a spectacular display on a buffet table. This

recipe is gauged to a home oven, but it's best in any case to measure your oven as well as the fish before you make your purchase. If you find that the salmon is still a tight fit for the oven, cut off the head and tail, steam them separately, and arrange them on the serving platter so that the fish appears whole.

For this menu, I had a freshly caught salmon flown in from Alaska. (For mail order, see page 187.)

> 1 **Alaskan king salmon (15 to 18 pounds), cleaned**
> ¼ **cup olive oil**
> 4 **tablespoons (½ stick) butter, melted**
> 1 **medium onion, coarsely chopped**
> 2 **sprigs of fresh tarragon**
> 2 **sprigs of fresh thyme**
> 2 **bay leaves**
> 10 **sprigs of fresh parsley**
> **Salt and freshly ground black pepper**
> ½ **cup dry white wine**
> 4 **cucumbers**
> **Enoki mushrooms, fresh sorrel leaves, and watercress, for garnish**
> **Sorrel Sauce (recipe follows)**

Preheat the oven to 400° F.

Lay the fish on a large piece of aluminum foil, and rub it thoroughly inside and out with a mixture of the oil and butter. Place the onion and herbs in the cavity and sprinkle with salt and pepper to taste. Bring the sides of the foil up around the fish and pour the wine over the top and into the cavity. Cover with another large piece of foil, and tightly pinch the edges of the 2 pieces of foil together.

Place the fish in the oven, turn the heat down to 375° F., and bake for 40 minutes, or until the juices run clear and the flesh at the thickest part near the backbone is opaque. Test for doneness with the point of a sharp knife. Do not overcook. Let the fish cool in the wrap, then refrigerate.

Before serving, scrape off all the skin, fat, and brown surface flesh.

Wash and score the cucumbers with the tines of a fork, then slice thinly. Cover the fish with the cucumber slices arranged in an overlapping pattern to resemble scales. Garnish with Enoki mushrooms, large fresh sorrel leaves, and watercress. Serve with Sorrel Sauce on the side.

Serves 30 to 40

. . . .

Sorrel Sauce

> 4 cups shredded fresh sorrel leaves
> 3 cups sour cream
> 1 cup heavy cream
> Salt and white pepper to taste

Combine all the ingredients and blend well with a fork. Refrigerate until ready to use. This sauce is also good with eggs or with other kinds of fish.

Makes about 5 cups

. . . .

BRIE EN BRIOCHE

> 2 packages active dry yeast
> ½ cup warm milk (105° to 115° F.)
> 1 teaspoon sugar
> 1½ cups (3 sticks) unsalted butter, at room temperature
> 6 cups presifted all-purpose flour
> 8 whole eggs
> 2 egg yolks
> 2 eggs plus 1 egg yolk, lightly beaten
> 1 (5½-pound) brie cheese with a solid crust, no cracks, and just at the point of ripeness
> Purple grapes, for garnish

Put the yeast and milk in a small bowl, mix with a fork, and set aside for 5 minutes to let the mixture work until bubbly.

Combine the sugar, butter, flour, whole eggs, and egg yolks in a large bowl of an electric mixer. Mix on slow speed until well blended. Add the yeast mixture, increase to medium speed, and beat for 5 to 6 minutes, stopping once to scrape the bottom and sides of the bowl. The dough should be very elastic and pull away easily from the sides of the bowl and from the beater.

Divide the dough into 3 parts. Roll out one part to a ¼-inch-thick round 1 inch larger around than the brie. Place the dough on a foil- or parchment-lined cookie sheet, put the brie in the center, and fold

the edges of the dough back against the sides of the brie.

Roll out a second piece of dough to a ¼-inch-thick round 2 inches larger around than the brie. Brush the entire surface with some of the egg wash and place the second dough round over the brie, egg-washed side down. Crimp the top and bottom edges of the dough together (like a pie crust), being sure to seal the brie well so that it won't leak while cooking. Brush the top and sides with the egg wash. Make decorations of your choice with the remaining piece of dough, place on or around the brie, and brush with the egg wash. (I like to make a braid to go all around the outer edge. For this wedding we also made hearts and doves and arranged them inside the braid.) Leave the brie at room temperature for 20 to 30 minutes.

Preheat the oven to 350° F.

Bake the brie for 25 to 30 minutes or until golden brown. To serve, slide onto a large platter or board and surround with purple grapes.

This keeps well at room temperature for several hours, or you can refrigerate or freeze it for several days and reheat in a 400° F. oven for 6 to 10 minutes, or just long enough to warm the crust without melting the cheese.

Serves 30 to 40

. . . .

Guests enjoyed the sunshine while the Alaska
king salmon was being prepared for baking.
Jacquot Chesnel, our inquisitive cat, took a
good look at this impressive display.

Family and friends gathered to share the occasion at a private log home, situated on a high ledge surrounded by the Sawtooth and the Whitecloud mountains. Everyone had a perfect day.

GREEN AND RED GOAT CHEESE TORTE

    1 pound firm white imported goat cheese
      (chèvre), such as Lezay
    1 pound cream cheese, softened
    3 cups (6 sticks) unsalted butter
    1 (6½-ounce) jar sun-dried tomatoes in oil,
      drained and finely chopped
    3 cups lightly packed fresh basil leaves
    ½ cup parsley sprigs
 1½ cups freshly grated Romano cheese
    ½ cup olive oil
    ¾ cup pine nuts
      Opal basil sprigs, for garnish

Combine the goat cheese, cream cheese, and butter in a food processor. Divide the mixture into 2 equal parts and place in separate bowls. Add the tomatoes to one part, combining well with a fork.

Make a pesto sauce by combining the basil, parsley, Romano cheese, oil, and half the pine nuts in the bowl of a food processor. Process just until well blended.

Butter an 8-inch springform pan (see Note). Add alternate layers of the red and white cheese mixtures, spreading the green pesto mixture between at least 2 of the layers. Sprinkle the remaining nuts on top. Cover with plastic wrap and chill for at least 2 hours. (This will keep for 5 days or more if refrigerated.) Unmold onto a chilled tray, garnish with opal basil.

Serves 30 to 35

Note: You can also use a charlotte mold, a small loaf pan, or any other smooth-sided mold. When using a mold without removable sides, line it with 2 thicknesses of dampened cheesecloth large enough to hang over the edge of the mold by 2 or 3 inches. Fold the excess cloth over the top after filling, and use it to pull the torte free of the pan, unmolding it very neatly.
....

RABBIT PÂTÉ

This is a country style pâté. You can increase the recipe to make two or more.

MARINADE
    ¼ cup cognac
    ¼ cup olive oil
      Pinch of dried thyme
      Pinch of poultry seasoning
    6 black peppercorns
    ½ teaspoon salt
    1 bay leaf
    ½ cup dry white wine
    1 medium carrot, chopped
    2 shallots, chopped
    1 garlic clove
    4 sprigs of fresh parsley

TERRINE
    2 pounds boneless rabbit meat, 1 pound cut
      into 1-inch strips and 1 pound ground
    ½ pound chicken livers, cut into ½-inch
      pieces
 2½ pounds ground pork
    1 pound ground veal
 2½ pounds thick-sliced bacon, boiled 10
      minutes, drained, and rinsed well under
      cold water
    ½ cup whole pistachios
    1 teaspoon fresh thyme, or ¼ teaspoon
      dried
    1 teaspoon salt
    ½ teaspoon freshly ground black pepper
    1 bay leaf

SEASONING MIX
    ½ teaspoon salt
    ⅓ cup Madeira
    2 pinches of poultry seasoning
    4 eggs, lightly beaten

      Buttered French bread
      Cornichons

Mix the marinade ingredients thoroughly in a glass or pottery bowl. Add the rabbit strips and chicken livers, and marinate for 6 hours or overnight. Drain, reserving the marinade.

Combine the ingredients for the seasoning mix and set aside. Put the ground meats in a separate bowl and mix thoroughly. Cut one pound of the bacon into small dice, and using your hands, mix it into the ground meats with the reserved marinade, seasoning mix, pistachios, thyme, and salt and pepper. Fry a small pattie and taste for seasoning.

Preheat the oven to 400° F.

Use several slices of the bacon to line a 2-quart terrine or two 9 x 5 x 3-inch loaf pans. Spread with one-third of the ground meat mixture, then with half the marinated meats. Repeat the layers, ending with the ground meat mixture. Top with the remaining bacon slices and the bay leaf, and cover tightly with foil. Place in a larger pan filled with enough boiling water to come halfway up the terrine. Bake for 2 to 2½ hours, or until the juices run clear. Let cool at room temperature.

Place a heavy weight (can, rock, or brick) on top of the foil and refrigerate for 24 hours or longer. Before serving, unmold and discard the bacon. Slice and serve with buttered French bread and cornichons.

Serves 25 to 30

. . . .

FRESHWATER BASS CEVICHE WITH HERBED TOAST ROUNDS

Freshwater bass fillets (4 pounds), cut into ½-inch cubes
2 pounds small fresh sea scallops, halved
1½ cups fresh lime juice
6 tablespoons olive oil
6 ripe medium tomatoes, chopped
¼ teaspoon dried red pepper flakes
2 cups minced fresh coriander (cilantro)
2 fresh red jalapeños, seeded and minced (see Note)
1 medium onion, minced
1 bunch scallions, finely chopped, including 1 inch of green parts
Salt to taste
Herbed Toast Rounds (recipe follows)

Put the bass and scallops in a large glass or pottery bowl and pour the lime juice over. Cover with plastic wrap and refrigerate for 2 to 3 hours.

Mix all the remaining ingredients into the fish and refrigerate for 1 hour before serving. Serve in the marinade with Herbed Toast Rounds.

Serves 25 to 30

Note: Chiles are very hot, so wear rubber gloves when preparing them to protect your hands.

. . . .

Herbed Toast Rounds

1½ cups (3 sticks) butter
½ cup olive oil
3 tablespoons minced fresh herbs; or 3 teaspoons dried thyme, rosemary, basil, or any combination you prefer
2 long baguettes (French bread), very thinly sliced

Preheat the broiler.

Melt the butter with the olive oil in a medium, heavy-bottom saucepan. Stir in the herbs. Using a pastry brush, butter the bread slices on one side and lay them on a cookie sheet buttered side up. Broil until golden, about 2 to 5 minutes on each side. Let cool before storing in an airtight container. These will keep for several days.

Serves 25 to 30

. . . .

HAM AND RICE PÂTÉ

This elegant free-form pâté is the perfect accompaniment to salmon. The pâté recipe makes enough to serve at least thirty people, but it can be easily cut to make just half or a third for a smaller gathering.

PASTRY (for each pâté)
1 egg
½ cup ice water
6 tablespoons solid vegetable shortening, chilled and cut into small pieces
1 cup (2 sticks) butter, chilled and cut into small dice
4 cups presifted all-purpose flour
½ teaspoon salt

PÂTÉ
½ cup plus 6 tablespoons (1¾ sticks) butter
24 canned or cooked frozen artichoke hearts, drained and chopped
2 (10-ounce) packages frozen peas, steamed and drained
3 tablespoons all-purpose flour
¾ cup heavy cream
2 teaspoons dried dill
Salt
1 teaspoon white pepper
1 tablespoon cider vinegar
1½ pounds baked ham, diced
1½ pounds fresh mushrooms, sliced
3 tablespoons minced fresh parsley
3 tablespoons minced fresh thyme, or 2 teaspoons dried
1 tablespoon lemon juice
Freshly ground black pepper
4½ cups cooked short-grain brown rice
1 tablespoon saffron threads (optional)
1 egg, lightly beaten

If making the full recipe, prepare 3 separate batches of pastry. For each one, beat the egg with the water in a small bowl. Put the rest of the ingredients in the bowl of a large food processor or mixer. Turn the machine on and off several times until the mixture forms small pea-size pieces. With the machine on, slowly add the egg mixture and process just until the dough starts to form a ball. Gather the dough into a ball, wrap, and chill for at least 3 hours.

To make the pâté, melt ½ cup (1 stick) of the butter in a large, heavy-bottom pot. Add the artichoke hearts and peas, sprinkle with the flour, and cook over low heat for 10 minutes, stirring once or twice. With the heat still on low, slowly add the cream, stirring constantly until the flour is incorporated and the sauce is smooth. Stir in the dill, 1 teaspoon salt, white pepper, vinegar, and ham. Set aside to cool.

Melt the remaining 6 tablespoons (¾ stick) of butter in another large, heavy-bottom pot. Add the mushrooms, parsley, thyme, lemon juice, and salt and black pepper to taste. Cook for 5 minutes, until the mushrooms are tender. Add the brown rice and the saffron, if using; blend well.

Preheat the oven to 375° F. Butter a cookie sheet.

On a floured surface, roll out half of 1 ball of pastry dough to a 6 x 14-inch rectangle. Lay the dough on the cookie sheet. Spread with one-third of the mushroom-rice mixture, leaving a ¾-inch border all around. Mound one-third of the artichoke-ham mixture over the rice. Roll out the other half of the dough to another 6 x 14-inch rectangle. Lay it over the filling and crimp the edges of the top and bottom together, rounding the corners to make a mounded oblong form. Use dough scraps to make decorations—either free form or with fancy cutters—for the top. Brush with beaten egg. Repeat the process with the other 2 batches of dough.

Bake for 30 to 40 minutes, or until nicely browned. Let cool at room temperature and slide onto a platter. Serve warm or at room temperature.

Serves 30 to 40

. . . .

BEEF TENDERLOIN WITH BÉARNAISE SAUCE

3 sprigs of fresh tarragon
1 (5-pound) beef tenderloin, trimmed
¼ cup cracked black peppercorns, or coarsely ground pepper

. . . .

An assortment of fresh fruits used to fill watermelon baskets.

2 tablespoons vegetable oil
2 tablespoons (¼ stick) butter
½ teaspoon salt
½ cup finely minced fresh parsley, for
   garnish
   Béarnaise Sauce (recipe follows)

Preheat the oven to 425° F.

Lay the tarragon down the middle of the tenderloin and fold the sides of the meat over it. Tie the meat snugly every 3 inches so that it will keep its shape while cooking (If your butcher has already tied the roast for you, poke some of the tarragon into the crevices between the string.) Spread the peppercorns on a wooden board or wax paper and roll the tenderloin on it to coat all sides.

Heat the oil and butter to sizzling in a skillet large enough to hold the length of the tenderloin. Sear the meat quickly on all sides, then using 2 spatulas, transfer it to a roasting pan. Sprinkle with salt.

Roast for 25 to 30 minutes for rare. When done, let the meat rest on a cutting board for 15 to 20 minutes. Garnish with minced parsley, and bring to the table on the board, decorated with leaves or other greens. Slice to preferred thickness and serve warm or cold with Béarnaise Sauce and baguette slices on the side.

Serves 25

Béarnaise Sauce

2 tablespoons white wine vinegar
¼ cup water
1 teaspoon ground white pepper
5 egg yolks
   Juice of ½ lemon (1 tablespoon)
1 cup (2 sticks) butter
3 tablespoons dry vermouth
3 tablespoons white wine or tarragon
   vinegar
2 shallots, minced
1 tablespoon minced fresh tarragon, or
   1 teaspoon dried

Combine the first 5 ingredients in a blender and blend for 1 minute on low speed.

Heat the butter to sizzling. With the blender on low speed, very gradually add the hot butter, continuing to blend until the mixture thickens. Pour into a small bowl and reserve.

Combine the vermouth, wine or tarragon vinegar, and shallots in a small, heavy saucepan and cook until the mixture is reduced to a scant tablespoon. Stir into the reserved sauce, then add the tarragon. Serve warm or at room temperature.

Makes 1½ cups

WATERMELON BASKETS

2 large watermelons
1 quart fresh blueberries or blackberries
8 cups sliced fresh fruit of your choice
1 quart fresh strawberries, hulled

To make a basket, draw a horizontal line with a sharp pencil around the watermelon one-third of the way down from the top. Draw 2 parallel lines across the top wide enough apart to form a handle.

Cut through the lines with either a heavy knife or a serrated, angled tool made for the purpose. If using a knife, push it through the rind, retract, and push it through again next to the first puncture. Repeat along the line, being careful not to cut through the base of the handle.

Scoop out the flesh from the melons and reserve it for another use. Chill the shells.

When ready to serve, fill the shells with the fruit. Tie a large bow on each basket handle and set the baskets out on platters.

Each basket serves 15 to 20

POPPYSEED WEDDING CAKE

This recipe makes a 10-inch tube cake or a 9-inch two-layer cake. To adapt it for the four-tiered wedding cake, you will need to make the recipe in four separate batches. Do not double the recipe. Each level consists of two layers of the same size put together with buttercream and secured with toothpicks. The two layers are then placed on a cardboard round (cut to size or purchased) and frosted and decorated with buttercream icing. Two layers for each tier, or level, give the cake a much better proportion than one layer per level.

Wooden dowels cut to the appropriate length can be inserted through each set of layers to support the tier above.

For a wedding cake to serve 70 or more people, you will need two 12-inch layers, two 10-inch layers, two 8-inch layers, and two 6-inch layers for the bride's cake at the top. Make the layers as follows:

1. Use one full batch of the cake batter to make one 12-inch layer and one 6-inch layer. Use 2-inch-deep pans and fill them two-thirds full. Then repeat, making another batch of batter for two more layers, one 12-inch and one 6-inch.
2. Use one full batch of the cake batter to make one 8-inch layer and one 10-inch layer. Make another full batch of batter to make one 8-inch layer and one 10-inch layer.

When the cakes are cool they can be wrapped in plastic and refrigerated for up to two days or frozen for up to a month. When ready to frost the cakes, make four times the amount given for the Buttercream Icing (recipe follows). Make it in a large mixer, or if you have a small mixer, double the recipe and make it twice. You will need this much icing for putting the layers together and for icing the cake. You may need more if you want to make elaborate decorations with a pastry tube, or decorate with fresh flowers, if you prefer.

CAKE
- ¾ cup poppy seeds
- 2 cups plain yogurt
- 2 cups (4 sticks) unsalted butter
- 3 cups sugar
- 8 eggs, separated
- 4¼ cups presifted all-purpose flour
- 4 teaspoons vanilla extract
- 4 teaspoons baking soda

BUTTERCREAM ICING
- 1 cup (2 sticks) unsalted butter
- 1 teaspoon orange extract
  Pinch of salt
- 2 tablespoons Cointreau liqueur (optional)
- 1 pound confectioners' sugar
- 6 to 8 tablespoons heavy cream, approximately

Preheat the oven to 375° F. Butter a 10-inch tube pan or two 9-inch round pans, line with wax paper, and butter the paper.

Soak the poppy seeds in the yogurt for 10 minutes. Cream the butter and sugar in a mixer until light and fluffy. Add the yogurt mixture. Beat the egg yolks in a small bowl and add to the yogurt mixture. Add the flour, vanilla, and baking soda, blending just until the dry ingredients are incorporated. In a separate bowl, beat the egg whites until stiff peaks form, then fold gently into the batter.

Pour the batter into the pan(s), spreading evenly with a spatula. Bake for 35 to 45 minutes in the tube pan, or 25 to 30 minutes in round pans—or until a cake tester comes out clean. Cool the cake in the pan(s) for 15 minutes before turning out onto a rack to cool thoroughly.

Whip the butter with an electric mixer until creamy and pale. Add the orange extract, salt, and Cointreau. Slowly beat in the confectioners' sugar. Add the cream, beating until smooth. More cream may be added if necessary to produce the proper consistency for icing the cake.

If baked in a tube pan, the cake can be served plain or iced. If baked in round layer pans, put one layer on a serving platter, spread it with icing, top with the second layer, and spread with icing.

Serves 16

Thanksgiving in the Rockies can bring snow, but an unseasonably warm day allows us to enjoy our feast on the beach at Redfish Lake in the Sawtooth Valley, Idaho.

LAKESIDE THANKSGIVING DINNER

. . . .

This menu is patterned after a dinner I and my staff catered in late fall at a U.S. Forest Service picnic area on the edge of a large alpine lake. Snow began falling as we approached the lake, but the roaring fires we immediately got going in the picnic area's open pits cheered and warmed us.

All the food was prepared ahead of time at home. At the site we built small charcoal fires in the barbecue pits to warm up the vegetables and sauce. We left the hot soup in its thermos and the turkey in an insulated carrier until carving time. Once unwrapped and carved, the turkey as well as the side dishes and store-bought hard rolls were kept warm over the coals.

As guests arrived, white wine was served and a tray of cheeses passed. When it was time to eat, everyone moved along the buffet tables decorated with the last of the season's wildflowers, whose beauty was doubly enhanced by the falling snow, their colors even more jewellike in the winter light.

Hot coffee (which we brought in a thermos, but which could have been made

MENU for 8
. . . .

Assorted Cheese Tray

Butternut Squash Soup

Roast Turkey with Wild Rice Stuffing

Cranberry-Apricot Chutney

Succotash

Hard Rolls

Homemade Mincemeat Pie with Hard Sauce

White Wine • Mineral Water Coffee • Tea

cowboy style or in a percolator over a fire hot enough to boil water) and mince pie, also warmed over the coals, made a satisfying end to a wonderful Thanksgiving.

Depending on where you live, you may choose to have your own Thanksgiving indoors or out. This menu can be easily served either buffet style or to family and friends gathered around the holiday table.

Our friend Edith Weithorn and her granddaughter, Elka.

BUTTERNUT SQUASH SOUP

This soup always gets raves! I concocted it one fall evening when I was thinking of ways to use dried calendula blossoms. Calendula are garden flowers of the marigold family, which I had grown to use as a substitute for costly saffron. Calendula are in fact sometimes called "poor man's saffron." The dried blossoms are also available in herb shops.

Try this soup as the first course of a special menu; the combination of chives, calendula, and squash produces a subtle flavor that is seductive.

2 tablespoons (¼ stick) butter
¼ cup minced onion
1 medium butternut squash, peeled, thinly sliced, and slices cut into lengths of 1 inch or less
2 tablespoons all-purpose flour
6 cups homemade or canned concentrated chicken stock
3 tablespoons minced fresh chives
1 dried calendula blossom, crumbled; or a large pinch of saffron threads
Salt and pepper

Melt the butter in a heavy-bottom pot. Add the onion and cook over low heat for 10 minutes, until soft. Add the squash and the flour, and stir constantly for about 5 minutes. Add the stock, 2 tablespoons of the chives, calendula, and salt and pepper to taste. Simmer over low heat for about 10 minutes, or until the squash is tender but not mushy. Ladle into warm bowls and sprinkle each serving with some of the remaining chives.

If you're going to an outdoor dinner, take the soup in a thermos, or carry it in a jar and heat it in a pot over the fire. Serve in insulated cups.

Serves 8

....

ROAST TURKEY WITH WILD RICE STUFFING

This recipe can be made with either a wild or domestic bird. The wild turkey is considered the most desirable of all game birds, for both its size and its flavor, which is distinctive but not gamey. Unfortunately, there are only a few markets in the West where wild turkeys can be found, but there are some game suppliers who offer wild turkeys seasonally by mail order (see page 187).

>   1 small turkey (about 8 pounds), domestic or wild
> ½ large lemon
> 1½ cups (3 sticks) butter, melted
>   1 teaspoon salt
> Freshly ground black pepper to taste
> Wild Rice Stuffing (recipe follows)
>   2 tablespoons Madeira
> Pinch of dried thyme
> Pinch of dried rosemary
>   2 tablespoons heavy cream

Preheat the oven to 500° F.

Rub the surface and cavity of the turkey with the lemon, then thoroughly coat the surface with some of the melted butter, using a basting brush. Salt and pepper the bird inside and out. Lightly stuff with the Wild Rice Stuffing and sew up the opening. Place the turkey in a roasting pan just large enough to hold it.

In a small saucepan, mix the Madeira with the rest of the butter and bring to a boil. Add the thyme and rosemary. Reserve for basting.

Roast the turkey uncovered for 10 minutes. Turn the heat down to 350° F. and continue to roast for 2 hours (15 minutes per pound), basting frequently until the turkey is nicely browned and tender. Dur-

ing the last 10 minutes of cooking, baste the bird with the cream.

To take to an outdoor dinner, transfer the turkey to a large piece of double-thickness foil and wrap well. Put into a plastic bag, wrap in several layers of newspaper, and place in an insulated carrier. The turkey will stay warm for up to 2 hours.

Serves 8 or more

....

Wild Rice Stuffing

A very good quality wild rice is grown in the northern panhandle of Idaho and is available by mail order (see page 190).

> ½ cup (1 stick) butter
>   4 chicken livers
>   2 tablespoons brandy
> ¼ cup finely chopped shallots
> ¼ cup finely chopped red onion
>   2 cups wild rice, well washed
> 4½ cups chicken stock
> ½ cup chopped celery
> ½ cup chopped green bell pepper
> 1½ cups coarsely chopped cooked chestnuts
> ½ cup minced fresh parsley
> ½ pound pork sausage, cooked, crumbled, and drained on paper toweling
>   1 cup toasted coarse bread crumbs
> ⅛ teaspoon cayenne (ground red) pepper
> ½ teaspoon salt
> Freshly ground black pepper

Melt 2 tablespoons of the butter in a small frying pan. Add the chicken livers and cook over low heat for 6 minutes, or until they are lightly browned and still pink inside. Remove the livers and deglaze the pan with the brandy. Add any liquid and browned bits to the chicken livers.

In a large, heavy-bottom pot, melt 4 tablespoons of the butter and cook the shallots and onion over gentle heat for about 5 minutes, or until they are soft. Stir in the wild rice, stock, celery, and green pepper. Bring to a boil, reduce heat, cover and simmer for 40 to 50 minutes, or until the rice is tender and the stock has been absorbed.

Off the heat, stir in the chestnuts, pars-

Some of the guests, and the family dog, test the waters of the lake, perhaps to further whet their appetites for the rice-stuffed turkey, succotash, and chutney, served in a hollowed-out squash.

ley, sausage, and remaining butter. Coarsely chop the chicken livers and stir them into the rice along with the bread crumbs, cayenne, salt, and pepper to taste.

Makes 8 cups

....

CRANBERRY-APRICOT CHUTNEY

3 tablespoons peanut oil
2 tablespoons yellow mustard seeds
½ pound fresh cranberries
1 pound dried apricots, cut into pieces
2 cups cider vinegar
¼ teaspoon ground cinnamon
1 tablespoon salt
¼ teaspoon ground cloves
1½ cups dark brown sugar, tightly packed
2 tablespoons molasses
¼ cup finely chopped fresh ginger
1 tablespoon garlic, finely chopped
½ cup golden raisins
½ cup apple juice, approximately

Put the oil in a small skillet and fry the mustard seeds quickly over high heat, for about 1 minute; set aside.

Combine the cranberries, apricots, vinegar, cinnamon, and salt in a heavy saucepan. Bring to a boil over medium-high heat, stirring constantly. Stir in the remaining ingredients. Lower the heat and cook for 5 minutes longer. Stir in the mustard seeds, raise the heat, and bring the mixture to a boil. Turn the heat down and simmer, stirring often, for about 10 minutes, or until the mixture thickens but is still moist, adding more apple juice if it seems dry. Let cool.

This chutney will keep well for about 3 to 4 weeks in the refrigerator, or it can be poured into clean jars, processed in a Hot-Water Bath (see page 170), and stored indefinitely in a cool, dark place.

Makes 2 pints

....

SUCCOTASH

Succotash is wonderful when made with fresh corn and a combination of green beans and lima beans.

1 cup (½ pound) dried baby lima beans
4 tablespoons (½ stick) butter
3 cups fresh corn cut from the cob (about 3 medium ears)
1 cup sliced fresh green beans, in ½-inch pieces
½ teaspoon salt
¼ teaspoon paprika
¼ cup chopped fresh parsley

Soak the lima beans overnight in cold water to cover.

Bring the beans to a boil in the water they soaked in, lower the heat, and simmer for about 30 minutes, until tender. Drain. Add 1 tablespoon of butter. Reserve.

Steam the corn kernels and green beans in separate pots, 5 minutes for the corn, 15 for beans, until tender. Combine with the lima beans. Stir in the salt, paprika, parsley, and remaining butter.

Serves 8

....

HOMEMADE MINCEMEAT PIE WITH HARD SAUCE

Here is my mother's mincemeat recipe. It's the real thing, unlike the commercial meatless kind.

MINCEMEAT
2 pounds lean ground beef (or venison or elk, if available)
1 pound ground beef suet
5 pounds tart apples (about 9 large), pared, cored, and finely chopped
3 cups brown sugar, tightly packed
1 cup molasses
1 quart apple cider
1½ pounds dried currants
2 pounds raisins
½ pound diced citron
1 teaspoon ground cloves
1 teaspoon ground cinnamon
1 teaspoon ground mace
1 teaspoon salt
Grated rind and juice of 1 lemon
1 pound walnuts, broken or coarsely chopped

CRUST
3⅓ cups presifted all-purpose flour
1 cup plus 2 tablespoons (2¼ sticks) unsalted cold butter, cut into cubes

⅛ teaspoon salt
1 tablespoon sugar
1 egg beaten with 2 tablespoons ice water
1 tablespoon milk

Combine the mincemeat ingredients in a large, heavy pot, and stir well. Cook over low heat for 2 hours, or until thick but not dry, stirring with a wooden spoon from time to time. Reserve 1 quart for the pie. Can remaining hot mincemeat according to the instructions below.

To make the pie crust, place the flour, butter, salt, and sugar in a food processor. Turn the machine on and off quickly several times until the mixture is in pea-size chunks. With the machine on, add the egg slowly and steadily, stopping as soon as the dough starts to cling together and comes away from the sides of the bowl. Use a bit more cold water if necessary. Form the dough into a ball, wrap in plastic wrap, and refrigerate for at least 30 minutes.

Preheat the oven to 350° F.

Cut dough in half and place half on a well-floured board and roll out a round large enough to line a 10-inch pie pan. To make a lattice-top crust, roll out the remaining dough to the same size. Cut it into long strips about ¾ inch wide, using a pastry crimper for pinked edges or a knife or pastry cutter for straight edges. Closely interweave the strips on wax paper or foil.

Fill the pie shell with the mincemeat. Invert the lattice crust on top and secure the ends to the bottom crust by dampening them with a little water. Crimp the crust all around. Brush with 1 tablespoon of milk. Bake for 30 minutes or until nicely browned. Serve warm or cold with Hard Sauce (recipe follows).

Serves 8

Hard Sauce

½ cup (1 stick) unsalted butter, softened
1 cup confectioners' sugar
1 tablespoon cognac
⅛ teaspoon salt

Cream the butter and sugar until thoroughly mixed. Beat in the cognac and salt. Chill in a shallow dish or in individual decorative molds until ready to use.

Makes about 1 cup

CANNING INSTRUCTIONS FOR MINCEMEAT

Wash four 1-quart jars and their lids in hot soapy water, rinse well, and let drain until dry. Spoon hot mincemeat into the jars to within ½ inch of the top, seal, and process for 20 minutes at 10 pounds pressure in a pressure cooker (240° F.).

If canning at high altitude, add ½ pound to the pressure gauge for each 1,000 feet above sea level. Directions for your pressure cooker should be followed exactly as to how much water to use, etc. The jars should be placed on a rack, but not touching each other. The air should be exhausted from the cooker for at least 10 minutes before closing the steam vent so that the heat will be uniform. Count processing time from the time pressure reaches 10 pounds, usually determined by a constant jiggle of the weight gauge.

Let pressure fall to normal before opening the cooker. Remove jars with tongs and set on a towel to cool. Test for seal after the jars have cooled. Push down the center of the dome. If it is already down or stays down, the jar is sealed. Wait 24 hours and test again if all jars do not seal. If a jar should fail to seal in 24 hours, refrigerate and use mincemeat within 2 days.

If you prefer, you can process mincemeat in a boiling water bath for 90 minutes. Screw the lids on the filled jars and place on a rack in a large pot, making sure the jars do not touch each other or the bottom or sides of the pot. Add enough water to come 2 inches above the tops of the jars. Bring to a full boil, cover the pot, and boil for 90 minutes. As soon as the time is up, remove jars with tongs and place on a cloth to cool. When cool, test for seal. The mincemeat can be kept in a cool, dark place for a year or more.

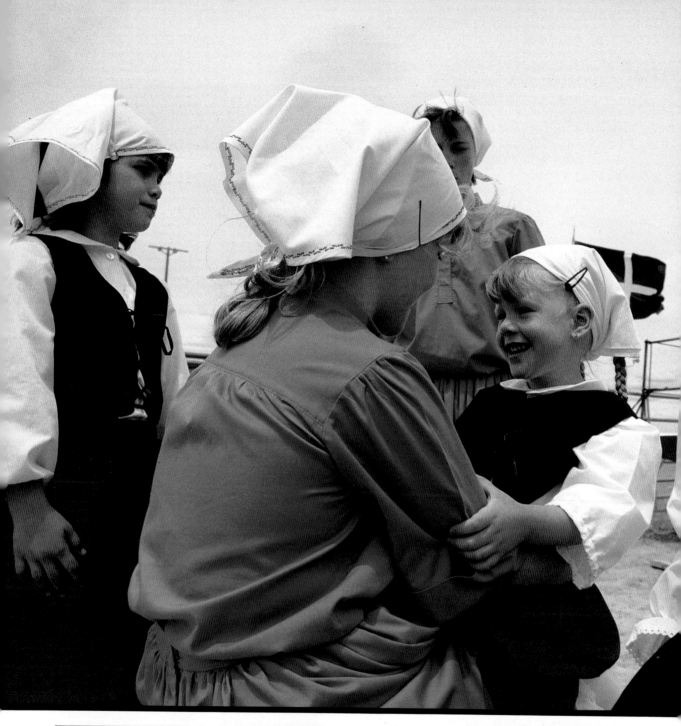

BASQUE FESTIVAL OUTDOOR DINNER

The end of the nineteenth century saw a large migration of Basques from the western Pyrenees to Western America—Idaho, Colorado, Utah, Nevada, and California. Today, second- and third-generation Basques still maintain many of the old ways, celebrating them at annual festivals throughout the West. While no two festivals are exactly alike, they all include marvelous displays of costumes, dancing, games, music, and Basque food, and they form one of the major events of the Basque year.

Although the public is invited to view the dancing and games at many of the festivals, the picnics held at the end are sometimes restricted to Basque participants and their families. An exception is the National Basque Festival in Elko, Nevada, held annually on July 3 and 4, when all events—including the final barbecue, for which tickets are sold—are open to the public.

The food is arranged on long buffet tables set up in a public park. Hundreds of people partake of this gargantuan meal, which goes on all afternoon.

Meat is the mainstay of the Basque diet, and a Basque festival menu almost always includes two meat dishes, usually lamb and beef. The men cook the meat over half-barrels made into barbecue grills. The side dishes, prepared in advance by the women, are flavored with generous quantities of

Young Basque dancers from Boise, Idaho, look fetching in their native costumes.

M E N U for 12

Grilled Beef Steaks

Roast Leg of Lamb

Red Beans with Homemade Chorizos

Chicory Salad

Sourdough Sheepherder Bread

Gâteau Basque

Red Wine • Coffee

Basque men come from many of the western states to help prepare steaks for the crowd.

garlic, red wine, and home-roasted pimientos, ingredients heavily used in the country food of Spain and France.

The usual dessert for a large festival, where the meal itself is so large and filling, is a compote of fruit cooked in red wine. But here I have included my personal favorite, Gâteau Basque. Except for the dessert, the menu that follows is typical for a Basque festival.

At a Basque festival, steaks are simply cooked on an outdoor grill. I have not included a recipe. Prepare your favorite cut on a barbecue grill, perhaps basting with a sauce.

ROAST LEG OF LAMB

    1 leg of lamb with shank (6 to 7 pounds)
    4 garlic cloves, cut in slivers
    1 cup hearty red wine
    ¼ cup olive or vegetable oil
    1 bay leaf
      Salt and freshly ground black pepper

Pierce the lamb in several places with the point of a sharp knife, and insert half the garlic slivers.

Mix the wine, oil, bay leaf, and salt and pepper to taste with the remaining garlic. Rub ½ cup of the mixture into the meat with your hands. Let the lamb rest at room temperature for at least 30 minutes, then rub in one-quarter more of the marinade.

Preheat the oven to 350° F.

Place the lamb in a shallow roasting pan and roast for approximately 90 minutes (15 minutes per pound) for medium but still pink. Baste several times during the roasting with the remaining marinade. Test for doneness with the point of a knife.

Serves 12 to 15

. . . .

RED BEANS WITH HOMEMADE CHORIZOS

2 pounds (5 cups) dried red beans
1 large onion stuck with 5 cloves
1 ham hock (about 1½ pounds)
1 (1-pound) can Italian plum tomatoes, chopped and with juice reserved
1 (8-ounce) can tomato sauce
1 (6-ounce) can tomato paste
2 garlic cloves, minced
2 bay leaves
5 chorizo sausages (about 1½ pounds), cut into ½-inch slices (recipe for Homemade Chorizos follows, or use any good-quality commercial brand)

Soak the beans overnight in enough cold water to cover.

Drain the beans and place in a large pot with the onion and ham hock; add cold water to cover by about 3 inches. Bring to a boil and skim foam off the top. Reduce the heat and simmer, uncovered, for 1½ hours.

Set the ham hock aside and discard the onion. Add the remaining ingredients, including the reserved tomato juice and the chorizos. Continue to simmer, uncovered, for 30 minutes, or just until the beans are tender.

Trim the fat and gristle from the ham hock; cut the meat from the bone and chop it into small pieces. Return the meat to the pot for the last 15 minutes of cooking.

Serves 12 to 15

. . . .

Homemade Chorizos

To make chorizos, you need to order 24 feet of medium sausage casings from your butcher. You also need a sausage stuffer. Attachments are available for various brand-name electric mixers as well as for hand-operated meat grinders. The Basques usually make at least 50 pounds of sausage at a time. This recipe makes 10 pounds, or around forty sausages. You can make half this quantity if you prefer.

1 pound large, dried sweet red chiles, or ½ cup sweet Hungarian paprika
10 pounds coarsely ground pork with some fat
1 small bulb garlic, ground to a pulp
¾ cup cold water
¼ cup salt, approximately

If using dried chiles, seed them under cold running water, put them in a large bowl with water to cover, and soak overnight.

Put the peppers through a food mill to remove the skins. You should have about 3 cups of pulp. Put the pulp in a large bowl, add the pork, and mix well with your hands. If using paprika, sprinkle it over the meat and mix in well. Cover the bowl with a clean dish towel.

Mix the garlic and water and pour onto the towel, letting the liquid drain into the meat. Take care that pieces of the garlic don't get into the meat; they will cause it to discolor and eventually spoil. When all the water has seeped through the cloth, scrape the garlic to the center, gather the cloth around it, and squeeze the remaining liquid into the meat. Discard the garlic. Add the salt to the meat, 1 tablespoon at a time, mixing well after each addition. Cover and refrigerate overnight.

The next morning make a small patty,

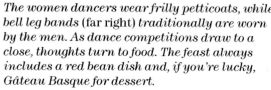

The women dancers wear frilly petticoats, while bell leg bands (far right) traditionally are worn by the men. As dance competitions draw to a close, thoughts turn to food. The feast always includes a red bean dish and, if you're lucky, Gâteau Basque for dessert.

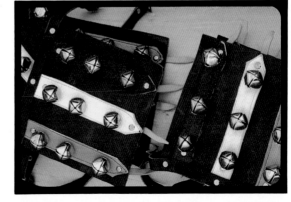

fry until well cooked, taste for seasoning, and add more salt to the mixture if needed, then refrigerate again overnight. Otherwise, proceed to make the chorizos.

Put the sausage casings in cold water to cover and soak for 30 minutes or more. Stuff the casings according to the instructions with your sausage stuffer, using kitchen twine to tie the casings every 6 inches. Puncture the sausages with the point of a knife every 2 inches all around to aid in the drying process.

Hang strings of 3 or 4 sausages each in a cool (40° to 50° F.), well-ventilated place to dry. A small fan to create air movement is helpful, but be sure it doesn't blow directly on the sausages and dry them too quickly on the outside. In cool weather, you can hang the sausages in a garage or basement with the door left open. Put a pan or papers under the sausages, since liquid will drain from the punctures in the casings. Let the sausages dry for 3 days, rotating away from air current if some are drying faster than others. If the temperature is not consistently cool, dry for 4 days. After they have dried, the sausages will be ready to cook with the red beans. They can also be steamed, baked, or fried for 20 to 30 minutes and eaten as is, or used in other dishes.

The chorizos can be stored in a container or plastic bag and refrigerated for 5 to 6 days, or put into freezer bags and frozen for up to 3 weeks.

Makes 40 sausages

CHICORY SALAD

2 medium cucumbers, peeled, halved
    lengthwise, seeded, and thinly sliced
    Salt
2 medium heads chicory, torn into bite-size
    pieces
2 medium red bell peppers, cut into
    julienne strips
1 cup cherry tomatoes, halved
¼ cup minced fresh parsley
6 radishes, thinly sliced
4 scallions, trimmed and thinly sliced,
    using 1 to 2 inches of green parts

DRESSING
1 tablespoon tarragon vinegar
1 small clove garlic, minced
½ teaspoon salt
    Freshly ground black pepper to taste
1 teaspoon Dijon mustard
½ cup olive oil

Put the cucumbers in a colander, sprinkle with salt, and let stand at room temperature for 30 minutes or more.

Mix the first 5 dressing ingredients in a small bowl with a whisk or fork. Slowly add the oil in a very fine stream, whisking constantly until well blended.

Rinse and pat cucumbers dry with a paper towel. Place in a large bowl, add the rest of the salad ingredients, and toss with dressing.

Serves 12 to 15

SOURDOUGH SHEEPHERDER BREAD

This is a modern version of the classic sheepherder's sourdough made in a Dutch oven. Take your starter (page 131) out the night before you intend to make the bread and increase it by adding 2 cups of warm water and 2 cups of flour. The next day, measure out the starter you need, and return the rest to the refrigerator.

2 cups Sourdough Starter
2 tablespoons olive oil
3 cups tepid water
8 cups bread or all-purpose flour
1½ teaspoons salt
    Cornmeal for dusting

Pour the starter into the bowl of a large mixer, and add the oil and water. Mix gently on slow speed, using the paddle attachment, while you add up to 7 cups of the flour, 1 cup at a time. If the dough seems too wet, add ½ cup more flour. (Be careful not to add too much flour, since the dough should remain sticky.) Add the salt and mix well. Change to a dough hook and knead for 6 minutes on medium speed.

Turn out the dough onto a lightly floured surface and knead by hand for about 3 minutes. The dough should be very elastic, soft, and smooth. Lightly oil and dust a 12-inch Dutch oven with cornmeal, put the dough in, cover with a cloth, and let rise in a warm place (70° to 80° F.) until it is doubled in size. This can take from 1½ to 3 hours, depending on the leavening effect of the starter.

Place a bowl of water in the bottom of the oven, and preheat the oven to 500° F. Slash a design in the top of the risen dough. Bake for 5 to 10 minutes, then reduce the heat to 400° F., remove the bowl of water, and bake the bread for 40 to 50 minutes, or until the bottom sounds hollow when tapped and the bread is golden brown. Let cool on a rack and wrap in a cloth or a paper—not plastic—bag.

Serves 12 or more

. . . .

GÂTEAU BASQUE

This is a specialty of Mireille and Alex Dusser of Alex's restaurant in Park City, Utah. Make two cakes to serve 12.

PASTRY CREAM
 ¾ cup milk
 ¼ cup sugar
 2 tablespoons flour
 2 egg yolks
 ½ teaspoon vanilla extract
 ¼ teaspoon almond extract
 ¼ cup finely chopped blanched almonds

CAKE
 2 cups all-purpose flour
 1½ teaspoons baking powder

 3 eggs
 1 cup sugar
 ¾ cup (6 ounces) unsalted butter, melted and cooled to room temperature
  Juice of ½ medium orange
 ½ teaspoon vanilla extract or anise extract
 ¼ teaspoon almond extract
 1 egg, beaten

Scald the milk in a small saucepan. Beat the sugar, flour, and egg yolks together until light in the top of a double boiler. Add the scalded milk gradually, blending well. Cook over medium heat, stirring constantly until the mixture begins to thicken. Remove from heat, add flavorings and almonds, and continue to stir for a few minutes. Cover and cool to room temperature. Meanwhile make the cake.

Mix flour and baking powder together in a small bowl. Beat the egg and sugar lightly in a medium mixing bowl. Slowly add the butter while stirring. Add the flour mixture a little at a time, mixing after each addition. Stir in the juice and flavorings. Let the batter rest, uncovered, for 15 minutes.

Preheat the oven to 400° F.

Butter a 9-inch springform or a 9-inch cake pan with removable bottom.

Divide the dough into 2 portions, one slightly larger than the other.

Place the larger portion of the dough in the pan, flattening and spreading with your fingers until it comes about 1½ inches up the sides of the pan. Pour in the cooled custard, spreading it to within ½ inch of the sides of the pan, taking care that it does not touch the sides at any point. Pipe the remaining dough through a pastry bag in a spiral pattern over the custard, making sure the batter touches the sides of the pan; or pat the batter into a circle large enough to touch the sides of the pan and place it on top of the custard. With the tines of the fork, lightly mark the top with two sets of diagonal lines in a crosshatch pattern. Brush with the beaten egg and bake for 40 minutes, or until nicely browned. Let the cake cool in the pan.

Makes 6 servings

SUPPER WITH A CROW INDIAN FAMILY

The powwow that takes place every August on the Crow reservation near Billings, Montana, site of Custer's Last Stand, is an opportunity to witness the magnificent pageantry of Native American costumes, music, and dance, and to eat some traditional food. Competitive dancing goes on for days and lasts far into the night. Music and movement both are so mesmerizing that an observer feels drawn in, as if these rhythms themselves could allow one to enter that sacred world the white man tried to destroy. Compelling and powerful, it is an awesome experience.

Winnona Plenty Hoops, Amy White Man, and Agnes Deer Nose, some of the elder ladies of the Yellowtail clan.

Christine Yellowtail with a platter of grilled buffalo steaks.

M E N U for 8

Grilled Buffalo Steaks

Corn on the Cob from the Garden

Oven-Roasted New Potatoes

Green Salad with Dill Dressing

Traditional Frybread

Fresh Berry Soup

Carbonated Beverages
Coffee

Circling the dance arena are stands selling jewelry, moccasins and other handwork, and tacos. These tacos make a substantial meal. Filled with the usual taco ingredients, they are nevertheless quite different from the familiar Mexican kind. The traditional frybread with which they are made seems a cross between a pancake and a large, flat biscuit. The taco filling is placed in the middle of the frybread, which is then folded over to form a thick sort of sandwich. Frybread is also eaten plain, spread with butter and honey, or with cooked berries. However it is served, it is always eaten hot.

Crows, like other Native Americans, often extend their families to include adopted sons and daughters who are not necessarily of their lineage. My husband, who is French, is the adopted grandson of Tom Yellowtail, a Crow medicine man and the patriarch of the Yellowtail family. Visiting the Yellowtails on the Crow reservation during tribal powwows or the Sundance ceremony, times when family get-togethers are traditional, we have been included in the family dinners, which are not public events.

The women do all the food preparation, and I usually help ready the meals for their large families and many friends. You never know how many people you will be feeding, so you always make more than you think

you need. You don't worry if you don't have enough; somehow, it works out. It doesn't seem possible, yet it happens. This was hard for me at first, since I am a careful planner, but it has taught me a great deal about the Native American culture, where things can simply happen like magic.

Meat is the staple food for the Crows, as it is for all Plains tribes. Preferring buffalo or venison to beef, they often raise buffalo to eat. Like many Americans, they grill meat over coals or open fires outdoors if the weather is nice. For them, cooking outside is traditional, and therefore preferred, but bad weather sends the cooks to indoor kitchens.

The emphasis on starchy side dishes is not unlike that of any Rocky Mountain menu in which meat and potatoes are the favored meal. The menu that follows is one that would be served for a family gathering. It can easily be increased for a larger group.

GRILLED BUFFALO STEAKS

Buffalo does not have a gamey taste so it need not be marinated, unless you wish. Grilled buffalo is best rare or pink, never well done.

> 8 buffalo sirloin or rib steaks (about 4 pounds), ¾ inch thick (see page 187 for suppliers)
> ¼ cup peanut oil
>   Salt and pepper
> 3 tablespoons butter
> 3 tablespoons minced fresh parsley
> 1 cup sour cream
> 2 tablespoons prepared horseradish

Rub the steaks with the oil. Sprinkle with salt and pepper to taste. Bring to room temperature while the barbecue is heating.

Place the steaks on an oiled grill about 6 inches above a single layer of white-hot coals or a hardwood fire. If the meat starts browning too fast, either raise the grill or remove the steaks and allow the coals to burn down a bit. The meat should cook gently, about 7 minutes per side for medium-rare.

Winnona Plenty Hoops is an adept breadmaker; no Crow feast is complete without freshly made frybread.

Young neighbors on the Crow reservation pause for a chat. Meanwhile, the feast is under way. Winnona and Agnes start the buffet line after overseeing the grilling of the meat. Tacos made with traditional Indian frybread are a popular accompaniment.

When the steaks are done to preference, arrange on a heated serving platter and top each with about 1 teaspoon of butter and a sprinkling of parsley. Serve with a mixture of sour cream and horseradish.

Serves 8

. . . .

CORN ON THE COB FROM THE GARDEN

8 ears fresh-picked corn, husked
½ teaspoon sugar
½ cup (1 stick) butter, melted
 Salt and pepper

Put the corn and sugar in a large pot of boiling water to cover. (The sugar brings out the corn's natural sweetness.) Boil for 5 minutes, turn off the heat, and cover the pot. Let it sit for 10 minutes. Drain.

Before serving, roll the corn in the melted butter and sprinkle with salt and pepper to taste. Serve immediately.

Serves 8

. . . .

OVEN-ROASTED NEW POTATOES

4 tablespoons (½ stick) butter
2 tablespoons vegetable oil
2 garlic cloves, minced
6 scallions, finely chopped, using about
 2 inches of the green parts

1 teaspoon paprika
½ teaspoon salt
 Freshly ground black pepper to taste
12 medium new potatoes (about 2½ pounds)

Preheat the oven to 375° F.

Heat the butter and oil in a medium roasting pan. Stir in the garlic, scallions, and seasonings. Add the potatoes, rolling them around to coat all sides.

Bake for 30 to 40 minutes, or until the potatoes are tender, stirring once or twice so that they brown evenly and are well-coated with the butter mixture.

Serve 8 to 10

. . . .

GREEN SALAD WITH DILL DRESSING

Our Crow friends raise a vegetable garden each year and have to contend with the short growing season that results from the early and late frosts that hit most of the Rocky Mountain region. Nonetheless, in late summer there are usually garden greens on the table.

DILL DRESSING
¼ cup vegetable or peanut oil
1 tablespoon cider vinegar
1 teaspoon chopped fresh dill, or
 ¼ teaspoon dried
 Salt and freshly ground pepper to taste

2 medium heads iceberg lettuce, washed
 and broken into bite-size pieces
1 cup shelled fresh peas
4 scallions, minced

1 medium tomato, diced
½ cup parsley sprigs

Put all the dressing ingredients in a small bowl and blend well with a fork.

Just before serving, toss the salad ingredients in a bowl with the dressing.

Serves 8

. . . .

TRADITIONAL FRYBREAD

Frybread is very popular with the Crow people. They make it often, and always for special occasions. It is much preferred to regular bread. It is usually eaten without butter as it is cooked in oil.

6 tablespoons nonfat dry milk
3 cups all-purpose bread flour
1 tablespoon baking powder
1 teaspoon salt
1½ to 2 cups lukewarm water
1 teaspoon vegetable oil
    Vegetable oil for frying

Blend the dry milk with the flour, baking powder, and salt in a large mixing bowl. With a wooden spoon, mix in the water in small amounts, using just enough to produce a soft, but not sticky dough. Stir in the oil. Knead the dough in the bowl for a few minutes until it is pliable.

Pull off egg-size pieces of dough and roll them into ¼-inch thick rounds about 5 inches in diameter. Fry the rounds one at a time in a deep skillet filled with ½ inch of sizzling hot vegetable oil, or in a deep-fryer half-filled with oil, for 3 to 5 minutes on both sides, until brown, turning once. Drain on paper towels and serve immediately while hot.

Serves 8

. . . .

FRESH BERRY SOUP

Susie Yellowtail, Tom's late wife, told me this story, and I always remember it when I go out to pick wild berries. Years ago, Susie and some other women of her tribe were picking blackberries in a tangled stand of bushes near the home of Chief Plenty Coup in Pryor, Montana. The women concentrated on picking for several hours, all the time aware of noises on the other side of the bushes. One of the women finally went around to see who was there, and to her great surprise it was a black bear! She ran to tell the others, and they all sped back to their truck, leaving the harvest baskets scattered.

Berry "soup" is a traditional native American way of using fresh berries, and is served as a snack or dessert.

4 cups fresh berries, such as blackberries
    or huckleberries
½ cup honey, or more if the berries are tart
¼ cup cornstarch or flour dissolved in ½ cup
    cold water

Put the berries in a large pot with fresh water to cover. Bring to a boil, turn the heat to low, and cook for about 5 minutes. Stir in the honey. Add the cornstarch mixture slowly, stirring constantly. Continuing to stir, cook the soup for a few minutes more until thickened. Pour into bowls and serve with hot frybread (recipe above) and additional honey for the soup or to spread on the bread.

Serves 8 to 10

. . . .

BEEF-TASTING POTLUCK SUPPER

Colorado is cow country, and the people of Custer County are proud of it.

Every year, the Custer County Cowbells, the ladies' auxiliary of the local Cattleman's Association, puts on a potluck supper at the Westcliffe Schoolhouse. It's a sort of combination celebration and fundraiser, and the proceeds of the dinner are used to promote the sale of Colorado beef. This informal affair draws as many as 300 people, who pay about $3.50 each for a dinner that is an old-fashioned potluck buffet, with all the ladies contributing their best culinary efforts. It is an event residents look forward to as a family occasion, as well as one many tourists consider an annual tradition on their vacations.

On long tables set up inside the schoolhouse, the Cowbells present a wonderful array of main dishes made with beef, along with a great variety of vegetable accompaniments, salads, beverages, and desserts. The menu that follows is a sampling of some of the dishes prepared for this festive event.

TOMATO ASPIC WITH SHRIMP

Anything made with shrimp is always a special treat in the Rocky Mountain West. Shrimp in a recipe usually means canned, although in many areas fresh baby shrimp are now available. They make this dish even more delicious.

 2 packages unflavored gelatin
½ cup cold water
 1 cup boiling water
2½ cups tomato juice
 2 tablespoons lemon juice
   Pinch of salt
 1 tablespoon Worcestershire sauce
 2 tablespoons ketchup
½ cup chopped green bell pepper
¼ cup chopped celery
 6 scallions, finely chopped, using 1 to 2 inches of green parts
 1 medium avocado, cubed
½ pound cooked baby shrimp, or 1 (7-ounce) can, drained well
 2 bunches fresh coriander (cilantro), stemmed and washed, for garnish

113

Stir the gelatin into the cold water, add the boiling water, and mix well to dissolve. Add the tomato juice, lemon juice, salt, Worcestershire, ketchup, vegetables, avocado, and most of the shrimp, stirring them in lightly with a fork.

Dampen a 6-cup ring mold with cold water, pour in the mixture, and chill for several hours or until set. Unmold onto a bed of parsley and complete the garnish with the reserved shrimp.

Serves 8 to 12

. . . .

CHILI CON CARNE COLORADO

Chili made with either beef, elk, or venison is definitely a staple in the diet of the modern-day mountain man. This recipe is my own concoction, the result of experiments with many a batch of chili. It's good with or without the beans.

      1 pound dried red or pinto beans
      3 dried whole large, red, mild ancho chiles
        (3 to 4 inches long) (see Note)
      2 small dried hot red chiles
      3 pounds top round beef, cut into ½-inch
        cubes (do not use ground beef)
      1 bay leaf
      4 garlic cloves, 3 minced and 1 left whole
    ¼ cup vegetable oil
      2 large onions, coarsely chopped
      2 tablespoons chili powder
    ½ teaspoon salt
      1 (28-ounce) can Italian plum tomatoes
      1 teaspoon dried oregano
      1 teaspoon cuminseed, lightly ground with
        a mortar and pestle
    ¼ teaspoon ground allspice
    ½ ounce dried wood ear or oyster
        mushrooms, crumbled
      2 bay leaves, crumbled
   1½ cups beer (12-ounce can)
        Freshly ground black pepper to taste
    ¼ pound sharp cheddar cheese, grated
        Sour pickles (sliced into sticks), or
        cornichons

Rinse the beans under cold running water and put them in a medium pot. Add enough cold water to cover and soak overnight.

Leave the beans in the water they soaked in, adding more water if necessary to cover by 3 or 4 inches. Bring to a simmer and cook uncovered for about 30 minutes, until the beans are tender but firm. Drain. Meanwhile, place the chiles in a small saucepan, add enough cold water to cover, and boil for 15 minutes, then let stand for at least 30 minutes. Drain, seed, and finely chop.

Put the meat in a large pot with water to cover by 2 inches. Add the bay leaf and whole garlic clove. Bring to a boil, skim, turn down the heat, and simmer for 20 minutes, skimming occasionally. Discard bay leaf and garlic clove.

Heat the oil in a 5-quart Dutch oven and sauté the onions, stirring occasionally, about 10 minutes, until soft and lightly browned. Add the minced garlic and cook for 1 minute. Add the chiles. Stir in the chili powder and salt. Add the meat, along with 3 cups of the cooking liquid.

Put the tomatoes with their juice through a food mill and add to the pot with the remaining ingredients except pickles. Cover and simmer for 1 hour. Add the beans and taste for seasoning. Simmer for 30 more minutes, adding cooking liquid from the meat or more beer if the chili seems too thick. If too thin, thicken with a little flour mixed with cold water. Serve with sour pickles or cornichons.

Serves 8

Note: Large mild dried chiles are available in Mexican food shops and usually in the Mexican food sections of supermarkets. If you can't find them, the chili will still be exceptionally good without.

. . . .

ROAST BEEF WITH HORSERADISH SAUCE

      1 beef sirloin roast (4 to 5 pounds)
      2 garlic cloves, peeled and slivered
        Salt and pepper to taste
        Horseradish Sauce (recipe follows)

Let the roast come to room temperature. Meanwhile, preheat the oven to 450° F.

With the point of a small, thin-bladed knife or a larding needle, poke holes in the meat and put a garlic sliver in each. Rub salt and pepper all over the meat and place it, fat side up, on a rack in a roasting pan just large enough to hold it. Roast for 10 minutes. Turn the oven down to 325° F. and roast for 1 to 2 hours (15 minutes per pound for rare, 20 minutes per pound for medium, and 25 to 30 minutes per pound for well done).

Let the roast rest at least 10 minutes before carving, then carve at the buffet table if possible. The meat tastes best warm or at room temperature. Serve with Horseradish Sauce on the side.

Serves 8 to 10

HORSERADISH SAUCE
    1 cup sour cream
    2 tablespoons prepared horseradish
      Dash of salt
    2 scallions, finely chopped

Thoroughly mix the sour cream, horseradish, and salt in a small bowl; sprinkle with the scallions.

Makes about 1 cup

MARGY'S OATMEAL BREAD

I got this recipe from a dude-ranch cook who swore by it!

    1 cup rolled oats
    2 cups boiling water
    2 tablespoons (¼ stick) unsalted butter, softened
    2 teaspoons salt
    3 tablespoons molasses
    1 package active dry yeast, dissolved in ¼ cup warm water (105° to 115° F.)
    2 cups whole wheat flour, approximately
    3 cups all-purpose flour, approximately

Place the oats in a large mixing bowl and add the boiling water. Let stand until cool. Add the butter, salt, molasses, and yeast.

Blend together, adding just enough whole wheat flour, about 2 cups, to make a sponge (a wet dough). Cover with plastic wrap and let rise in a warm place for about 30 minutes.

Punch down the dough, adding enough white flour, ½ cup at a time, to make handling easy. Form into a ball and place on a floured surface. Knead the dough until smooth and elastic, about 15 minutes. Replace in the bowl, cover with plastic wrap, and let rise for 60 minutes, until doubled in size.

Grease two 9 x 5 x 3-inch loaf pans.

Divide the dough in half and put into the pans. Let rise for 60 minutes, until doubled in size.

Preheat the oven to 350° F. Bake loaves for 45 to 55 minutes, or until nicely browned.

Makes 2 loaves

LEMON-APPLE CRISP

    6 cups sliced, pared apples (about 3 large apples)
    ¼ cup fresh lemon juice
    ⅔ cup light brown sugar, tightly packed
    ⅓ cup all-purpose flour
    2 teaspoons grated lemon rind
    ⅓ cup butter
    ½ cup lightly toasted sliced almonds
    1 cup heavy cream

Preheat the oven to 375° F. Butter an 8-inch square baking dish.

Arrange the apple slices in the baking dish. Sprinkle with the lemon juice.

Put the brown sugar, flour, and lemon rind in the bowl of a food processor. Turn the machine on and off quickly several times to blend. Add the butter and blend just until the mixture is crumbly. Stir in the almonds with a fork.

Spoon the mixture evenly over the apples. Bake for 35 minutes, or until browned. Serve with the cream.

Serves 6 to 8

CHRISTMAS DAY WILD GAME BUFFET

C hristmas is a special time in the mountains. Ski resorts are going full tilt, with visitors and residents alike energized by the beauty and bustle of the season. Towns, hung with elaborate decorations, sponsor special celebrations. Christmas lights, strung on isolated ranch houses in remote valleys, sparkle in the winter night. Snow covers everything, from the mountains to the valleys. Frost glitters on windowpanes. In rooms warmed by roaring fires and filled with inviting aromas,

M E N U for 8

Marinated Trout Spanish Style

Roast Wild Ducks with Green Chutney and Red Pepper Jam

Roast of Venison with French Marinade

Piquant Onion Salad

Carrot Salad with Honey Dressing

Rustic Whole Wheat Sourdough Bread

Almond Bread

Brazo de Gitano

Pumpkin Chiffon Pie

Fresh Fruit • Nuts Dried Figs

Champagne • Red and White Wines • Mineral Water Coffee • Tea

friends and families gathered to celebrate the season indulge in all the splendors of holiday food—the festive breads and special cakes, the lavish menus that only happen now.

A Christmas day buffet table offers country cuisine at its most sumptuous. It is likely to include game—birds or venison or both—complemented with exotic condiments. Side dishes, breads, and desserts are all worthy of the holiday table. Even when the menu is kept simple, there is a special quality that looks and feels and smells like Christmas.

Typical of Rocky Mountain menus, this one is diverse. The Brazo de Gitano, a Spanish Basque cake, is similar to the traditional French Christmas dessert, *bûche de Noël,* a rolled sponge cake made to resemble a log. The Carrot Salad, Red Pepper Jam, and Pumpkin Pie are all American. You can make many of these recipes ahead, freeing yourself to pay full attention to the last-minute details without having to deny yourself your own place at the table.

MARINATED TROUT SPANISH STYLE

Fresh mountain trout are almost daily fare in the Rocky Mountains. Rather than freezing excess fish in the day's catch, I like to marinate them for use over the next few days. Trout marinated this way should be eaten within four days. They make an elegant first course for dinner and are also good to take on a picnic or to a barbecue.

    4 small trout (about ½ pound each),
        cleaned
    ½ medium lemon
    ½ cup olive oil
    2 garlic cloves, minced
    ¾ cup dry white wine
    1 teaspoon minced fresh chervil or parsley
    1 tablespoon thin orange peel curls
    1 tablespoon thin lemon peel curls
        Juice of 1 lemon, strained
        Juice of 1 orange, strained
    1 teaspoon salt
        Freshly ground black pepper to taste

Do not wash the trout. Wipe them with the cut lemon, then pat dry. Sauté in ¼ cup of the olive oil over medium heat for about 4 minutes per side until brown, turning once. Add more oil if necessary.

Lay the trout in an oblong glass or pottery baking dish large enough to hold them in a single layer. Combine the rest of the ingredients, including the remaining olive oil, and mix well with a whisk. Pour over the trout, cover with plastic wrap, and refrigerate for at least 24 hours. Bring to room temperature before serving.

Serves 8

ROAST WILD DUCKS WITH GREEN CHUTNEY AND RED PEPPER JAM

This is one of the best—and simplest—ways to prepare wild ducks. If you use domestic ducks, you will have to adjust the roasting time because they are much larger and take longer to cook—about 7 minutes per pound for medium rare.

    4 wild ducks (about 2 pounds each),
        dressed
    ¼ pound salt pork, cut into small strips
        (optional)
    5 tablespoons crushed juniper berries
    ½ teaspoon freshly ground black pepper
    ½ cup soy sauce
    6 tablespoons vegetable oil
    2 tablespoons (¼ stick) butter
    4 shallots, minced
    2 medium onions, coarsely chopped
    2 tart apples, coarsely chopped
        Celery leaves
    ½ cup brandy, warmed
        Green Chutney (recipe follows)
        Red Pepper Jam (recipe follows)

If you want to lard the duck breasts, boil the salt pork in water for 10 minutes, drain, rinse with cold water, and insert into the breasts with a larding needle.

Mix the juniper berries with the pepper and soy sauce, then rub about 2 tablespoons into the ducks. Pour the remaining mixture over the ducks and refrigerate for at least 30 minutes, or up to several hours.

Preheat the oven to 450° F.

Heat the oil and butter in a large, heavy skillet until sizzling. Brown the ducks quickly on all sides until they turn a dark golden color. Reserve the butter and oil.

Stuff each duck loosely with one-quarter of the shallots, onions, apples, and some of the celery leaves. Roast untrussed in an open roasting pan for 35 minutes. Baste a couple of times with the reserved butter-oil mixture, melting more butter in the pan if necessary. Test for doneness with a fork or the point of a knife. Wild duck should always be served pink or medium rare, but if you prefer the meat very rare, roast for 20 to 25 minutes only.

Flame the brandy and pour over the ducks. Cut ducks in half and arrange on a warmed serving platter. Serve with Red Pepper Jam or Green Chutney on the side.

Serves 8

Green Chutney

    2 cups finely chopped fresh parsley
      Salt
1½ teaspoons coarsely chopped fresh ginger
¼ cup finely chopped unpeeled green apple
    4 to 6 garlic cloves, coarsely chopped
    3 tablespoons finely chopped fresh mint
    2 tablespoons lemon juice
½ cup plain yogurt
      Pinch of cayenne (ground red) pepper

Put all the ingredients in a food processor and turn the machine on and off a few times just until blended. Refrigerate in a covered jar. This will keep for a week or more. Bring to room temperature before serving.

Makes 1 cup

Red Pepper Jam

12 large red bell peppers
 1 tablespoon salt
 3 cups sugar
 2 cups distilled white vinegar

Remove the seeds and pith from the peppers, cut the flesh into chunks, and grind in a food processor or chop finely. If you use a food processor, be careful not to grind to a mush, but only to the finely chopped stage so that the jam will have the consistency of a relish. Add the salt and let stand for 3 to 4 hours.

Pour the peppers into a strainer, rinse under cold water, and drain. Place in a heavy kettle with the sugar and vinegar. Boil gently until the mixture thickens, about 45 minutes for long-term storage, pour into clean jelly jars, leaving ½- inch head space, and process in Hot-Water Bath (see page 170).

Makes 3 half-pints

ROAST OF VENISON WITH FRENCH MARINADE

This recipe was given to me by my French mother-in-law. I was surprised to discover that her marinade is almost exactly the same as that used by cooks in this country for game or red meat.

FRENCH MARINADE
    4 cups good-quality red wine
    1 cup red wine vinegar
      Several sprigs of fresh parsley
    2 sprigs fresh of thyme, or 1 teaspoon dried
    3 large bay leaves
    2 large onions, thinly sliced
    2 medium carrots, scrubbed and sliced
½ cup olive oil
      Salt and freshly ground pepper to taste

    1 haunch of venison, 10 to 12 pounds
¼ pound salt pork, cut into strips,
      parboiled 10 minutes, and rinsed in cold water
    3 tablespoons all-purpose flour
½ cup cold water
      Salt and pepper

Place the marinade ingredients in a bowl and mix with a fork.

Remove the skin from the venison and lard the meat with the strips of salt pork. Use a larding needle, or pierce the meat in

Top: *Lambs from a local sheepherder's flock.*

Above: *Eugene Le Breton of Pierre Country Bakery in Utah displays one of his Rocky Mountain loaves, a must for a hearty winter menu.*

Views of the Wasatch mountain range before the first heavy snowfalls of winter blanket the slopes.

121

several places with the point of a sharp knife, and push in the strips. Put the roast in a crock or a large pottery or glass bowl and pour over the marinade. Cover with plastic wrap and refrigerate for 5 to 6 days, turning the meat at least once a day. Before cooking, bring to room temperature.

Preheat the oven to 450° F.

Place the roast on a rack in a roasting pan and cook for about 2½ hours (15 minutes per pound), basting often with the marinade. Use a long pronged fork or tip of a sharp knife to test for doneness. When the meat is ready, remove to a platter and cover with foil to keep it warm while you make the gravy.

Place the roasting pan with drippings over very low heat. Make a paste of the flour and cold water, then add to the drippings, stirring with a whisk until smooth. Add enough leftover marinade to give the gravy the desired consistency. Strain and season with salt and pepper to taste.

Carve the roast into slices of desired thickness. Arrange overlapping slices on a serving dish and serve gravy on the side.

Serves 8 to 14

. . . .

PIQUANT ONION SALAD

This is very good served as a side dish with other meats and game as well.

    ½ **cup olive oil**
    3 **large onions, thickly sliced and slices quartered**
    2 **garlic cloves, put through a press**
    ½ **cup sherry wine vinegar**
    Salt
    Freshly ground black pepper
    2 **teaspoons Dijon or other strong mustard**
    ¼ **teaspoon ground cloves**
    ¼ **teaspoon ground cinnamon**
    ½ **cup golden raisins, plumped in hot water and drained**

Heat the olive oil in a large, deep skillet; add the onions and cook over medium-low heat, stirring often, for 20 minutes. When the onions start to turn golden, add the remaining ingredients. Cover and simmer for

5 minutes more, until the onions are barely tender. Check to be sure there is enough moisture during cooking, and add a little hot water if necessary. Serve cold or at room temperature.

Serves 8

. . . .

CARROT SALAD WITH HONEY DRESSING

    6 **large carrots, peeled and thinly sliced**
    ¼ **cup sunflower seeds**
    1 **large red onion, thinly sliced and slices quartered**
    1 **medium green bell pepper, seeded and finely chopped**
    ¼ **cup honey**
    2 **tablespoons fresh lemon juice**
    ¼ **cup vegetable oil**
    Salt and pepper
    Several red cabbage leaves, for garnish

Cook the carrots in boiling water for 3 minutes. Drain and rinse under cold water.

Spread the sunflower seeds in a shallow pan and toast in the oven for a few minutes, until lightly browned. Add to the carrots, onion, and pepper in a large mixing bowl.

Combine the honey, lemon juice, and oil in a small saucepan, bring just to a boil, and pour over the carrots. Add salt and pepper to taste.

This salad is best served at room temperature. It looks very pretty in a bowl lined with red cabbage leaves.

Serves 8

. . . .

RUSTIC WHOLE WHEAT SOURDOUGH BREAD

SPONGE
    Sourdough Starter (page 131)
    1 **cup warm water**
    1 **cup flour**

DOUGH

    1 tablespoon active dry yeast
    ¼ cup lukewarm water (105°–115° F.)
    3 cups water, at room temperature
    3 cups whole wheat flour
    1 tablespoon plus 1 teaspoon salt
    ¼ cup whole wheat berries, soaked in water
        for several hours or overnight (available
        in health food stores), optional
        Cornmeal

To make the sponge, the night before increase your starter by adding the warm water and flour. Let it sit at room temperature for 8 hours or more.

The next day, measure out ¾ cup of starter, return the rest to the starter container, and return to the refrigerator.

In a small bowl, dissolve the yeast in the warm water. Set aside.

In the bowl of an electric mixer, with a dough hook, mix the starter and 3 cups of water on the lowest speed for 5 minutes. Add the flour and mix on low speed for 4 minutes. Cover the bowl with plastic wrap, then with a dish towel, and let rest for 30 minutes.

Add the yeast mixture, salt, and wheat berries; mix for 10 minutes on low speed. Recover with plastic wrap and the dish towel; let rise for 30 minutes.

Turn on the machine briefly (30 seconds) just to deflate the dough, recover, and let it rest again for 30 minutes.

Turn out the dough onto a lightly floured board, punch down, and form into a large round ball. Place the ball into a large mixing bowl lined with a floured kitchen towel. Cover the entire bowl with plastic wrap and let the dough rise for 1 hour, or until doubled in size.

Place a small heat-proof bowl of water in the bottom of the oven.

Preheat the oven to 400° F. Sprinkle a baking sheet or baking stone with cornmeal.

When the dough has risen, gently invert bowl so that the dough is placed in the center of the baking sheet. Slash any pattern you like on the top with a razor blade. Sprinkle with flour. Remove the bowl of water from the oven. Bake the bread for 20 minutes at 400° F., then reduce the heat to 350° F. and bake for 30 to 40 minutes more, or until the bread sounds hollow when tapped on the bottom and is nicely browned on top. Spray the top and sides of the oven with a fine spray of water 3 times during the first 10 minutes of baking to give the loaf a rustic crustiness.

When done, cool on a rack, then wrap in a dishcloth or a paper—not plastic—bag.

Makes 1 large loaf

. . . .

ALMOND BREAD

Here's a special bread that's not too sweet to serve with a holiday meal. It's also good for breakfast or for tea, spread with preserves.

    2 tablespoons active dry yeast
    4 cups all-purpose flour
1½ teaspoons salt
2¼ cups milk
    4 tablespoons (½ stick) unsalted butter
1½ cups chopped blanched almonds
    1 cup wheat germ
    1 cup medium rye flour
    1 teaspoon fennel seeds
⅓ cup molasses
    1 egg, lightly beaten

Combine the yeast, 2 cups of the flour, and the salt in the bowl of an electric mixer. Warm the milk with the butter in a small saucepan and pour into the flour mixture. Beat for 2 minutes with the dough hook on low speed. Add 1 cup of the flour and beat on medium speed for 1 minute. Add the almonds, wheat germ, rye flour, fennel seeds, and molasses; mix just to blend.

Turn out onto a floured board and knead in the remaining cup of flour for about 7 minutes. Place the dough in an oiled bowl, cover loosely with a cloth, and set in a warm spot to rise for about 1 hour, until doubled in volume.

Punch down the dough and form 2 loaves to fit 8- x- 4-inch loaf pans. Brush the tops with the beaten egg. Let the dough rise in a warm spot for 30 minutes, or until doubled in volume again.

Preheat the oven to 375° F. Bake for 25 to 30 minutes, or until nicely browned.

Makes 2 small loaves

Note: This bread can also be made into a braided loaf, which is especially nice for Christmas. Divide the dough into thirds and shape into three 12-inch strips. Join the strips at one end and braid. Brush the top with egg and place on an oiled baking sheet. Let rise for 30 minutes in a warm spot. Bake for 40 minutes until nicely browned.

. . . .

BRAZO DE GITANO

BASQUE CAKE WITH CUSTARD FILLING

This festive recipe was given to me by Gloria Batis, who is Spanish Basque and has prepared many traditional Basque meals, both privately and professionally. Gloria frosts the cake with chocolate to resemble a *bûche de Noël,* but it can also be served unfrosted and just sprinkled with fine sugar. Make this cake for a special occasion any time of the year.

CUSTARD
   3 egg yolks
   7 tablespoons sugar
   2 tablespoons cornstarch
   2 cups milk, scalded
   1 tablespoon light rum, or flavoring of choice
   1 tablespoon butter

CAKE
   8 eggs, separated
   ½ cup sugar
      Zest of 1 lemon
   ¾ cup presifted all-purpose flour
   ½ teaspoon baking powder
   ⅛ teaspoon salt

   4 ounces almond paste (marzipan), red food coloring, green food coloring (optional)

CHOCOLATE FROSTING
   ½ cup milk
   1 cup sugar
   4 ounces unsweetened chocolate, melted
   4 tablespoons (½ stick) butter, in pieces

To make the custard, mix the egg yolks, sugar, and cornstarch with a whisk in a small, heavy saucepan. While whisking, slowly pour in the scalded milk and cook over medium heat, whisking constantly, until the mixture is thick. Stir in the rum. Float the butter on top to melt and to keep a skin from forming. Cool for 30 minutes or more before making the cake.

   Preheat the oven to 350° F.

   With an electric beater, beat the egg yolks with the sugar and lemon zest until very light in color. Put the egg whites in a large bowl and beat until soft peaks form. Gently fold into the yolks with a spatula. Sift the flour with the baking powder and salt, and lightly fold it in, a little at a time.

   Line a buttered 12 x 16 x 1-inch jelly-roll pan with a sheet of wax paper large enough to extend over the ends of the pan, then butter the paper. Spread the batter in the pan and bake for 10 to 12 minutes, or until the cake starts to pull away from the sides of the pan. Loosen edges and unmold the cake onto a floured dish towel. Immediately remove paper and trim crusty edges with a sharp knife.

   Spread the custard on the hot cake and roll the cake jelly-roll fashion, using the towel under the cake to assist the rolling motion. Let the cake cool on the towel to room temperature, wrap it in wax paper or plastic wrap, and refrigerate while you make the marzipan leaves and berries, if using, and the frosting.

   To make marzipan leaves and berries, mix about 1 ounce of the almond paste with the red food coloring, and form small berries. Mix green food coloring with the remaining almond paste and form leaves by rolling the paste to about ¼-inch thickness and cutting leaf shapes with a small sharp knife. Use the knife tip to draw veins on the leaves. Set aside.

   To make the frosting, combine the milk and sugar in a small saucepan, and bring to a boil. Stirring well, add the chocolate, then the butter, a small piece at a time, continuing to stir until the butter is completely melted.

Cool in the refrigerator until the mixture is of spreading consistency.

Spread the frosting over the top and sides of the chilled cake. Make wavy lines in the chocolate with a fork so that the finished cake resembles a log. Decorate with marzipan leaves and berries. Refrigerate until ready to serve.

Serves 12

....

PUMPKIN CHIFFON PIE

Chiffon pies are reminiscent of old-fashioned cookbooks, but I feel they are light and elegant enough to be included in today's menus. This pie has a cinnamon-nut crust with a mousselike filling piled high and decorated for the holiday table with whipped cream rosettes.

CINNAMON-NUT CRUST
  1 cup whole wheat pastry flour
  1 cup pastry or presifted all-purpose flour
  ⅛ teaspoon salt
  1 teaspoon sugar
  ½ cup (1 stick) unsalted butter, chilled and cut into pieces
  ¼ cup finely chopped toasted pecans
  ¼ teaspoon ground cinnamon
  4 to 5 tablespoons ice water

FILLING
  1 tablespoon unflavored gelatin
  ¼ cup cold water
  4 eggs, separated
  ½ cup light brown sugar, loosely packed
  1¼ cups puréed pumpkin, fresh cooked or canned
  ½ cup milk
  ¼ teaspoon salt
  ½ teaspoon ground cinnamon
  ½ teaspoon grated nutmeg
    Pinch of cream of tartar
  3 tablespoons granulated sugar
  1 cup sweetened whipped cream, for garnish

To make the crust, place the flours, salt, sugar, and butter in the bowl of a food processor and turn the machine on and off quickly several times until the mixture is like coarse meal. With the machine off, add the pecans and cinnamon. Turn on the machine and slowly pour in the ice water in a steady stream. Stop processing just as soon as the dough holds together and starts to draw away from the sides of the bowl. Wrap in plastic wrap and chill for at least 30 minutes.

Preheat the oven to 375° F.

On a floured surface, roll out dough to a round large enough to fit a 9-inch pie pan. Bake for 12 minutes, poking any bubbles that form as the crust bakes. Cool to room temperature. Meanwhile, make the filling.

Dissolve the gelatin in the cold water and set aside. Combine the egg yolks, brown sugar, pumpkin, milk, salt, cinnamon, and nutmeg in a medium saucepan. Cook over low heat, stirring constantly until the mixture comes to a boil. Remove from the heat and stir in the gelatin mixture. Cool for 10 minutes. Place the pan over ice cubes and continue to stir until the mixture holds its shape in a slight mound when dropped from a spoon.

Combine the egg whites with the cream of tartar and beat until frothy. Add the granulated sugar little by little, beating constantly until the mixture stands in soft peaks. Fold half the whites into the pumpkin mixture, then fold in the second half and pour filling into the prepared shell. Chill for 3 hours or more before serving. The pie can be decorated with whipped cream rosettes before chilling or just before serving.

Serves 6

....

Mountain Recipes

SOURDOUGHS AND OTHER BREADS

....

In the nineteenth-century Rocky Mountains, sourdough starter was one of the ingredients that could be easily transported, assuring sourdough bread an integral place in the lives of prospectors, cowboys, and homesteaders. With a history dating back to 4000 B.C., starters had already been transported through considerable space and time just to *get* to the Rockies. In the era before the advent of commercial yeast, sourdough starter provided the staff of life.

A starter was one of the few things a man could count on, besides the fact that life in the wilderness was hard. It was a very personal possession, a source of pride to the owner. The longer the starter's history, the more potent it was considered to be. The mystique surrounding sourdough—which lingers still—was so vital that magical powers were attached to some starters. North of the Canadian border, the word *sourdough* stuck to the men who carried it, becoming an all-inclusive name for those nineteenth-century prospectors who braved the rigors of life in the north to follow the dream of gold in their hearts.

A man's starter was usually carried inside his bedding, so it would stay neither too hot nor too cold. Once he set up camp, he would mix the starter with the flour, salt, and sugar he carried in his saddlebags, cover the dough loosely, then leave it to rise near the fire (but not right next to it, where it would get too hot). Once risen, the dough was put into a Dutch oven, then buried in the fire's coals to bake all day.

Sourdough is a healthful food, which is one reason for its current renaissance.

Yeast cells collected from the air react with flour, producing microorganisms that aid the digestive process. Sourdough's quite distinctive taste has many partisans. Recipes like those for bread, flapjacks, waffles, biscuits, muffins, and even banana bread show sourdough's versatility.

Sourdough shares top billing with oatmeal, whole wheat, cornmeal, and bran when it comes to the kind of wholesome baked goods that suit the Rocky Mountain taste. In the recipes that follow it combines with such local foods as pine nuts, blueberries, and raspberries to make some delicious treats. Most of these freeze well, making them good recipes to double, so there is always something special on hand when you need it. They also make wonderful gifts.

....

SOURDOUGH STARTER

The first chapter of *The Complete Sourdough Cookbook* by Don and Myrtle Holm, published by Caxton Printers Ltd., Caldwell, Idaho, is entitled, "Sourdough May Save the World." It says: "On the frontier, a sourdough starter was the most important possession a family could have, next to the Holy Bible; it was something to be guarded at the expense of almost everything else, and many a tale has been told of this. The starter was the wellspring of every meal. From it one could not only make bread, biscuits, and flapjacks, but feed the dogs, treat burns, chink the log cabin, brew a form of hootch, and, some say, even re-sole one's boots. It was the mainstay of the "Cowboy West," and no chuckwagon would leave the home ranch for the roundup without a keg of starter and the "makin's." It became the *pièce de résistance* of the Basques who migrated to America from the mountain regions of the Spanish-French border. . . ."

A sourdough starter is simple to make; and baked goods made with it are the most flavorful, satisfying, and nourishing, with the added advantage of improving with age.

STARTER

1 package active dry yeast
2¼ cups lukewarm water (use water potatoes have been boiled in for faster results)
2 cups all-purpose flour

You can mix your starter right in the container you are going to store it in. Use either a glass or a pottery jar, never a metal bowl. Scald the container with boiling water. Add the yeast and mix in ¼ cup of water. Add the rest of the water and the flour, stirring with a fork just until blended.

Cover the container with a clean cloth, but loosely so as to expose the mixture to the yeast spores that are in the air. These will react with the mixture causing it to "work" (bubble and grow). Set the container in a warm spot, around 70° to 80° F., for a minimum of 24 hours. Be careful not to put your starter in a place that is too warm while it is working. Temperatures above 90° F. kill the yeast spores and ruin the starter. Skim off the top from time to time. The mixture will become bubbly and sour smelling, at which point use what you need and store the rest, or refrigerate all of it until needed. You will have from 1 to 2 cups after skimming. If the starter turns orange at any time, discard.

You should use your starter at least once a week. However, unused starter will remain "alive" for several weeks if refrigerated. Some people freeze the starter if they won't be using it for longer than this. If you don't use your starter for more than a month, you may find that it no longer works and bubbles, in which case, discard it and start over.

The starter must be brought to room temperature, covered with a cloth, and left to work in a warm place for at least 8 hours before adding it to recipes.

It's important to remember never to overmix any sourdough batter. Overmixing breaks down the bubbles in the starter and makes the batter heavy.

I admit I enjoy using a starter that has a history. I am still getting excellent results from the starter I ordered several years ago from Salmon, Idaho. This starter originated in 1880 in Bayhorse, Idaho, once a booming mining community that is now a ghost town. I have also made my own starter, which seems to work as well but somehow doesn't produce as good a taste as one with an interesting history.

Starter with directions and recipes is also available by mail order (see page 190).

SUSAN'S SOURDOUGH BREAD

This recipe was given to me by my friend, Susan Peterson, who makes wonderful, crusty loaves of bread. The key to successful sourdough breadmaking is an active, very bubbly starter; Susan keeps her starter alive by using it to make pancakes between bread batches. I "feed" my starter 24 hours before making bread so that it will have time to absorb a lot of yeast spores and become very active and bubbly. However, if you have been using your starter at least once a week, you can increase it the night before.

SPONGE
Sourdough Starter
3 cups lukewarm water
3 cups presifted all-purpose flour

DOUGH
2 tablespoons sugar
6 to 6½ cups bread or presifted all-purpose flour
1½ cups warm milk
2 tablespoons (¼ stick) unsalted butter, melted
2 teaspoons salt

To make the sponge, increase, or "feed" your starter by transferring it to a medium glass or pottery bowl and stirring in water and flour. Cover loosely with a clean cloth and let sit in a warm place for 8 hours or overnight.

The next day, measure out 3 cups of the sponge into a large mixing bowl. Return the rest to the starter container, and refrigerate. This is very important, as you lose your starter if you forget to set aside the original quantity (about ¾ cup) before mixing in the other ingredients.

Mix the sugar and 1 cup of flour into the sponge, then mix in the milk, melted butter, and salt; add 4 cups of flour. Knead, adding remaining flour, either by hand or in a mixer with a dough hook, until the dough is smooth and elastic but not too stiff. Cover the bowl loosely with a clean cloth and place in a warm spot to rise for 2 hours. (I use my unlit gas oven for this because the pilot light provides just the right temperature, but a sunny spot in the kitchen works as well.)

Punch the dough down and let rise for 30 more minutes. Divide the dough in half and place in 2 oiled 9 x 5 x 3-inch loaf pans. Let the dough rise for another 1½ hours or until doubled.

Preheat the oven to 375° F. Bake the loaves for approximately 45 minutes, or until nicely browned. (For a crusty loaf, spray the oven very lightly with cold water twice during the first 10 minutes of the baking period.) Remove from the pans and place on a rack to cool. Sourdough bread improves with age, and it makes the best toast imaginable.

Makes 2 large loaves

. . . .

SOURDOUGH BANANA BREAD

SPONGE
  Sourdough Starter (page 131)
  1 cup presifted all-purpose flour
  1 cup warm water

BATTER
  2 to 2½ cups presifted all-purpose flour
  1 teaspoon baking powder
  1 teaspoon salt
  ½ teaspoon baking soda
  ½ cup (1 stick) unsalted butter, softened
  1 cup light brown sugar, loosely packed
  2 eggs, beaten
  2 medium, very ripe bananas, mashed to make 1 cup purée
  1 teaspoon vanilla extract
  ½ cup chopped pecans

To make the sponge, increase your original starter by transferring it to a glass or pottery bowl and mixing in flour and warm water. Cover the bowl loosely with a clean cloth and set it in a warm place to "work" for 8 hours or overnight.

Preheat the oven to 375° F. Butter and lightly flour a 9 x 5 x 3-inch loaf pan. Measure 1 cup of the sponge, return the rest to the starter container, and refrigerate.

Combine the flour, baking powder, salt, and baking soda in a medium bowl; stir to blend thoroughly.

Cream the butter and brown sugar in a large bowl. Stir in the eggs, sponge, and banana purée. Add the dry ingredients, stirring until well blended. Stir in the vanilla and pecans.

Pour the batter into the pan and bake for about 1 hour, or until the bread slightly draws away from the sides of the pan and a cake tester comes out clean. Cool the loaf in the pan for 10 minutes before turning out onto a rack. Delicious served warm with butter, or sliced thin and spread with jam for afternoon tea.

Makes 1 large loaf

Note: This keeps very well, as do all sourdough breads. You don't need to refrigerate, but wrap well in plastic or foil. It also freezes well.

. . . .

SOURDOUGH BISCUITS

Biscuits and gravy are standard breakfast fare in some homes and restaurants in the Rocky Mountain West, but more often biscuits are served with just butter and honey or jam.

SPONGE
  Sourdough Starter (page 131)
  1 cup lukewarm milk (or water)
  1 cup presifted all-purpose flour

BATTER
  1½ cups presifted all-purpose flour
  3 teaspoons baking powder
  1 teaspoon salt
  2 tablespoons sugar

¼ cup solid vegetable shortening, in pieces
1½ teaspoons baking soda, mixed with a little warm water to a smooth paste
¼ cup (½ stick) unsalted butter, melted

To make the sponge, increase your original starter by transferring it to a glass or pottery mixing bowl and mixing in lukewarm milk and flour. Cover loosely with a clean cloth and set in a warm place to "work" for 8 hours or overnight. The next day, measure out 1½ cups, then return the rest to the starter jar and refrigerate.

Combine the flour, baking powder, salt, and sugar in a mixing bowl. Work the shortening in with a fork or a pastry cutter until the mixture resembles coarse meal. Add the sponge and the baking soda paste, and blend well.

Turn the dough out onto a floured board and knead 10 or 15 times—no more—until it has a satiny texture. Roll out to ½-inch thickness and cut out rounds with a 2-inch biscuit cutter or the rim of a glass dipped in flour. Dip both sides of each round in the melted butter and place on a buttered baking sheet with the sides of the rounds barely touching. Cover loosely with a dish cloth and set in a warm place to rise for 45 minutes.

Preheat the oven to 375° F. Bake biscuits for 30 to 35 minutes, or until browned.

Makes about 16 biscuits

SOURDOUGH CINNAMON ROLLS

Cinnamon rolls are a Rocky Mountain institution. These are the best!

SPONGE
Sourdough Starter (page 131)
1 cup presifted all-purpose flour
1 cup lukewarm water

BATTER
½ cup milk
6 tablespoons (¾ stick) unsalted butter
2 teaspoons salt
2 tablespoons granulated sugar
1 tablespoon dry yeast
2 cups bread or all-purpose flour

½ cup buckwheat flour or whole wheat pastry flour
1½ teaspoons baking soda
½ cup raisins
½ cup coarsely chopped walnuts
¼ cup plus 2 tablespoons light brown sugar, tightly packed
1½ teaspoons ground cinnamon
1 tablespoon strong coffee

To make the sponge, increase your starter the night before by transferring it to a glass or pottery mixing bowl and mixing in flour and water. Cover loosely with a clean cloth and set in a warm place to "work" for 8 hours or overnight. The next morning, measure out 1 cup of sponge, return the rest to the starter jar, and refrigerate.

Scald the milk and add 2 tablespoons of the butter, salt, and granulated sugar, stirring to melt the butter. Let cool to room temperature. Stir in yeast. Put in a medium bowl with the sponge. Using a wooden spoon, stir in the flours and baking soda, and continue stirring until a soft dough forms.

Put the dough in an oiled bowl, cover with plastic wrap, and let rise in a warm place for 1 hour. Punch down the dough and roll out a ¼-inch-thick rectangle approximately 10 x 16 inches. Dot with 2 tablespoons of the butter, sprinkle with the raisins, nuts, and ¼ cup of the brown sugar and 1 teaspoon of cinnamon. Roll up from the long end like a jelly roll and cut into 1-inch-thick slices. Melt the remaining 2 tablespoons of butter in a 9 x 5-inch baking pan and stir in the remaining ½ teaspoon of cinnamon, the remaining 2 tablespoons of brown sugar, and the coffee. Place the rolls cut side up (not too close) on the butter mixture. Cover with plastic wrap and let rise for 1 to 2 hours, until doubled in bulk.

Preheat the oven to 375° F. Bake the rolls for 15 to 20 minutes, until nicely browned. Turn out onto a serving plate immediately. Serve warm for a real Rocky Mountain treat!

Makes 10 rolls

SOURDOUGH MUFFINS

SPONGE
2 cups all-purpose flour
2 cups warm milk (or water)
½ to 1 cup Sourdough Starter (page 131)

BATTER
2 cups presifted all-purpose flour
½ cup whole wheat pastry flour
½ cup peanut oil
½ cup condensed milk
1 egg, beaten
1 teaspoon salt
1 teaspoon baking soda
1 teaspoon sugar or honey

Mix the sponge ingredients in a glass or plastic bowl. Cover with a dish towel and let the mixture ferment overnight.

Preheat the oven to 400° F. Butter and flour 2 large muffin tins.

Measure out 1½ cups of fermented sponge and put it into a medium mixing bowl. Put the rest in a glass, crockery, or plastic container, cover, and refrigerate for future use.

Add the rest of the ingredients to the sponge and mix lightly only until blended.

Spoon into muffin cups, filling each three-quarters full. Bake for 35 to 45 minutes, or until muffins are nicely browned. Serve immediately.

The recipe can be easily cut in half.

Makes 18 large muffins

. . . .

SOURDOUGH SESAME WAFFLES

You will find that these waffles are the lightest and tastiest you have ever eaten, and they are nutritious as well. Serve with real maple syrup or a berry syrup.

SPONGE
Sourdough Starter (page 131)
1 cup whole wheat flour
1 cup presifted all-purpose flour
1 cup warm water

BATTER
2 eggs, separated
6 tablespoons (¾ stick) unsalted butter, melted and cooled

1 teaspoon baking soda
1 teaspoon salt
2 teaspoons baking powder
¼ teaspoon cream of tartar
2 tablespoons white sesame seeds

To make the sponge, increase your original starter by transferring it to a large glass or pottery bowl and mixing in whole wheat flour, all-purpose flour, and warm water. Cover loosely with a clean cloth and set in a warm place to "work" for at least 8 hours or overnight.

About 30 minutes before using, measure out 2 cups of sponge into a medium bowl. Return the rest of the sponge to the starter jar and refrigerate.

Add the egg yolks, butter, baking soda, baking powder, and salt to the sponge, mixing lightly just to combine. Be sure the butter is lukewarm, and don't overmix. Hot butter and overmixing stop the action of the yeast. Set the batter in a warm place to "work" for a few minutes.

Meanwhile, beat the egg whites with the cream of tartar until soft peaks form. Fold into the batter just before cooking.

Preheat a waffle iron, then pour on sufficient batter to cover the surface. Sprinkle immediately with sesame seeds, close the lid, and bake for about 5 minutes, until the steaming stops. Remove waffle and keep warm while you bake remaining waffles.

Makes 6 large waffles

. . . .

SOURDOUGH FLAPJACKS

Flapjacks are probably the most familiar and most popular form of sourdough cookery in the Rocky Mountain West. In the early days, wherever kitchens were established—on farms, in settlement houses, in boardinghouses, in logging and mining camps—sourdough flapjacks were served. These "sourdoughs," as they came to be called, are much lighter in texture and far superior in flavor to flapjacks made without a starter. This recipe is the one still used today for an old-fashioned Rocky Mountain sourdough flapjack feed.

SPONGE
Sourdough Starter (page 131)
2 cups lukewarm milk (see Note)
2 cups presifted all-purpose flour

BATTER
2 teaspoons baking powder
2 teaspoons sugar
1 teaspoon salt
1 teaspoon baking soda
2 eggs, separated
2 tablespoons vegetable oil

To make the sponge, increase your original starter by transferring it to a medium glass or pottery mixing bowl and stirring in lukewarm milk and flour. Cover loosely with a clean cloth and set it in a warm place to "work" for at least 8 hours or overnight.

The next day, measure out 2 cups of sponge, return the rest to the starter container, and refrigerate.

Add the dry ingredients, egg yolks, and oil to the sponge. In a separate bowl, beat the egg whites until stiff, then stir lightly into the batter just before cooking.

Preheat a griddle. When a drop of cold water bounces and sizzles on the griddle, it is ready to use.

Butter the griddle and pour on ¼ cup of batter for each flapjack. When bubbles appear on top (about 3 minutes), turn and cook for about 3 minutes more, until brown. Keep warm while you make remaining flapjacks. Serve with maple syrup or huckleberry syrup for an authentic Rocky Mountain breakfast. Huckleberry syrup is available in limited quantities from specialty food stores. For mail order, see page 189.

For a delicious variation for a special breakfast or brunch, add ½ banana, cut into very thin slices and the slices cut in half, to the batter.

Makes 12 flapjacks

Note: For this recipe, my family and our Basque friends add milk instead of water to the starter. However, if you want to keep your starter pure water and flour, which some cooks feel works better for bread,
then substitute water for the milk and add ½ cup of milk and more flour, if needed, when mixing the batter.

....

BLUEBERRY NUT BREAD

Toni Smith, a fellow caterer in Ketchum, Idaho, is the originator of this recipe. I have used it often for brunches and picnics.

2 cups presifted all-purpose flour
¾ cup sugar
1½ teaspoons baking powder
½ teaspoon baking soda
½ teaspoon salt
Juice and zest of 1 orange
2 tablespoons (¼ stick) unsalted butter, melted
1 egg, lightly beaten
1 cup chopped pecans
1 cup fresh blueberries

Preheat the oven to 350° F. Butter a 9 x 5 x 3-inch loaf pan.

Sift 1¾ cups of flour with the sugar, baking powder, baking soda, and salt into a medium mixing bowl. Pour the orange juice into a measuring cup. Add the zest, butter, and enough boiling water to make ¾ cup liquid. Add to the dry ingredients. Add the egg and mix until thoroughly blended. Put the pecans, remaining ¼ cup flour, and blueberries in a small bowl and mix lightly with a fork. Add to the batter, mixing lightly.

Pour batter into the loaf pan and bake for 1 hour, or until a cake tester comes out clean and the loaf is nicely browned. Cool in the pan for 5 minutes, then turn out onto a rack to cool completely.

Makes 1 large loaf

....

FINNISH COFFEE BREAD

PULLA

Over the years many Finns have settled in the Rocky Mountains, perhaps because of the climate. This is one of their wonderful breads. You might want to try it the next time you have friends in for coffee or tea.

>   2 eggs
>   ¾ cup sugar
>   2 cups lukewarm milk (105°–115° F.)
>   1 teaspoon salt
>   1 envelope yeast
>   2 teaspoons ground cardamom
> 5½ cups presifted all-purpose flour
>   ½ cup (1 stick) unsalted butter, melted
>   1 tablespoon sugar
>   ¼ cup finely chopped blanched almonds

Beat 1 egg with the sugar in a small bowl and set aside. Mix the milk and salt in a large bowl. Add the yeast. When the yeast has dissolved, add the cardamom and the egg mixture. Stirring by hand or using an electric mixer with a dough hook, add enough of the flour to make a smooth, elastic dough. Add the melted butter and the remaining flour and knead by hand for 10 to 15 minutes, or continue using the electric mixer until the dough is pliable, about 10 minutes.

Place the dough in a large oiled bowl, cover with a clean cloth, and let rise in a warm spot for 1 to 1½ hours, until doubled in size.

Knead the dough for a few minutes on a floured surface, then divide into 3 equal parts and braid. Place the braid on a buttered baking sheet and let rise for 30 minutes in a warm spot.

Preheat the oven to 400° F. Lightly beat the remaining egg and brush the braid with it. Sprinkle with sugar and almonds. Bake for 10 minutes, then lower the heat to 350° F. and bake for about 20 minutes, or until nicely browned.

Makes 1 large braided loaf about 15 to 16 inches long

ROCKY MOUNTAIN CORN BREAD

This quick and easy recipe is a wholesome version of an old favorite.

>   4 tablespoons (½ stick) butter, melted
>   1 cup yellow cornmeal
>   1 cup whole wheat pastry flour
>   ½ teaspoon salt
>   1 tablespoon honey
>   ½ cup plain yogurt
>   ½ cup milk
>   1 egg, lightly beaten
>   4 teaspoons baking powder

Preheat the oven to 425° F. Butter an 8-inch square baking pan.

Put all the ingredients in the order given into a large mixing bowl or in a food processor. Mix lightly just until blended.

Pour the batter into the baking pan. Bake for 20 to 25 minutes, or until lightly brown and bread has drawn away from the sides of the pan.

Serve warm with butter and honey.

Serves 8

RASPBERRY COFFEECAKE

This colorful coffeecake is good for breakfast, tea, or dessert.

>   ¾ cup light brown sugar, loosely packed
>   1 cup (2 sticks) butter, melted
>   4 eggs
>   1 cup buttermilk
>   2 cups whole wheat pastry flour
>   1 cup pastry or presifted all-purpose flour
>   3 teaspoons baking powder
>   1 teaspoon baking soda
>   ½ cup finely chopped dried apricots
>   ¼ cup finely chopped walnuts
>   ¼ cup raspberry jam

Preheat the oven to 350° F. Generously butter a 10-inch bundt pan.

Mix the brown sugar and melted butter in a large bowl. Add the eggs and the buttermilk, and beat well until the mixture is thoroughly blended and creamy.

Combine the dry ingredients in a separate bowl. Add to the liquid mixture, stirring well. Stir in the apricots and nuts.

Spread half the batter in the bundt pan. Drop the raspberry jam by teaspoonfuls at intervals on top of the batter. Pour the rest of the batter over, spreading it with a spatula. Bake for 40 to 45 minutes, or until a cake tester comes out clean.

Serves 10 to 12

ELEANOR'S RYE MUFFINS

These are the prize-winning muffins at our house, made from friend Eleanor Burke's recipe. They make a wonderful breakfast treat spread with honey or berry jam.

> 1 cup buttermilk
> 2 eggs
> 2 tablespoons walnut or peanut oil
> 2 tablespoons honey
> 1 cup medium rye flour
> ⅔ cup whole wheat pastry flour
> 1½ teaspoons baking powder
> ½ teaspoon baking soda
> ½ teaspoon salt
> ½ teaspoon caraway seeds
> 6 tablespoons chopped walnuts

Preheat the oven to 400° F. Butter and lightly flour 2 large-cup muffin tins.

Put the first 4 ingredients in a large bowl and mix with a whisk. Mix all the dry ingredients, except the seeds and nuts, in a separate bowl. Make a well in the center and add the liquid mixture all at once, stirring only enough to blend. Immediately and quickly stir in the seeds and nuts.

Spoon the batter into the muffin tins, filling the cups two-thirds full. Bake for 15 minutes, or until lightly browned.

Makes about 12 large muffins

SWEDISH OATMEAL PANCAKES

Sourdough starter added to any batter will lighten it and give a superior flavor. These pancakes, however, are superb with or without the sourdough. And they provide a wonderful way to add nutritional oats to your family's diet. The recipe makes 20 pancakes but can be easily cut in half for less.

SPONGE (optional)
> Sourdough Starter (page 131)
> ½ cup presifted all-purpose flour
> ½ cup lukewarm water

BATTER
> 2 cups rolled oats
> 1 cup milk
> 1 cup plain yogurt
> ½ cup presifted all-purpose flour
> 1 teaspoon baking soda
> 1 teaspoon baking powder
> 2 eggs, separated
> 1 tablespoon honey
> 4 tablespoons (½ stick) butter, melted and cooled
> Lukewarm milk, if needed

If using the sourdough sponge, increase your original starter by transferring it to a glass or pottery bowl and mixing in flour and lukewarm water. Cover loosely with a clean cloth and set in a warm place to "work" for 8 hours or overnight.

Combine the oats, milk, and yogurt in a mixing bowl, cover, and let sit at room temperature overnight.

The following day, measure out ½ cup of the sponge, return the rest to the starter jar, and refrigerate.

Combine the oatmeal mixture with the dry ingredients, egg yolks, honey, and melted butter. Mix lightly only until blended. (Add up to ½ cup of lukewarm milk if the batter is too thick. It should be the consistency of heavy cream.) Stir in sponge if using. Beat the egg whites until they hold soft peaks, and fold into the batter just before cooking.

Preheat the griddle, but not as hot as for other batters since these thin pancakes burn easily. Test the heat first with a small amount of batter. Pour a scant ¼ cup for each pancake onto the grill, cook until holes appear (about 3 to 5 minutes), turn and cook for 3 to 5 minutes more, until nicely browned. Serve with berry syrup. Huckleberry syrup is available; to order, see page 189.

Makes 20 medium pancakes

CORNMEAL PANCAKES WITH YOGURT

These pancakes are not only wholesome, they are absolutely delectable! Serve them with berry syrup or real maple syrup and your preference of sausage—or try the homemade sausage on page 99.

1¾ cups yellow cornmeal
1½ teaspoons salt
¾ teaspoon baking soda
⅓ cup brown rice flour or whole wheat pastry flour
2 eggs, separated
2¼ cups plain yogurt
⅓ cup safflower oil

Preheat a pancake griddle until medium hot.

Combine the cornmeal, salt, baking soda, and flour; sift into a large bowl.

Mix the egg yolks, yogurt, and oil in a small bowl. Pour into the flour mixture, stirring just until blended. Stir in a little warm water just until the mixture has the consistency of heavy cream. Beat the egg whites until stiff and fold into the batter.

Measure out ¼ cup of batter for each pancake; cook for about 3 minutes per side, until golden brown.

Makes 18 medium pancakes

. . . .

ODETTE'S BUCKWHEAT CREPES WITH APPLE FILLING

GALETTES NORMANDE

Buckwheat pancakes have always been popular in the Rocky Mountains. They were my father's favorite breakfast food, and he often made them as a Sunday morning treat when I was young. Many years later, I was surprised to learn that buckwheat cakes are just as popular in other parts of the world. My French mother-in-law gave me this recipe, which makes an elegant dessert. Omit the Calvados or brandy if making for breakfast.

APPLE FILLING
4 tablespoons (½ stick) butter
2 pounds tart cooking apples, peeled and thinly sliced
2 tablespoons heavy cream
2 tablespoons Calvados or brandy (optional)

CREPES
1½ cups buckwheat flour
1 cup presifted all-purpose flour
Pinch of salt
3 eggs, separated
1 cup milk
1 cup water, as needed
1 tablespoon butter, melted
Lemon juice
Sugar

To make the filling, melt the butter in a large, heavy-bottom pan and cook the apples for about 10 minutes, until they are tender and lightly browned. Add the cream and brandy, and cook for 2 minutes. Reserve while you make the crepes.

Combine the flours and salt in a large mixing bowl. Put the egg yolks and milk in a small bowl, and whisk until well blended.

Make a well in the center of the flour and slowly pour in the egg mixture, stirring with a wooden spoon to form a thick, smooth paste. Add the water a little at a time, just until the batter is the consistency of heavy cream. Cover the bowl loosely with a cloth and let sit for 3 hours at room temperature. Add more water if necessary to bring the batter to the consistency of heavy cream.

Beat the egg whites until stiff, then fold them into the batter. Heat a heavy 8- to 10-inch skillet with slanted sides, or a conventional crepe pan. Brush pan with some melted butter, and pour in about 2 tablespoons of batter, tilting the pan very quickly to spread it in a thin, even film before it sets.

Cook the crepes for about 2 minutes. Loosen the edges with a knife and flip them over with a long narrow spatula. Cook for an additional 2 minutes, until golden. As they are cooked, stack the crepes on a plate, and keep them in a warm oven.

Warm the apple filling and place 2 tablespoonfuls in the middle of each crepe. Fold over the side edges of the crepe about 1½ inches, then fold the top and bottom over the filling, overlapping to form an oblong envelope. If the crepes have cooled during the filling process, rewarm in a 300° F. oven before serving. Sprinkle some lemon juice and sugar over each crepe just before serving.

The crepes can be made ahead and refrigerated for up to a week. Stack between sheets of wax paper and wrap airtight in plastic wrap.

Makes 15 to 20 large crepes, depending on pan size

SOUPS AND SIDE DISHES

Nothing is more welcome on a chilly evening than a warming, good bowl of soup. In the mountains, where even hot summer days turn into crisp nights, it owns a special place.

While big meals beginning with soup are primarily a European tradition, Europeans are hardly the only people to relish soup. Among the recipes in this chapter are several Mexican soups spicy enough to be doubly warming. The Chili con Queso Soup, for instance, is equally good cold, ample proof that soup can be as much a treat on a hot summer day as on a cold winter night. Other soups—such as the Basque Garbure, a thick vegetable soup, and the Potage, made with brown rice and lentils—are hearty enough that, accompanied by a good, crusty loaf and a salad, they make meals in themselves.

Stock for these soups is often made with the bones and carcasses left over from the game animals or wild fowl—perhaps from a roast saddle of venison or the grilled breast of mallard that was cooked for dinner—but the bones of domestic livestock do as well.

Side dishes, which is what we here in the Rocky Mountains call vegetable dishes and salads, are often as hearty as the soups and, like them, can serve as one-dish meals.

Many side dishes are based on indigenous Rocky Mountain vegetables: corn and beans. Because corn can also be ground for meal, it may well be the single most vital food of the Rockies. Chiles, tomatoes, and potatoes—all historic mountain foods—figure prominently here, too. Maria's Vegetarian Stuffed Peppers, with bulgur in the filling, make delicious modern use of the traditional bell pepper. Mushrooms are abundant, especially the wild ones, and are available in a few scattered markets here and in large cities outside the region. Shaggy manes, the most easily identifiable of all wild mushrooms, are used in one of the salads in this section, but the recipe can also be made with other wild varieties or those commercially grown.

Until recent years, salad in the Rocky Mountains consisted of iceberg lettuce, and even that was considered a delicacy, available only with the advent of refrigerated trains bringing it from California. But these days a splendid variety of greens are grown in the Rockies. Butter lettuce, green and red leaf lettuce, endive, escarole, arugula, and radicchio can be found in farmers' markets, supermarkets, and home gardens. More exotic produce like fennel, jicama, shallots, and Enoki mushrooms are regularly sold in supermarkets, and the availability of fancy oils and flavored vinegars has revolutionized our whole concept of salad. Ranging beyond greens, it includes a wide variety of interesting and unusual combinations of foods, seasonings, and flavorings.

Other side-dish recipes run the gamut from all-American corn pudding to a molded Basque-style rice salad that offers a typically Basque taste that is rare in most of America.

Within this section, many combinations are interchangeable. For instance, the Green Goddess Dressing for the Cauliflower Salad can be used in a multitude of salads.

Highly versatile, these recipes can serve any number of people.

. . . .

CHILI CON QUESO SOUP

This is a good, warming soup for winter, but it is also delicious served very cold. Try it as a starter for a summer Mexican meal.

 1 quart well-seasoned chicken stock, or
  2 (11-ounce) cans chicken broth mixed
  with water to make 1 quart
 4 tablespoons (½ stick) butter
 1 cup minced onions
 2 tablespoons all-purpose flour
 1 medium tomato, peeled, seeded, and
  chopped
 2 fresh, mild green chiles, sliced very fine
 6 ounces mild cheddar cheese, grated
 6 ounces sharp cheddar cheese, grated
 1 cup half-and-half
 1 teaspoon minced fresh chives
 ⅛ teaspoon cayenne (ground red) pepper
  Salt and pepper

Heat the chicken stock to boiling.

Melt the butter in a large, heavy-bottom pot. Add the onions and cook for 10 minutes over medium-low heat, until soft but not brown, stirring occasionally. Stir in the flour and cook for 1 minute. Add the tomato and chiles. Slowly pour in the hot stock, stirring constantly. Simmer for 10 minutes.

Add the cheese and stir until melted. Stir in the half-and-half and chives. Remove from the heat and add the cayenne. Season to taste with salt and pepper.

To reheat soup made in advance, bring it to the desired temperature over low heat. Do not let it boil.

Serves 6

. . . .

BASQUE GARBURE
Vegetable Soup

The Basques are very fond of soup and serve it at the beginning of every meal. This recipe is a Rocky Mountain version of a well-known *garbure* from the French

Pyrenees. Rich, thick, and hearty, it can serve as a meal in itself. It tastes best when made two or three days in advance.

 1 pound dried Great Northern (white)
  beans
 2 smoked ham hocks, cut into pieces (about
  3 pounds)
 1 medium onion, stuck with 5 cloves
 2 teaspoons salt
 10 black peppercorns
 1 bay leaf
 ½ medium head green cabbage, shredded
 3 tablespoons olive oil
 2 leeks, washed and thinly sliced; or 2
  onions, diced
 8 small garlic cloves
 3 medium tomatoes, peeled, drained, and
  chopped; or 1 (16-ounce) can whole
  tomatoes, drained and chopped
 2 medium carrots, scraped and diced
 1 medium turnip, scrubbed and diced
 ½ teaspoon dried basil, or 1 tablespoon
  fresh minced basil
 ½ teaspoon dried thyme
 ½ teaspoon dried marjoram
 ½ teaspoon ground cloves
 ¼ cup minced fresh parsley
 1 large red bell pepper
 1 cup fresh string beans, cut into 1-inch
  pieces
 ½ cup corn, fresh-cut from the cob, or 1
  (10-ounce) package frozen
 2 small dried hot red chiles, soaked in
  warm water, then seeded and chopped
  (optional)
 1 teaspoon red wine vinegar
 1 teaspoon salt
  Freshly ground black pepper

Soak the beans overnight.

Drain the beans, and place in a large pot with the ham hock, onion, and 1 teaspoon of the salt. Tie the peppercorns and bay leaf in a piece of cheesecloth and add to the pot. Add cold water to cover by 2 inches. Bring to a boil, then lower the heat and simmer for about 1 hour, or until the beans are tender. Reserve the beans in the cooking liquid. Discard the onion and the peppercorns and bay leaf, and set ham hock aside.

In a separate pot of boiling salted water, blanch the cabbage for 5 minutes.

Preheat the oven to 425° F.

Heat the olive oil in a 10-quart heavy-bottom pot and sauté the leeks or onions and the garlic for a few minutes until soft. Stir in the cabbage, tomatoes, carrots, turnip, basil, thyme, marjoram, cloves, and parsley. Add the beans with cooking liquid and enough additional water to cover. Bring to a boil over high heat. Reduce the heat, cover, and simmer for ½ hour.

Meanwhile, roast the red pepper in the oven for about 15 minutes, turning often until it is blackened on all sides. Close it in a paper bag for 20 minutes to cool and soften. Peel, cut in half, and discard the seeds and white pithy veins. Cut flesh into narrow, 2-inch-long strips. Trim the fat and gristle from the ham hock, then cut the meat into small chunks. After the beans have cooked for ½ hour, add the ham, red pepper strips, string beans, and corn; continue cooking for about 10 minutes, or until string beans and corn are tender.

Just before serving, add the hot red peppers, if using, and the vinegar, 1 teaspoon salt, and pepper to taste.

Serves 10 to 12

POTAGE

This hearty soup is substantial enough to serve as a main course. The recipe supposedly originated in biblical times. It was known in medieval England as potage, a thick "peasant" soup. Perhaps the miners who came to the Rockies from the British Isles brought the recipe with them.

    7 cups water
    1 cup dried lentils
    ¾ cup raw brown rice
    ¾ cup olive oil
    4 medium onions, sliced
      Salt and pepper

Place the water and 1 tablespoon salt in a large pot and bring to a boil. Rinse the lentils under cold water and add to the pot. Simmer gently over low heat for 15 minutes. Add the rice and continue to simmer for 1 to 2 hours, or until the mixture is quite thick, like pea soup.

Meanwhile, heat the oil and sauté the onions for 10 minutes on medium-low heat, until they are transparent but not browned. When the soup is done, stir in the onions and season with salt and pepper to taste.

Serves 6 to 8

TORTILLA SOUP

La Montana, a Mexican restaurant in Steamboat Springs, Colorado, serves mesquite-grilled meats with freshly made guacamole, beans, and Spanish rice. While the meats are being grilled to order, diners are offered the soup of the day. Tortilla soup is a favorite. It is highly spiced, but you can use half the quantities of chili powder and cumin for a milder but still spicy soup.

    2 tablespoons olive oil
    ⅓ cup minced onion
    1 teaspoon minced garlic
    2 quarts rich chicken stock
    1 large tomato, peeled and diced
    ½ cup tomato juice
    2 tablespoons hot chili powder
    1 tablespoon ground cumin
    2 teaspoons dried oregano
    2 tablespoons fresh chopped coriander
      (cilantro) leaves
    2 tablespoons vegetable oil
    2 6-inch corn tortillas, cut into strips
    2 tablespoons grated Monterey Jack cheese

Heat the oil in a 4-quart heavy-bottom saucepan, and sauté the onion and garlic for 10 minutes on low heat, until soft and transparent.

Add stock to the onion and garlic along with the tomato, tomato juice, and herbs and spices except coriander. Bring to a boil and simmer for 20 minutes. Stir in the coriander. While the soup is simmering, heat the vegetable oil in a skillet and fry the tortilla strips for 10 minutes, until crisp. Drain on paper towels. When ready to serve, put several tortilla strips in individual bowls, pour the soup over, and garnish with the cheese.

Serves 8 to 10

MOLDED RICE SALAD, BASQUE STYLE

Rice salad made with a variety of ingredients and salad dressing made with a lot of garlic both are typically Basque. This salad tastes as good as it looks and is a wonderful dish to take to a potluck supper or to serve at a buffet.

   1 medium red bell pepper
   3 cups cooked short-grain brown rice (Tsuru Mai brand from California is excellent; see Note)
   2 (5-ounce) cans artichoke hearts, drained; or 6 to 8 cooked fresh or frozen artichoke hearts
   4 scallions, minced, including some green part
  ½ cup fresh or frozen peas, cooked and drained (do not use canned)
   3 tablespoons good-quality olive oil
   8 ounces boiled ham, cubed
   1 tablespoon white wine vinegar
    Salt and freshly ground pepper to taste
    Garlic Dressing (recipe follows)
    Salad greens and cooked artichoke leaves (if using fresh artichokes), for garnish

Place the pepper in a 450° F. oven or under the broiler, and roast until it begins to turn black, turning often. Put the pepper in a paper bag, close tightly, and set aside until the salad is mixed.

Put the rice in a large bowl, add the next 7 ingredients, and mix lightly with a fork. Peel the red pepper, discard the white pith and seeds, and cut into long strips. Oil a 6-cup mold (I like a ring or long loaf form) and arrange the pepper strips decoratively on the bottom. Combine the rice mixture with half the Garlic Dressing, spoon it into the mold, and chill until ready to serve.

To serve, unmold the rice onto a bed of salad greens and garnish with additional greens and cooked artichoke leaves. Spoon the rest of the dressing over the salad.

Serves 6 to 8

Note: I find it best to use the steaming instructions given on the package, decreasing the cooking time by 5 minutes so that the rice remains slightly chewy.

Garlic Dressing

   3 garlic cloves, put through a press
  ¼ cup minced fresh parsley
   1 tablespoon fresh lemon juice
    Salt and pepper
  ¼ cup olive oil
  ¼ cup heavy cream
   4 ounces cream cheese, softened

In a small bowl, blend the garlic and parsley with the lemon juice and salt and pepper to taste. Pour in the oil drop by drop, stirring constantly with a fork to blend well. Continuing to stir, blend in the cream a little at a time, then the cream cheese a little at a time until the mixture is smooth. Taste for seasoning.

Makes 1½ cups

SHAGGY MANE SALAD

Mushroom hunting is one of the great pleasures of living in the Rocky Mountains. Shaggy manes are easy to identify with a mushroom hunter's guide, but many wild mushrooms are toxic, even deadly. So if you gather mushrooms, be sure you know what you're picking.

This recipe for shaggy manes is my own invention, and I think exceptionally good. The recipe also works well with other wild mushrooms or with mushrooms from the supermarket. Alcoholic drinks and shaggy manes should not be consumed at the same meal. Some people have a reaction from the combination.

  12 shaggy manes, or ½ pound other wild or commercial mushrooms
   1 tablespoon minced fresh parsley
   2 tablespoons finely snipped fresh chives
    Vinaigrette Dressing (recipe follows)

Use only very young mushrooms with firm white flesh. Do not wash, instead wipe the caps and stems with a damp paper towel. Cut into ¼-inch-thick slices and drop immediately into a pot of boiling salted water. Boil for 3 minutes, then rinse under cold running water and drain. Just before serving, toss lightly with parsley, chives, and ¼ cup Vinaigrette Dressing.

Serves 4

....

Vinaigrette Dressing

    2 tablespoons fresh lemon juice
    1 tablespoon Dijon mustard
    **½ teaspoon minced fresh tarragon, or a
        pinch of dried tarragon
        Salt and freshly ground pepper**
    ½ cup peanut oil

Combine the lemon juice, mustard, tarragon, and salt and pepper to taste in a small bowl and stir with a fork or tablespoon. Continuing to stir, slowly pour in the oil until the dressing is thick and creamy.

Makes ¾ cup

....

CAULIFLOWER SALAD

    **1 large head cauliflower, washed, trimmed,
        and broken into florets**
    **1 cup Green Goddess Dressing (recipe
        follows)**
    1 bunch watercress, stemmed and washed

Steam the cauliflower for 10 minutes, until tender but still firm; be careful not to overcook. Rinse immediately under cold running water, and drain well. Chill.
    When ready to serve, toss with Green Goddess Dressing and arrange on a bed of watercress.

Serves 6

....

Green Goddess Dressing

    3 cups mayonnaise
    ¼ cup tarragon vinegar
    **1 scallion, including 1 to 2 inches of green
        part**
    ½ cup chopped fresh parsley
    **2 tablespoons chopped fresh tarragon, or
        1 tablespoon dried tarragon**
    ¼ cup minced fresh chives
    1 garlic clove
    8 to 10 anchovy fillets, chopped

Place all the ingredients in a blender or a food processor and blend just until mixed.

Makes 3½ cups

....

SWEET RED CABBAGE

This is a perfect side dish to complement wild duck and other game birds. Serve it with something sour, such as pickled onions or pickled crabapples.

    2 tablespoons olive oil
    **1 medium head red cabbage (about 2½
        pounds), finely sliced**
    **½ teaspoon salt
        Freshly ground black pepper to taste**
    ½ cup sugar
    ½ cup sweet vermouth or Dubonnet

Heat the olive oil in a heavy-bottom pot, and add the rest of the ingredients except the vermouth or Dubonnet. Cover and simmer over low heat for 1 hour. Add the vermouth, cover, and simmer for 1 hour more. The cabbage should be cooked at the lowest possible simmer for the entire cooking time.

Serves 6 to 8

....

SCALLOPED TURNIPS

    **4 pounds young white turnips, scrubbed
        and thinly sliced**
    ½ teaspoon salt
    ½ teaspoon white pepper
    ½ teaspoon fresh thyme, or pinch of dried
    2 tablespoons (¼ stick) butter, in pieces
    2 tablespoons dry bread crumbs
2½ cups light cream, heated
    3 tablespoons grated Monterey Jack cheese
    ¼ teaspoon paprika

Preheat the oven to 350° F. Butter a shallow 3-quart casserole.
    Layer half the turnips, salt, white pepper, thyme, butter, and bread crumbs in the casserole. Repeat the layers. Pour hot cream over, and sprinkle with cheese and paprika. Bake for 45 minutes, or until turnips are tender and the top browned.

Serves 8 to 10

MARIA'S VEGETARIAN STUFFED PEPPERS

Like many young people, my daughter Maria has new-age tastes, and leans toward vegetarianism rather than the predominantly meat diet traditional in the Rockies. She is also a very good cook. This recipe, a family favorite, is her own creation.

    6 medium green bell peppers, tops cut off
      and seeds and pith removed
 1½ cups cooked bulgur (cracked wheat)
    1 medium carrot, grated
    4 scallions, minced, including 1 to 2 inches
      green part
    1 large handful fresh spinach leaves,
      chopped
    1 large tomato, peeled, seeded, and
      chopped
  ½ cup cooked corn kernels
  ¾ cup chicken or vegetable stock
  ½ cup freshly grated Parmesan cheese
  ¼ teaspoon freshly grated nutmeg
    1 tablespoon olive oil
      Fresh Tomato Sauce (recipe follows)
      Minced fresh parsley

Preheat the oven to 350° F.

Blanch the peppers in boiling water for 5 minutes and drain.

Combine the next 10 ingredients in a large bowl. Place the peppers close together in a baking pan and fill with the mixture. Add ¼ cup of water to the pan. Bake for 30 minutes. Garnish with Fresh Tomato Sauce and sprinkle parsley on top. Serve either hot or warm.

Serves 6

Fresh Tomato Sauce

    3 ripe medium tomatoes, or 2 cups canned
      Italian plum tomatoes, coarsely chopped
    2 tablespoons olive oil
    2 tablespoons minced fresh oregano
    2 tablespoons minced fresh basil
      Piece of dried orange peel
    2 garlic cloves, minced
      Pinch of sugar
  ½ teaspoon salt
  ½ teaspoon white pepper

In a 1-quart heavy-bottom pot, cook the tomatoes in the oil over very low heat for 5 minutes. Add the rest of the ingredients and continue to cook at a gentle simmer for 20 minutes. When done, put the sauce through a food mill. This will keep refrigerated for a week or more.

Makes 1½ cups

BAKED POLENTA GRATIN

Polenta is a cornmeal dish native to the mountain regions of Europe. It was introduced to the Rocky Mountain West by the many Italians, Swiss, and French who left their alpine homes to settle here. This simple, traditional recipe is originally from the Italian Alps. It is even better made a day ahead and reheated in a moderate oven. It seems to get crustier and tastier with each reheating.

 1½ cups yellow cornmeal, preferably stone-
      ground
    1 cup cold water
 3½ cups clear beef stock
    1 teaspoon salt
    4 tablespoons (½ stick) butter, in pieces
  ½ to 1 cup milk or light cream
  ¾ cup grated Gruyère cheese

Mix the cornmeal and cold water in the top of a double boiler. Heat the stock to boiling, and mix it thoroughly into the cornmeal mixture. Add the salt. Place the upper pot directly on the burner on low heat and cook until the mixture comes to a boil.

Add only enough water to the lower half of the double boiler to barely touch the bottom of the upper pot. Put upper pot in place and continue cooking the cornmeal over simmering water for 1 hour, stirring occasionally. Stir in the butter and enough milk or cream to give mixture the consistency of a thick, creamy purée.

Preheat the oven to 300° F.

Spoon a layer of the cornmeal mush into a buttered 2-quart casserole. Sprinkle on the cheese. Bake for 40 minutes, or until bubbly and lightly browned. Let the dish cool for at least 10 to 15 minutes before serving.

Serves 6 to 8

....

BRAISED CELERY

Celery as a cooked vegetable is often overlooked. This recipe is especially good with game dishes.

 4 tablespoons (½ stick) butter
 1 tablespoon minced onion
 8 small celery stalks, cut in half
   lengthwise, tender leaves left on (see
   Note)
 2 cups hot beef stock
   Salt and freshly ground black pepper
 ½ cup dry white wine

Melt the butter in a heavy-bottom medium saucepan. Add the onion, celery, beef stock, and salt and pepper to taste. Cover and cook over low heat for about 20 to 25 minutes, or until the celery is tender.

Preheat the oven to 350° F.

Transfer celery and broth to a 1-quart casserole. Add the wine, place uncovered in the oven, and cook until the liquid is almost evaporated, about 40 minutes. Serve hot with the pan juices or cold with a vinaigrette dressing.

Serves 4 to 6

Note: You can also use large stalks, in which case remove the leaves, cut the stalks in half lengthwise, then crosswise.

....

GREEN RICE WITH CHEESE

 4 cups cooked short-grain brown rice (see
   Note)
 ½ cup (1 stick) butter, melted
 3 eggs, lightly beaten
 1 to 1½ cups minced fresh parsley
 1 teaspoon minced fresh oregano
 2 tablespoons minced fresh chives
 2 teaspoons salt
 ½ cup chicken stock
 4 ounces cream cheese, softened
 4 ounces sharp white cheddar, grated

Preheat the oven to 350° F. Butter a 9 x 5 x 3-inch loaf pan.

Combine the first 7 ingredients in a large mixing bowl.

Pour the chicken stock into the loaf pan. Spoon in half the rice mixture and spread the cheeses over the top, breaking the cream cheese into small chunks. Spread with the rest of the rice.

Cover the pan with aluminum foil and bake for 30 minutes. Cut into slices and serve hot or warm.

Serves 8 to 10

Note: You can use long-grain white rice if you prefer. Cook it until tender but still chewy and firm.

....

NICK'S MOUNTAIN POTATOES

My son Nick, who was a ski racer before becoming a professional ice skater, says he owes his stamina to his steak-and-potatoes diet. This is a dish he created and often makes for himself.

 2 tablespoons (¼ stick) butter
 1 tablespoon peanut oil
 3 medium baking potatoes (about 1½
   pounds), scrubbed and cut into ½-inch
   cubes
 1 teaspoon curry powder
 ½ teaspoon salt
 ¼ teaspoon cayenne (ground red) pepper
 ¼ teaspoon Tabasco
 4 ounces Monterey Jack cheese,
   shredded

Heat the butter and oil over low heat in a heavy, nonstick skillet. Add the potatoes, curry powder, salt, cayenne, and Tabasco. Cover and cook for 20 to 25 minutes, or until the potatoes are tender, stirring occasionally. Uncover, turn the heat to high, and brown the potatoes, stirring constantly. Sprinkle with the cheese and heat for about 30 seconds longer, or until the cheese melts.

Serves 4

....

STRING BEAN AND POTATO PIE

This is an Italian-style recipe, very good with roast meats.

 2 medium potatoes (about 1 pound)
 1 pound string beans
 1 cup fine dry bread crumbs
 3 ounces cream cheese, softened
 ½ cup milk
 3 eggs, lightly beaten
 1 garlic clove, put through a press
 3 tablespoons minced fresh parsley
   Dash of dried marjoram
   Pinch of dried oregano
 ¼ teaspoon salt
   Freshly ground black pepper
 1 teaspoon crushed dried mushrooms
   (optional)
 3 tablespoons olive oil

Peel the potatoes and cut into quarters. String and break the beans into 1- to 2-inch-long pieces. Boil the potatoes and beans together in water to cover for 15 to 20 minutes, until tender. Drain.

Preheat the oven to 350° F. Oil a 9-inch deep-dish pie pan, then sprinkle with half the bread crumbs.

Mash the potatoes with the cream cheese, add the milk, and whip until creamy and smooth. (It's easiest to use an electric mixer to mash the potatoes. Do not use a food processor.) Chop the beans coarsely and mix into the potatoes. Combine the eggs, garlic, parsley, marjoram, oregano, salt, pepper to taste, and mushrooms, if using. Add to the potatoes and mix thoroughly.

Spread the potato mixture in the pan and cover with the rest of the crumbs, spreading evenly over the surface. Sprinkle top with the olive oil. Bake for 35 to 45 minutes, until the pie is nicely browned.

Serves 6

MEXICAN SPOON BREAD

There are many versions of spoon bread, but this is my own creation, which is spicier and more breadlike than the traditional custard kind. Served freshly baked from the oven, it is especially good with chorizo sausages and a crisp green salad.

 1 cup yellow cornmeal
 1 (16-ounce) can corn, with liquid
 1 (4-ounce) can chopped green chiles,
   drained
 1½ cups shredded cheddar cheese
 2 eggs, lightly beaten
 ¾ cup milk
 ½ cup vegetable oil
 ½ teaspoon baking soda
   Salt and pepper to taste
   Pinch of dried basil
   Pinch of dried red pepper flakes
 6 scallions, chopped, using 1 to 2 inches of
   green part

Preheat the oven to 350° F. Butter a shallow 2-quart baking dish.

Combine all the ingredients in a large bowl and mix well. Pour into baking dish and bake for 30 to 40 minutes, or until lightly browned and a testing knife comes out clean.

Serves 4

SUMMER SQUASH WITH CHEDDAR

This simple, hearty casserole can be served as a main dish for lunch or supper, or as part of a more elaborate menu. Always use fresh squash and a good, aged cheddar.

 2 medium summer squash (or yellow
   crookneck or scallopini), unpeeled
 1 cup grated cheddar cheese
   Pinch of dried savory
   Pinch of dried thyme
   Freshly grated nutmeg
 ½ cup finely minced fresh parsley
 ¼ cup minced scallions
   Salt and white pepper to taste
   Cayenne (ground red) pepper to taste
 4 eggs, lightly beaten
 ½ cup peanut oil
 2 tablespoons (¼ stick) butter, in pieces

Preheat the oven to 350° F. Butter a 2-quart casserole.

Grate the squash to measure 4 loosely packed cups. Place in a large bowl, and add all the ingredients except the butter. Mix lightly with a fork. Pour into the casserole, dot with the butter, and bake for 30 minutes. Serve with a spinach salad for an attractive contrast of colors.

Serves 4 to 6

. . . .

SQUAW CORN

I don't know how this dish got its name, but it is an old Western recipe and very good!

8 slices lean bacon, coarsely chopped
3 medium onions, thinly sliced
   Kernels cut from 8 ears of corn, to make 4 cups (see Note)
   Salt and pepper

Fry the bacon for 5 minutes over medium-low heat, until half done. Add the onions and sauté for 10 minutes on low heat, until light brown. Add the corn and cook for 10 minutes, until tender, stirring occasionally. Before serving, add salt and pepper to taste.

Serves 8

Note: You can also use thawed frozen corn or canned corn that has been drained well.

. . . .

CORN PUDDING

2 large ears fresh corn, or 2½ cups frozen corn, thawed and drained
1 medium leek, washed well and chopped
3 tablespoons butter
4 eggs
3 tablespoons all-purpose flour
1 tablespoon sugar
   Salt and freshly ground pepper
2 tablespoons finely chopped red bell pepper, or canned, drained pimiento
1 cup light cream

Preheat the oven to 325° F. Butter a 2-quart casserole.

If using fresh corn, cut the kernels from the cobs and measure 2½ cups.

Over low heat, sauté the leek in 2 table-spoons of the butter for 15 minutes, or until soft. Beat the eggs in a mixing bowl. Add the corn and leek, and blend well. Combine the flour, sugar, and salt and pepper to taste, and add to the egg mixture. Add the pepper or pimiento, slowly stir in the cream, and mix thoroughly with a fork. Pour the mixture into the casserole, and sprinkle with the remaining tablespoon of butter.

Bake for 1¼ hours, or until a knife inserted in the center comes out clean. Serve warm or at room temperature.

Serves 6

. . . .

GIANT STUFFED ZUCCHINI

1 giant zucchini (about 4 pounds)
2 tablespoons olive oil
½ cup onion, finely chopped
1 garlic clove, finely minced
6 tablespoons finely chopped green bell pepper
   Salt and freshly ground black pepper
1 teaspoon dried oregano
½ pound ground beef
¼ cup pine nuts
1 egg, lightly beaten
6 tablespoons fresh fine bread crumbs
2 tablespoons grated Parmesan cheese
   Fresh Tomato Sauce (page 144)

Cut the zucchini in half lengthwise. Scoop out the flesh with a spoon, leaving shells about ¼ inch thick. Chop the pulp coarsely and set aside.

Place the zucchini shells in a large pot with cold water and bring to a boil. Lower the heat and simmer for 30 minutes. Drain and run under cold running water. Drain well again.

Preheat the oven to 400° F.

Heat 1 tablespoon of the oil in a skillet. Add the onion, garlic, green pepper, and zucchini pulp; cook for about 5 minutes, stirring constantly. Add salt and pepper to taste, and then the oregano. Remove from the heat and cool briefly.

Stir in the beef, pine nuts, egg, and 4 tablespoons of the bread crumbs; blend well. Spoon the mixture into the zucchini shells, place in a shallow baking pan large enough to hold them side by side, and sprinkle with salt and pepper. Blend the remaining bread cumbs with the grated cheese and sprinkle over the top. Drizzle over the remaining oil. Bake for 30 minutes, or until the top is browned.

Using spatulas, transfer the zucchini to a serving platter, cut into thick slices, and serve with Tomato Sauce passed separately.

Serves 8

FISH, FOWL, AND GAME BIRDS

F ew things are as mouth-watering as the aroma of freshly caught fish frying in a skillet. In the Rockies, a fish and fowl lover's paradise, cooking the day's catch over an outdoor fire is a frequent event. Trout, salmon, bass, whitefish, and other fish fill the region's blue-ribbon streams, while the upland fields offer a sufficiency of pheasant, quail, blue grouse, sage hen, chukar, dove, and Hungarian (gray) partridge. In autumn, ducks and geese abound on lakes and rivers.

While the Rocky Mountain native is apt to cook his fish in the simplest of ways, some frills, like the Red-and-Green Tomato Sauce accompanying the Cornmeal-Coated Fried Freshwater Bass or the Mexican Green Sauce for the baked striped bass, are very much in keeping with the mountain taste.

Cooking game birds is only slightly more complex than cooking fish. Always flavorful, game birds lack the fat of domestic fowl, which can cause them to be dry unless cooked in a liquid, larded, or basted. The oven-bag method used for the Roast Wild Goose on page 156 is another good, moisture-retaining technique.

The texture of a game bird depends in part on its age and sex, but since even a tough old goose can be rendered tender by marinating it, marinades are popular. Marinades also lend good flavor and texture to domestic fowl and those tenderer game birds specially raised for the market. These are frequently sold in specialty markets in large cities, but are also available by mail order; see page 187. Or domestic fowl can be nicely substituted for wild in any of the game bird recipes. The end result is a dish as typically Rocky Mountain, or Rocky Mountain ethnic, as these recipes describe.

FRESHWATER BASS WITH RED-AND-GREEN TOMATO SAUCE

CORNMEAL COATING
 1 cup yellow cornmeal
 ¼ teaspoon freshly ground black pepper
 ⅛ teaspoon cayenne (ground red) pepper
 1 teaspoon sea salt

RED-AND-GREEN TOMATO SAUCE
 2 fresh medium tomatoes, peeled, seeded, and chopped
 6 fresh tomatillos, chopped; or 1 cup canned, drained and chopped
 ½ cup minced fresh parsley
 2 tablespoons minced fresh chives
  Pinch of dried red pepper flakes
 1 tablespoon chopped fresh oregano
 ¼ cup lime juice
 2 tablespoons olive oil

 ¼ cup peanut or olive oil
 6 bass fillets, about 1 inch thick

Mix all the ingredients for the cornmeal coating in a shallow bowl, and set aside.

Mix all the sauce ingredients (use an additional tomato if tomatillos are not available) in a heavy medium saucepan and simmer for 10 minutes. Remove the tomatillo skins with a fork. Reserve the sauce.

Heat the peanut or olive oil in a large skillet. Coat the fillets with the cornmeal mixture and sauté for about 4 minutes per side, until nicely browned. Drain on paper towels. To serve, arrange on a warm platter and pass the tomato sauce separately.

Serves 6

INDIAN SALMON

This method of cooking salmon is known to fishermen in the Northwest and in the Rocky Mountains wherever salmon run the mountain streams. The fish is usually cleaned and filleted immediately after it is caught, and cooked over an open fire for an impromptu meal on the banks of the stream. You might want to prepare salmon this way at the beach or a campground. Choose a good hardwood for your fire (available in bags at barbecue supply stores) or, if necessary, use commercial charcoal and sprinkle on some mesquite or other wood chips which have been soaked in water for 30 minutes so as to give an interesting flavor. Fresh salmon cooked over aromatic wood is truly a culinary treat.

> **6 fresh salmon fillets, 8 to 10 inches long and 1½ to 2 inches thick, skin on (see Note)**
> **Salt and pepper**
> **Lemon wedges**

Use sharp-pointed flat sticks or heavy skewers at least 28 inches long and run them in and out of the center of each fillet at intervals of about 3 inches. The sticks or skewers must be long enough so you can leave 6 to 8 inches of one end bare to plant in a mound of earth or sand.

Dig a 1 x 2-foot pit about 6 inches deep and build a fire in it, preferably with alderwood, mesquite, or applewood. When the fire has turned to glowing embers, push them all to one side of the pit. Build up a mound of sand or earth about 1½ to 2 feet high down the length of the coals.

Plant the ends of the sticks or skewers in the mound so that they slant toward the pit and the skin side of the salmon is about 1½ feet from the fire. Cook the salmon for 6 to 8 minutes, until the skin starts to brown and the juice on the flesh side still

runs clear. The thin layer of fat just under the skin will be turning white and show as a thin line the length of the fillet. Turn the sticks around and cook for 5 minutes more, only until the juice from the flesh turns from clear to white. Season with salt and pepper to taste and serve with wedges of fresh lemon.

Serves 6

Note: To fillet a salmon, cut off the head and tail, then cut down along the backbone, freeing one side of the fish from the bone at a time. If the fillets are longer than 10 inches, cut in half crosswise before skewering.

DEEP-FRIED TROUT IN BEER BATTER

> **BATTER**
> **1 (12-ounce) can beer**
> **1½ cups presifted all-purpose flour**
> **2 teaspoons paprika**
> **½ teaspoon salt**
> **¼ teaspoon white pepper**
>
> **12 trout fillets (each fillet one side of a boned 5- to 6-inch fish)**
> **Oil for deep-frying**
> **Parsley sprigs and lemon wedges, for garnish**

Mix the batter ingredients in a medium bowl. Dip each fillet in the batter and fry in a deep-fryer or in a deep pan in 1 inch of hot oil at 370° F., turning once. Cook for 6 to 10 minutes, until nicely browned.

To serve, arrange on a platter garnished with parsley and lemon wedges.

Serves 6

BAKED STRIPED BASS IN MEXICAN GREEN SAUCE

Bass can be found in many areas of the Rockies where they have been planted in freshwater lakes. I especially like to bake the fish whole in a Mexican Green Sauce prepared with tomatillos, which have a distinctive flavor. If fresh tomatillos are not available in your part of the country, you can use canned ones available in shops that carry Mexican foods.

½ cup olive oil
2 cups fresh or 1 (3-ounce) can tomatillos, cut in half
1 fresh striped bass (3 to 4 pounds), cleaned
2 large onions, chopped
2 garlic cloves, mashed
¼ cup fresh lemon juice
¾ cup minced fresh parsley
½ teaspoon salt
Freshly ground black pepper
Several pimiento-stuffed green olives, for garnish

Preheat the oven to 350° F. Butter a large baking dish.

Heat 2 tablespoons of the oil in a large, heavy-bottom skillet. Add the fresh tomatillos and cook for about 10 minutes, until soft. (If using canned tomatillos, eliminate this step.)

Place the fish in a buttered pan and rub the surface and cavity with some of the oil. Add to the tomatillos the rest of the oil and the remaining ingredients except the olives. Spoon the sauce around the fish and into the cavity. Cover the pan completely with foil, tucking the edges under.

Bake for 10 minutes. Remove the foil, increase the heat to 400° F., and bake for 10 to 15 minutes more, testing for doneness near the backbone with the point of a knife. The flesh should be white, not translucent. Do not overcook. Striped bass is a moist and soft fish, delicious if properly cooked. With 2 spatulas, remove the fish to a platter, spoon sauce around it, and garnish with olives.

Serves 6 to 8

. . . .

TROUT WITH TARRAGON CREAM

During trout season in Idaho, I often serve the freshly caught fish with this cream sauce, which originated in Normandy. Al-

though I prepare fresh trout in almost every way imaginable, this recipe is my favorite.

¼ cup vegetable oil
1 medium tomato, diced
½ cup (1 stick) butter
8 fresh trout, 1 pound or less each
2 cups milk
1 cup all-purpose flour
2 teaspoons cornstarch
1½ cups heavy cream
Salt and pepper
2 tablespoons chopped fresh tarragon leaves
2 sprigs of fresh tarragon, for garnish

Heat 1 tablespoon of the oil in a small skillet. Saute the tomato briefly over medium heat, until softened. Remove from the heat and reserve.

Heat the butter with the rest of the oil in a large, heavy skillet until hot but not smoking. Dip the trout in the milk to which a little salt has been added (this helps to seal in the natural flavor of the fish and seasons it at the same time), then dust with the flour, shaking off any excess. Fry over moderate heat, turning only once, for about 6 to 10 minutes per side depending on size, or until the fish flake when pricked with a fork and are nicely browned on both sides.

While the fish are cooking, in a small, heavy saucepan, dissolve the cornstarch in the cream. Blend well. Season with salt and pepper to taste. Add the chopped tarragon. Stirring constantly over low heat, cook just until the sauce begins to simmer. Remove from the heat immediately.

Arrange the trout on a heated platter and pour over the sauce. Garnish with the tarragon sprigs and cooked tomatoes.

Serves 8

. . . .

OYSTER STEW

Oyster stew is basic fare in the Rocky Mountains. It can be found on the menus of most small-town cafes and has always been a quick supper favorite with home cooks. Because of the lack of fresh shellfish in the mountains, we used to have to rely on canned oysters for our taste of the sea. Now, improved shipping methods make it possible to buy fresh oysters in season in some local markets. Oyster stew made with fresh oysters is, of course, the best.

      6 tablespoons (¾ stick) butter
      1 garlic clove, minced
      4 scallions, minced, including some green
     16 to 24 small fresh oysters, shucked, with
          liquor reserved; or canned oysters with
          liquor
     1½ quarts milk
      1 cup heavy cream
          Salt and pepper
          Cayenne (ground red) pepper

Melt 2 tablespoons of the butter in a heavy-bottom saucepan. Add the garlic and scallions, and sauté over low heat for 5 minutes, until soft. Add the oysters and their liquor, and cook only until heated through. Remove the oysters with a slotted spoon and place equal portions in 4 or 6 warmed bowls.

Heat the milk and cream in the pan in which the oysters were cooked, being careful not to let them boil. When the milk is very hot, add salt and pepper to taste, and ladle it over the oysters. Garnish each bowl with a dab of the remaining butter and a pinch of cayenne.

Serves 4 to 6

. . . .

CHINESE CHICKEN WITH WALNUTS

      4 large whole chicken breasts (about 4
          pounds), skinned, boned, and split
     ¾ cup dry sherry
     ½ cup soy sauce
      1 tablespoon honey
     ½ teaspoon salt
      2 tablespoons cornstarch
      2 eggs, lightly beaten
      2 tablespoons oil, approximately
     1½ cups walnut halves
     ½ teaspoon finely chopped peeled fresh
          ginger (see Note)

      3 garlic cloves, minced
     ¾ cup water
      1 cup drained, sliced canned bamboo
          shoots

Lightly flatten the chicken breasts between sheets of wax paper. Cut the chicken into 1-inch squares and place in a ceramic or glass bowl. Add the sherry, soy sauce, honey, and salt. Cover with plastic wrap and refrigerate overnight.

Drain the chicken and reserve the marinade. In a separate bowl, toss the chicken with the cornstarch until the pieces are evenly coated. Add the eggs and toss the mixture again until the egg is evenly distributed.

Heat the oil in a wok or heavy skillet. Add the walnuts and sauté, turning them often, for 1 to 2 minutes, or until they are hot and crisp. Remove with a slotted spoon and drain on paper towels. Add the ginger and garlic to the pan. Add the chicken in batches and sauté for 5 minutes, until browned, using more oil if necessary. Remove the pieces with a slotted spoon as they are done.

Add the water and the reserved marinade to the pan. Over moderate heat, scrape and stir up the brown bits clinging to the bottom and sides of the pan. Add the chicken, cover, and simmer for 5 to 7 minutes, or until the chicken is tender. Add the bamboo shoots and the walnuts, and simmer for 2 to 3 minutes more, or until heated through.

Serves 8

Note: I keep a chunk of fresh ginger in my freezer and slice a piece off whenever I need it.

. . . .

BASIL CHICKEN WITH RED PEPPER SAUCE

This dish is adapted from a French recipe called *poule à la basilic*. I have used a rich aromatic vinegar in place of wine, and added a Red Pepper Sauce garnish, which makes for a wonderful combination of colors and flavors.

- 1 **large frying chicken (about 4 pounds), cut up**
- ½ **large lemon**
- ¼ **cup olive oil**
- 2 **garlic cloves, sliced**
- ¼ **cup good-quality aromatic red wine vinegar**
  Salt and pepper
- 1½ **cups chicken stock**
- ½ **cup minced fresh basil, or 2 tablespoons dried mixed with enough minced fresh parsley to make ½ cup**
- 4 **anchovy fillets, mashed**
- 2 **tablespoons tomato paste**
- 12 **imported pitted black or green olives**
  Red Pepper Sauce (recipe follows), for garnish

Rub the pieces of chicken with half a lemon and pat dry. Heat the oil in a deep, heavy pot. Add the chicken and brown on all sides. Drain off all oil. Turn the heat down very low, and add the garlic, vinegar, and salt and pepper to taste. Cover the pot tightly and cook for 5 minutes, until the vinegar has completely evaporated. Add the chicken stock, cover, and cook at a steady simmer for about 30 minutes, or until the chicken is tender, adding water if needed to keep the liquid to at least a ½-inch level in the bottom of the pot.

When the chicken is done, stir in the basil, anchovies, tomato paste, and olives. Cook for a few minutes more just to blend the ingredients and heat the dish through.

Arrange the chicken on a warmed platter. Boil down the cooking liquid to thicken it, degrease, and pour a little over the chicken. Serve the rest in a separate dish. Garnish the platter with spoonsful of Red Pepper Sauce.

Serves 4

Red Pepper Sauce

- 1 **large red bell pepper**
- 1 **tablespoon olive oil**
- 1 **small garlic clove, minced**
  Dash of red wine vinegar

Salt to taste
Dash of white pepper

Wash the pepper and cut it into large pieces, removing the white pith and the seeds. Put the pepper in a food processor and purée by turning the machine on and off quickly several times.

Heat the olive oil in a small skillet. Add the pepper purée and the remaining ingredients. Cook over medium heat, stirring constantly until all the liquid from the pepper has evaporated.

Makes ½ cup

MEXICAN-STYLE CHICKEN IN OLIVE SAUCE

This dish can also be made with pork chops or beef steaks. Just cook the meat by your preferred method, whip up the sauce, spoon it over the meat when you're ready to serve, and there you have it—another good potluck entrée.

- 1 **frying chicken (3 to 4 pounds), cut up**
- ½ **medium lemon**
- 2 **tablespoons (¼ stick) butter, melted and mixed with 2 tablespoons peanut oil**
  Salt and pepper

OLIVE SAUCE
- 1 **cup chicken stock**
- 1 **(6-ounce) can tomato paste**
- 1 **medium onion, finely chopped**
- 1 **small green bell pepper, seeded, pith removed, and chopped**
- 15 **pitted green or pimiento-stuffed olives**
- 15 **pitted black olives**
- 3 **small dried red chiles (if *very* hot, use only 1)**
- 1 **teaspoon ground cumin**
- 2 **tablespoons fresh coriander (cilantro), or 1 teaspoon dried**
- ½ **teaspoon ground cinnamon**
- 1 **garlic clove, crushed**

  Several sprigs of fresh coriander (cilantro), for garnish

Preheat oven to 350° F.

Rub the chicken pieces with lemon half, brush with the oil and butter mixture, and sprinkle with salt and pepper to taste. Place in a shallow pan just large enough to hold the pieces and bake for about 40 minutes, until brown and tender, brushing several times with the oil and butter.

Mix the ingredients for the Olive Sauce in a blender or a food processor. Heat the sauce and spoon some over the chicken during the last 10 minutes of cooking. When ready to serve, garnish with fresh coriander. Serve the rest of the sauce separately.

Serves 4 to 6

. . . .

MARINATED ROAST DUCK

Here is a wonderful way to prepare all domestic and game birds. It is a favorite of Herman and Marian Maricich; Herman is a fine amateur chef. The marinade is also a good poaching medium for small game birds or for duck or chicken breasts, so you might want to make a double batch. It can be kept refrigerated for about 2 weeks or frozen indefinitely.

MARINADE
1 cup mushroom soy sauce, preferably
  Pearl River Bridge brand
½ cup honey
¼ cup imported dry sherry
3 slices fresh ginger
4 garlic cloves, unpeeled and mashed
2 star anise, crushed
1 (11-ounce) can chicken broth

1 domestic duck (4 to 5 pounds), dressed

Combine ingredients for the marinade in a small saucepan. Bring to a boil and simmer for 5 minutes. Cool to room temperature, and refrigerate if not using right away.

Place the duck in a deep glass or pottery dish, pour the marinade over, cover with plastic wrap, and refrigerate for several hours, turning the bird from time to time.

Transfer the duck to a pot just large enough to hold it, pour the marinade over, cover, and simmer on top of the stove for 30 minutes. (The recipe can be made several hours or a day ahead to this point, in

which case let the duck cool in the poaching liquid, cover, and refrigerate. Bring to room temperature before final cooking.)

Preheat the oven to 400° F. Remove the duck from the marinade, place it on a rack in a roasting pan, and cook for 30 minutes, testing for doneness with the sharp point of a knife. The meat should remain pink, but if you prefer it rarer, test after 15 or 20 minutes. Cut the duck into serving pieces. Serve with Baked Polenta Gratin, page 144.

Serves 3 to 4

. . . .

GAME HENS WITH SAVORY STUFFING

This recipe, given to me by Sharon Ikauniks, originated with her mother-in-law, who is Canadian. It is a fine addition to Rocky Mountain cookery.

4 Cornish game hens with livers
½ medium lemon
4 tablespoons (½ stick) butter
4 shallots, finely chopped
½ pound cottage cheese
¼ cup fine dry bread crumbs
¾ teaspoon salt
  Freshly ground black pepper
  Dash of grated nutmeg
½ teaspoon ground cloves
¼ teaspoon dried thyme
1 tablespoon finely chopped fresh parsley
¾ cup dry sherry
2 tablespoons olive oil
1 cup chicken stock
2 bay leaves
4 slices thin white bread with crusts
  removed, browned in butter
3 tablespoons heavy cream
2 teaspoons cornstarch, dissolved in 2
  tablespoons water (optional)

Rub the hens with the lemon half and set aside.

Heat 2 tablespoons of the butter in a heavy skillet. Add the livers and sauté for 5 minutes over low heat. Add the shallots and cook for 5 minutes, until lightly browned. Remove the livers, cool, and finely chop.

In a small mixing bowl, combine the

shallots and livers with the cottage cheese, bread crumbs, ½ teaspoon salt, pepper to taste, nutmeg, cloves, thyme, parsley, and 1 tablespoon of the sherry. Mix thoroughly.

Stuff hens with mixture (do *not* stuff tightly) and close cavities with skewers.

Put the remaining butter and the oil in a heavy, flame-proof casserole just large enough for the hens. Heat until sizzling. Brown hens, 2 at a time, on all sides. Pour out the oil, return birds to the casserole, and add the remaining sherry, chicken stock, bay leaves, and remaining salt. Bring to a simmer. Drape buttered wax paper over the birds, cover the pot, and cook slowly for about 45 minutes, or until tender.

Place browned bread slices on a warm serving platter. Remove the skewers from the hens, and place a hen on top of each bread slice.

Skim off any fat from the liquid left in the pot, discard the bay leaves, and bring the liquid to a rapid boil over high heat. Add the cream and continue to boil gently until slightly syrupy. If desired, thicken with the cornstarch mixture. Pour a little of the sauce over each hen, and serve the rest separately.

Serves 4

. . . .

BRAISED SAGE HENS

Sage hens are so called because their habitat is the sagebrush-covered foothills of the Rockies. The meat of these hens is dark, with a rich and distinctive flavor enhanced by fresh or dried herbs. You can also make this recipe with pheasant or partridge.

    4 strips bacon, diced
    3 sage hens, dressed and cut into quarters
      Salt and freshly ground pepper
    2 tablespoons all-purpose flour
 1½ cups dry white wine
  12 garlic cloves, unpeeled and split
    1 orange, sliced and slices quartered
      Juice of 1 orange
    2 cups boiling water
    4 sprigs of fresh parsley
    2 fresh sage leaves, chopped, or ¼ teaspoon dried
    1 sprig of fresh thyme, or ⅛ teaspoon dried

    1 bay leaf
    2 tablespoons tomato paste
    2 tablespoons cornstarch, mixed with ¼ cup cold water (optional)
      Several fresh sage sprigs and orange peel or slices, for garnish

Cook the bacon in a large, heavy-bottom pot for 10 minutes, until lightly browned and crisp. Reserve the fat. Drain the bacon on a paper towel and set aside.

Season the birds with salt and pepper to taste and dust with the flour. Heat the bacon fat to sizzling and brown the birds on all sides. Place in a roasting pan that will hold them snugly. Add the wine, garlic, orange slices and juice, and boiling water. Add the herbs, tomato paste, and bacon. Cover tightly and simmer for about 45 minutes, until the birds are tender.

Transfer the birds to a warm platter and cover with foil to keep them warm until ready to serve.

Strain the sauce and thicken, if desired, with cornstarch mixture. Arrange the birds on a warmed platter with a little sauce spooned over. Garnish with fresh sage and orange peel curls or orange slices. Serve the rest of the sauce on the side.

Serves 6

. . . .

GRILLED BREAST OF MALLARD WITH RED-HOT GINGER SAUCE

This is my adaptation of a recipe created by caterer Selene Isham of Delightful Occasions, Sun Valley, Idaho. Selene is an artist with food and seasonings. Her Red-Hot Ginger Sauce was just what I had been looking for to accompany succulent slices of wild duck breasts—my favorite entrée. If mallards aren't available at your local market or butcher shop, other types of duck will work as well.

    6 mallards, dressed, or other wild or domestic ducks

    4 medium onions, quartered
    4 medium carrots, scraped and thickly sliced

1 medium white turnip, peeled and thickly
   sliced
4 celery stalks, thickly sliced
4 garlic cloves, mashed
1 small bunch parsley, including stems
2 sprigs of fresh thyme, or 1 teaspoon dried
2 bay leaves
4 whole cloves
2 teaspoons dried basil
8 black peppercorns
   Fresh sage leaves, for garnish
   Red-Hot Ginger Sauce (recipe follows)

Place the mallards breast side up on a flat
surface. Cutting close to the breastbone
with a very sharp knife, separate the breast
in 1 piece from each side of the bone. You
will have 2 fillets from each bird. Reserve
the giblets and trimmings. Refrigerate the
breasts until ready to use.

Put the carcasses into a stockpot and
break them up with a wooden spoon. Add
the remaining ingredients along with the
giblets and trimmings. Add enough water
to cover by 2 inches. Bring to a boil, and
skim off foam. Cover and simmer for 2
hours. Strain and return the stock to the
pot. Boil until reduced to 6 cups, then
strain again through a cloth. Cool to room
temperature, and reserve 3 cups for sauce.
Refrigerate or freeze the remaining stock.

Bring the duck breasts to room temperature while you prepare the fire. Spread
enough charcoal in an outdoor barbecue to
make a bed the same size as the duck
breasts when placed side by side. Push the
charcoal into a pile and heat for 20 to 30
minutes, or until the coals are partially
covered with white ash. Spread them out
again in a single layer.

Season the duck breasts with salt and
pepper to taste and lay them skin side
down about 4 to 6 inches above the coals.
Cook for 5 to 7 minutes per side, watching
carefully to avoid overcooking. These are
best served very rare, like steak.

To serve, slice the breasts on the diagonal. Lay overlapping slices on a warmed
platter, garnish with fresh sage, and pass
the Red-Hot Ginger Sauce separately.

Serves 6

Red-Hot Ginger Sauce

1 teaspoon freshly ground black pepper
¾ teaspoon salt
½ teaspoon white pepper
1 teaspoon dried thyme
¼ teaspoon cayenne (ground red) pepper
¾ teaspoon Hungarian sweet paprika
½ teaspoon dry mustard
2 tablespoons (¼ stick) butter, softened
1 tablespoon vegetable oil
1 teaspoon minced fresh garlic
½ cup finely chopped onions
¼ cup finely chopped celery
3 cups reserved duck stock
½ teaspoon ground ginger, approximately
½ teaspoon dried sage
⅛ teaspoon ground cumin
¼ cup dark brown sugar, tightly packed
1 teaspoon minced candied ginger

Make a seasoning mixture by stirring the
first 8 ingredients together with a fork.

Heat the oil in a large, heavy-bottom pot.
Add the garlic, onions, and celery, and cook
for about 10 minutes, until soft. Add the
seasoning mixture and cook for 5 minutes
longer, stirring occasionally. Add the stock,
bring to a boil, and cook over high heat
until reduced to 1½ cups. Add the remaining ingredients, and simmer for 5 minutes.
Taste for seasoning. If the ginger flavor is
not pronounced enough, add additional
ground ginger to taste.

Makes about 1¾ cups

QUAIL WITH GARLIC BREAD SAUCE AND FRIED PARSLEY

Quail have a delicate flavor and are delicious morsels if you watch them carefully
while they are cooking, and baste often so
they don't dry out. Allow two quail per per-
son, more for large appetites.

You can order fresh quail from your
butcher or buy them frozen in some supermarkets. They are also available by mail
order (see page 187).

GARLIC BREAD SAUCE

    3 tablespoons butter
10 to 12 garlic cloves, crushed
1½ cups day-old white bread crumbs
    2 cups chicken stock
    3 tablespoons cream cheese, softened
      Salt and white pepper to taste
      Pinch of cayenne (ground red) pepper
      Pinch of grated nutmeg

  10 quail
  ½ medium lemon
    4 tablespoons (½ stick) butter
    2 tablespoons olive oil
  ½ teaspoon crumbled dried rosemary
      Salt and pepper
    2 cups parsley sprigs
      Oil for deep-frying

To make the bread sauce, melt the butter in a deep skillet. Add the garlic cloves and cook, covered, over very low heat for 30 minutes. If necessary, to keep the garlic from scorching add 2 tablespoons of hot water to the skillet. When the garlic is soft, add the bread crumbs and brown them for a few minutes. Stir in the remaining sauce ingredients. Remove the sauce from the heat, let it cool for a few minutes, then blend in an electric blender until smooth. Return to the skillet and set aside.

Preheat the oven to 450° F.

Rub the birds all over with lemon half. Place in a shallow roasting pan just large enough to hold them.

Melt the butter in a small saucepan, stir in the olive oil, rosemary, and salt and pepper to taste, then warm slightly. Brush each bird with the mixture.

Roast the birds for 5 minutes, then turn the oven down to 300° F., and continue roasting for 15 to 20 minutes, until the birds are tender. Baste thoroughly with the butter mixture every 5 minutes to keep them succulent.

While the quail are cooking, stem, wash, and thoroughly dry the parsley. Add 2 to 3 inches of oil to a saucepan and heat until a piece of parsley sizzles loudly when dropped in but does not turn dark when cooked for 30 seconds. (If it does, the oil is too hot.) Cook several sprigs at a time, removing them with a slotted spoon or tongs.

The parsley should be crisp and bright green. Drain on paper towels.

Arrange the quail on a heated platter. Warm the bread sauce in the skillet. Spoon a little on each bird, and top with the fried parsley. Serve the remaining sauce and parsley on the side.

Serves 5

ROAST WILD GOOSE WITH CORN-BREAD STUFFING

This is my favorite recipe to serve for Christmas dinner. A wild goose weighing five pounds or under is probably a young bird and will be tender and succulent cooked this way. The recipe is equally good made with a domestic goose.

    2 ounces salt pork, cut into ¼- to 1-inch
      strips
    1 small wild goose (4 to 5 pounds), dressed
      Salt and pepper
      Corn-Bread Stuffing (recipe follows)
    1 cup chicken stock
    1 cup dry white wine
    1 tablespoon all-purpose flour, mixed with
      3 tablespoons cold water
      Cranberry-Apricot Chutney (page 94)

Preheat the oven to 375° F.

Boil the salt pork for 10 minutes, rinse, and drain. Using a larding needle, lard the breast of the goose with the salt pork. Salt and pepper the goose, and stuff lightly with Corn-Bread Stuffing. (Bake leftover stuffing in a separate small buttered casserole.) Close the cavity with skewers. Place in an oven roasting bag and add the stock and wine. Secure the end of the bag tightly with a twist-tie and prick top of bag in about 10 places. Roast for 1 to 1½ hours.

Cut the bag open and discard. Drain off all the pan juices and reserve. Raise the oven temperature to 500° F. and roast the bird for 15 to 25 minutes more, until brown. Remove to a carving board and let rest while you make the gravy.

Place the reserved juices in a small saucepan and slowly stir in flour mixture.

Simmer for a few minutes until thickened. Season to taste.

Serve the goose with the gravy on the side and with a separate dish of Cranberry-Apricot Chutney.

Serves 6

. . . .

Corn-Bread Stuffing

½ **pound pork sausage**
6 **tablespoons (¾ stick) butter**
1 **medium onion, finely chopped**
1 **celery stalk, finely chopped**
1 **shallot, finely chopped**
3 **cups white corn bread crumbs**
½ **teaspoon salt**
1 **tablespoon dried sage**
½ **teaspoon dried thyme**
1 **egg, lightly beaten**

Brown the sausage in a small skillet, breaking it up with a fork as it cooks. Drain on paper towels.

Melt the butter in a medium skillet. Sauté the onion, celery, and shallot for 10 minutes on low heat, or until soft and the onion begins to turn golden.

Combine the crumbs and seasonings in a large bowl. Stir in the egg, add the sausage and the sautéed vegetables, and mix well.

Makes 4 cups

CASSEROLES AND MAIN-DISH PIES

. . . .

asseroles and main-dish pies are among the most versatile entrées in the Western cook's repertoire. They can be prepared a few days or a few weeks ahead and stored in the refrigerator or freezer until needed. Some are perfect to carry to the potluck dinners, which are popular here. Many, such as the zucchini

and tamale pies, the Chiles Rellenos Casserole, and the Smoked Salmon Quiche with Yogurt Crust make complete meals once you add bread and a salad. The Casserole of Venison and Partridge, a very special dish, is one that any cook with access to specialty meat markets can put together.

The focus in these recipes is on traditional Western foods—beans, chiles, corn, squash, and the spices of the region's Mexican heritage—used in ways not entirely traditional.

Ever since shellfish have been available in many Rocky Mountain markets, our cuisine has included dishes using crab and shrimp. Crab enchiladas take a traditional Mexican dish to a new elegance. For the salmon pie, the fresh salmon that is now available in supermarkets and fish markets throughout most of the country might also be caught in some areas of the Rockies in freshwater lakes where they have been landlocked or at spawning time when ocean fish return to mountain streams, or brought in from the West Coast. At least one fishmonger makes a monthly trip in his refrigerated wagon from Oregon to the Rockies, stopping at towns along the way to deliver his fresh fish. The Basque Casserole of Cod and Red Peppers is made with salt cod, once the only fish able to survive the long, unrefrigerated journey to the Rockies from the East Coast. Today, when it is possible to choose salt cod for reasons other than necessity, it has a brand-new appeal.

In the following recipes, the amalgam of native foods, European influence, and modern tastes (in the use of bulgur and yogurt) is pure Rockies. Nothing could show more clearly the region's melting-pot cuisine than these one-pot dishes, or display its broad range from down-home substantial to hunger-satisfying elegance.

. . . .

CASSEROLE OF VENISON AND PARTRIDGE

Several years ago I received this recipe along with Christmas greetings from Hildegard Raeber, who is known in and around Sun Valley, Idaho, for her superlative cuisine.

  3 partridges (12 to 16 ounces each),
    cleaned and dressed
  3 strips bacon
¼ cup vegetable oil
  2 tablespoons (¼ stick) butter
    Green leafy tops from 2 celery stalks,
    chopped to make about ½ cup
  1 large carrot, thinly sliced
  1 large onion, chopped
    Salt and pepper
  2 pounds boneless venison, shoulder or
    leg, fat and sinew trimmed
  2 tablespoons all-purpose flour
  2 cups beef broth, approximately 1
    (11-ounce) can, plus ½ cup water
½ cup dry red wine
  1 bay leaf
    Pinch of dried thyme
¼ teaspoon grated nutmeg
  1 teaspoon ground ginger
¼ teaspoon freshly ground black pepper
  2 tablespoons lingonberries
  3 large mushrooms, thinly sliced
  1 goose liver, cubed, or 6 chicken livers,
    left whole but trimmed
  3 tablespoons sour cream
    Lemon juice

Salt the insides of the birds and wrap a strip of bacon around each. In a large, heavy-bottom pan with a lid, heat 2 tablespoons of the oil with 1 tablespoon of the butter. Brown the birds on all sides, turning often. Add the celery tops, carrot, onion, and salt and pepper to taste. Cover and cook for 15 to 20 minutes, until partially done.

Remove the birds and discard the bacon. When cool enough to comfortably handle, cut birds into quarters and trim off all the bony parts, such as wings and necks. Save the trimmings.

Slice the venison into ½-inch-thick steaks. Heat the remaining butter and oil in a separate heavy-bottom pan. Dip one side of the steaks in the flour and brown on both sides. Remove from the pan and cut into cubes. Add the bird trimmings, vegetables, and any drippings from the pan in which the birds were browned to the venison pan with any trimmings from ven-

ison. Sprinkle 1 tablespoon of flour over and cook a few minutes more, stirring. Add the consommé, stirring and scraping the pan to loosen any brown bits. Continuing to stir, add the wine, the spices and herbs, and the lingonberries. Cover and simmer for 30 minutes. Add more wine or consommé, if the pot seems dry.

Place the birds, venison cubes, sliced mushrooms, and liver in the 4-quart Dutch oven. Using a strainer, pour the sauce from the venison pan over the meat to barely cover. (The dish can be cooked up to one day ahead to this point and refrigerated until ready to use.) Bring the pot to a boil, cover, reduce the heat, and simmer for 30 minutes. Just before serving, remove from the heat and stir in the sour cream and lemon juice to taste. Taste for seasoning.

Serves 6 to 8

. . . .

NAN'S FONDUE

This is a wonderful dish for fall or winter menus. It contains the basic ingredients of a Swiss fondue and bakes to a smooth soufflé consistency. It is even good reheated. Nan Crocker is owner of Epitome, a charming tea room and restaurant in Ketchum, Idaho.

  4 cups cubed good-quality French bread,
    loosely packed
  4 eggs
2½ cups milk
½ teaspoon salt
½ teaspoon white pepper
    Dash of cayenne (ground red) pepper
  6 ounces Gruyère cheese, grated (about 2
    cups loosely packed)
    Freshly grated nutmeg
  2 tablespoons kirsch or cognac

Place the bread cubes in a shallow 2-quart casserole. Mix the eggs and milk in a medium bowl. Add the rest of the ingredients in the order given, stirring just enough to blend. Pour over the bread cubes, cover, and refrigerate for several hours or overnight.

Preheat the oven to 350° F.

Bring the casserole to room temperature. Bake for 40 minutes, until a knife inserted comes out clean. Turn the heat up to 400° F. and bake for 5 to 10 minutes more, until the top is nicely browned. Serve immediately.

Serves 6

Note: To reheat leftover portions, cover with foil and place in a 350° F. oven for 15 minutes, or until heated through.

CASSEROLE OF SALT COD AND RED PEPPERS

BACALÃO A LA VIZCAINA

An authentic Basque meal always includes a cod dish. Salt cod is delicious when properly prepared, and it is especially good cooked with peppers and garlic, as in this traditional recipe. Serve it for supper in fall or winter to satisfy sharpened appetites.

> 1 large piece salt cod (about 1 pound)
> 6 medium red bell peppers, or 1 cup drained and chopped canned pimientos
> ¾ cup olive oil
> 4 garlic cloves, mashed
> 2 slices stale white bread, crusts removed and cubed
> 1 (14-ounce) can Italian plum tomatoes, drained and chopped

Preheat the oven to 350° F.

Rinse the cod well under cold water, then soak for about 8 hours in cold water to cover. Rinse again under cold water, drain, and pat dry. Cut the fish into 2-inch chunks.

If using fresh peppers, place them in a shallow baking pan and roast in the oven until charred, turning several times. Reserve any juice for later use. Place the peppers in a paper bag, close tightly, and let them steam for about 30 minutes. Peel, seed, and chop to make 1 cup.

Heat ¼ cup of the olive oil in a large, heavy skillet and sauté the garlic for a few minutes. Discard the garlic, add the fish, and cook gently over low heat for 10 min-

utes. Add the peppers and their juice. (If using canned pimientos, do not use the juice.)

In an oiled 2-quart casserole, layer the fish and the bread cubes. Pour the tomatoes over, then the remaining olive oil. Bake for 20 minutes, or until thoroughly heated.

Serves 4 to 6

SHEEPHERDER CASSEROLE

This is the kind of dish the sheepherders in Idaho leave over a campfire to cook all day while they're off on their rounds. The Basques often feature it at outdoor meals, accompanied by a crusty loaf of French bread and a hearty red wine. I often take it to picnics and reheat it either on a Coleman stove or over an open fire.

> 2 tablespoons olive oil
> 4 pounds lamb shanks, cut into 4-inch pieces; or lean lamb ribs, cut into single rib sections
> ¼ cup chopped fresh parsley
> 3 garlic cloves, chopped
> 1 large onion, quartered
> 1 large carrot, cut into 3-inch lengths
> 1 large potato, cut into 3-inch chunks
> 2 large green bell peppers, seeds and pith removed and cut into ½-inch strips
> ½ teaspoon salt
> Freshly ground black pepper to taste
> 1 cup beef stock
> ¼ cup dry red wine
> 6 bacon strips

Preheat the oven to 350° F.

Heat the oil in a large Dutch oven and brown the lamb on all sides. Add the rest of the ingredients except the bacon, and stir lightly with a fork. Lay the bacon slices over the top, cover the pot, and bake for 2 hours.

Serves 4

RANCH-STYLE BARBECUE BEANS

A plate of these beans, topped with raw onion rings and served with hot corn bread and a green salad, makes a satisfying meal. They are also very good as a side dish with grilled or roasted meats.

4½ cups (2 pounds) dried red beans
1 smoked ham hock
2 tablespoons vegetable oil
2 medium onions, coarsely chopped
2 large garlic cloves, chopped
1 tablespoon dark brown sugar
½ cup Dijon mustard
2 (12-ounce) bottles ale
3 tablespoons tomato paste
1 tablespoon salt
1 teaspoon fennel seeds
   Pinch of ground cloves
¾ cup barbecue sauce, preferably homemade (page 167), or Tabasco to taste
¼ teaspoon liquid smoke (optional)

Soak the beans overnight in cold water to cover.

Drain the beans and place in a large pot. Add water to cover by 2 inches. Bring to a boil, drain, and return the beans to the pot. Add the ham hock and water to cover by 2 inches. Bring to a boil, reduce the heat, and simmer, uncovered, for 1½ to 2 hours, until the beans are tender.

Meanwhile, heat the oil in a medium frying pan and cook the onions and garlic over low heat for about 10 minutes, until soft.

Preheat the oven to 250° F.

Remove the ham hock from the pot, trim off all fat, skin, and gristle, and cut the meat from the bone in chunks. Reserve.

Drain the beans and mix with the remaining ingredients in a 6-quart casserole. Stir in the ham, onions, and garlic. Bake for approximately 4 hours, or until most of the liquid is absorbed and the top is browned. Check the pot from time to time, adding water if the beans become dry. Don't overcook; the beans should remain moist. Serve topped with raw sweet onion rings. (Walla Walla Sweets from Washington are superb!)

Serves 12 to 14

. . . .

CRAB ENCHILADAS VERDE

CRAB FILLING
2 cups crabmeat
2 tablespoons oil
2 medium onions, finely chopped
1 medium tomato, chopped
8 ounces Monterey Jack cheese, grated
   Salt and freshly ground pepper

GREEN SAUCE
3 tablespoons vegetable oil
2 (13-ounce) cans tomatillos, with juice
2 garlic cloves, minced
1 (4-ounce) can chopped green chiles, drained

3 tablespoons vegetable oil
12 6-inch corn tortillas
½ cup sour cream, at room temperature
1 (2-ounce) jar red lumpfish caviar, for garnish

To make the crab filling, first pick over the crabmeat, removing any cartilage. Set aside. Heat the oil and gently sauté the onions for 10 minutes, until transparent. Reserve half the onions for the sauce. Place the rest in a small mixing bowl, add the crabmeat, tomato, and cheese, and mix lightly with a fork. Add salt and pepper to taste. Set aside.

To make the sauce, warm the oil in a large skillet (don't let it get too hot). Add the tomatillos with their juice, and mash with a fork. Simmer for 5 to 10 minutes, until the skins separate from the pulp. Remove the skins with a fork. Add the garlic, chiles, and reserved onions, and cook at a bare simmer for about 15 minutes, or until thickened.

Preheat the oven to 350° F.

Prepare the tortillas. Heat the oil in a medium frying pan. Dip in one tortilla at a time and fry quickly so that it remains soft. As each tortilla is fried, lay it on paper toweling, put on a generous dollop of crab filling, roll it up, and place it seam side down in a shallow baking pan large enough to hold the enchiladas in neat rows, but not too snugly. Pour the Green Sauce evenly over the enchiladas. Bake for 20 to 30 minutes, or until heated through. Do not overcook or the enchiladas will become mushy. When done, put a dab of sour cream on each and garnish with the caviar. Serve immediately.

Serves 6 to 8

Note: Canned tomatillos are available in the Mexican food sections of many markets.

ZUCCHINI PIE

Serve this with cold vegetables and vinaigrette or a sliced tomato and avocado salad for lunch or a light supper. Be sure to make the crust ahead; it must be thoroughly chilled before you roll it out.

CREAM CHEESE CRUST
½ cup (1 stick) unsalted butter, chilled and cut into pieces
4 ounces cream cheese, chilled and cut into chunks
1½ cups presifted all-purpose flour
½ teaspoon baking powder
¼ teaspoon cider vinegar
2 to 4 tablespoons ice water

FILLING
½ cup (1 stick) butter
1 cup chopped onions
4 cups thinly sliced zucchini (about 3 medium)
½ teaspoon salt
½ teaspoon freshly ground black pepper
½ cup minced fresh parsley
¼ teaspoon dried thyme
2 eggs, lightly beaten
⅛ teaspoon freshly grated nutmeg
4 ounces Swiss cheese, grated
¼ cup heavy cream

To make the crust, put the butter, cream cheese, and dry ingredients in the bowl of a food processor. Turn the machine on and off quickly until the mixture has a coarse, mealy texture. Add the vinegar, then add the ice water by tablespoonfuls and process only until the dough starts to pull away from the sides of the bowl. Wrap and chill the dough for at least 30 minutes.

Preheat the oven to 375° F.

Roll out the dough large enough to line a 10-inch pie pan or a 9-inch square baking dish. Refrigerate while you make filling.

Melt the butter in a deep, heavy-bottom pan. Add the onions and zucchini and cook over medium-low heat for about 10 minutes, until soft. Stir in the salt, pepper, parsley, and thyme.

Combine the eggs with the remaining ingredients in a medium bowl. Mix into the zucchini mixture, blending well with a fork. Pour into the pastry-lined pan and bake for 30 minutes, or until set and a testing knife comes out clean.

Serves 8 to 10

TAMALE PIE

Tamale pie is a favorite one-dish meal in the Rockies. This is my own version, made with a spicy meat mixture called picadillo, instead of the usual chili-flavored beef.

5 cups water
1½ teaspoons salt
1½ cups yellow cornmeal
3 tablespoons vegetable oil
1 medium onion, chopped
1 medium green bell pepper, chopped
1 pound lean ground beef
1 (16-ounce) can Italian plum tomatoes, chopped, with the juice
¼ cup raisins, soaked in ¼ cup hot beef stock
8 to 10 whole canned artichoke hearts (in water, not with spices), drained and halved
½ cup chopped toasted almonds
1 teaspoon ground cinnamon
Pinch of ground cloves
¼ teaspoon ground cumin
White pepper to taste
6 pitted black olives and remaining artichoke hearts, for garnish

Bring the water to a boil in a 3-quart pot, add 1 teaspoon of the salt, and slowly stir in the cornmeal. Cook for 30 minutes at a bare simmer, stirring occasionally.

Preheat the oven to 350° F. Butter a 2-quart casserole.

Heat 2 tablespoons of the oil in a large frying pan and sauté the onion and green pepper until soft over medium heat, about

10 minutes. Sauté the meat in a separate pan in the remaining 1 tablespoon of oil, crumbling the meat with a fork until smooth. When the meat has just turned pink, remove from the heat and drain on paper towels.

Stir the remaining ½ teaspoon of salt and the rest of the ingredients, including the juice from the tomatoes, into the onion and pepper mixture, reserving a couple of artichoke halves for garnish. Simmer for about 10 minutes, then stir in the meat.

Pour half the cornmeal mush into the casserole, smoothing a thin layer partway up the sides of the dish with the back of a spoon. Add the meat-vegetable mixture and smooth the remaining mush over to cover. Cut the remaining artichoke hearts in half. Arrange artichoke halves and olives in a decorative pattern on top. Bake for 30 minutes, or until thoroughly hot.

Serves 6

. . . .

FRESH SALMON PIE WITH FENNEL

This delicious pie is elegant enough for a special occasion.

CREAM CHEESE CRUST
½ pound (2 sticks) unsalted butter, chilled
    and cut into pieces
3 cups presifted all-purpose flour
½ teaspoon baking powder
8 ounces cream cheese, cold or frozen
½ teaspoon cider vinegar
6 to 8 tablespoons cold milk
    Milk for brushing top

FILLING
1½ cups chicken stock
½ cup bulgur (cracked wheat) or short-
    grain brown rice
2 tablespoons (¼ stick) butter
2 tablespoons vegetable oil
1 medium onion, finely chopped
¾ pound mushrooms, sliced (5 loosely
    packed cups)
2 pounds poached fresh salmon, skinned,
    boned, and broken into 1-inch chunks
¼ cup chopped fresh parsley
½ teaspoon dried dill

1 teaspoon fennel seeds, preferably
    coarsely ground but can be used whole
2 hard-cooked eggs, chopped
    Salt and pepper
½ teaspoon paprika

To make the crust, place the butter and the dry ingredients in a food processor, then add the cream cheese in small chunks. Turn the machine on and off quickly until the mixture has a mealy texture. With the machine running, add the vinegar and milk gradually, processing just until the pastry pulls away from the sides of the bowl. Wrap and refrigerate until thoroughly chilled, at least 30 minutes.

Divide the dough in two, with one part slightly larger. Roll out the larger part to fit a shallow 9-inch square or 7 x 11-inch baking dish, allowing 1-inch overhang. Chill crust while you make the filling.

Bring the stock to a boil in a medium saucepan. Stir in the bulgur. Cover and steam over very low heat for 10 to 15 minutes. Reserve. (If using rice, cook according to package instructions, using chicken stock instead of water.)

Meanwhile, heat the butter and oil in a heavy skillet, and sauté the onion and mushrooms for 10 minutes, until soft. Add the salmon, stirring lightly. Add the bulgur or rice, then lightly stir in the parsley, dill, fennel seeds, chopped eggs, and salt and pepper to taste.

Preheat the oven to 350° F.

Sprinkle the prepared crust with half the paprika and spoon in the salmon mixture, spreading it evenly to the corners. Sprinkle with the rest of the paprika.

Roll out the remaining pastry to make a top crust. Lay it over the top of the dish, and crimp the edges together. Make several small slits in the top, then brush with a little milk. Bake for 30 minutes, or until the crust is browned.

Let the pie cool for at least 15 minutes before serving. It is good at room temperature, or it can be made ahead, refrigerated, and rewarmed, covered with foil.

Serves 8 to 10

. . . .

QUICK DEEP-DISH QUICHE

This is very easy to make and delicious for breakfast, lunch, or a light supper.

 2 tablespoons (¼ stick) butter
 1 large potato, peeled, boiled until tender, and thinly sliced
 ½ pound bacon, cooked, drained, and crumbled; or cooked ham, finely diced
 1 large tomato, diced
 1 teaspoon dried basil
 ½ cup minced fresh parsley
 4 scallions, minced (with some green part)
 ¾ cup presifted all-purpose flour
 1 teaspoon baking soda
 2 tablespoons vegetable or olive oil
 4 eggs
 1 cup heavy cream
 1 cup milk
 ½ teaspoon salt
 ¼ teaspoon white pepper
 1 cup grated cheddar cheese
 1 cup grated Swiss cheese

Preheat the oven to 350° F. Butter an 8- or 9-inch deep-dish pie pan.

Heat the butter to sizzling in a medium frying pan and sauté the potato slices quickly, until lightly browned. (You can eliminate this step if you wish.) Layer the bacon, potato, and tomato in the pie dish. Sprinkle with the basil, parsley, and scallions. Mix the rest of the ingredients except the cheeses in a blender for a few minutes, then pour over the top. Sprinkle on the cheeses and bake for 1 hour, or until the top is nicely browned and a knife comes out almost clean when inserted into the middle. Do not overcook; the quiche should be moist.

Serves 8 to 10

Note: You can substitute other vegetables such as green or red bell peppers and use sausages or seafood in place of the bacon with equally good results.

. . . .

ZUCCHINI AND GREEN CHILE QUICHE

CRUST
 1¼ cups pastry or presifted all-purpose flour
 ½ teaspoon salt
 ½ cup (1 stick) butter, chilled and cut into pieces
 ¼ cup ice water

FILLING
 2 small zucchini (about ¾ pound total)
  Salt and pepper
 1 (4-ounce) can whole green chiles, drained
 1½ tablespoons butter
 ¾ cup sliced scallions (with green part)
 1 tablespoon all-purpose flour
 1 cup grated cheddar cheese
 ½ cup grated Monterey Jack cheese
 3 eggs
 1½ cups evaporated milk or light cream
  Salt and pepper

To make the crust, place the flour, salt, and butter in a food processor. Turn the machine off and on quickly until the contents are the consistency of coarse meal. With the machine still on, slowly add the ice water and process just until the dough starts to pull away from the sides of the bowl. Form the dough into a ball, wrap in plastic wrap, and refrigerate for at least 1 hour.

Roll out the pastry to line a 9-inch pie pan, and chill while you prepare filling.

Coarsely grate the zucchini onto a sheet of foil to yield 3 cups. Sprinkle with some salt. Let stand for 30 minutes. Preheat the oven to 400° F. Squeeze out excess moisture from zucchini and blot dry. Rinse and seed the chiles, then cut into ½-inch pieces and set aside.

Heat the butter in a large skillet and slowly cook the scallions for 5 to 7 minutes, until soft. Stir in the zucchini, heat for a few minutes, then blend in the flour. Spread the mixture in the prepared pie shell; sprinkle with the chiles and half the cheese. Beat the eggs with the evaporated milk or cream, add salt and pepper to taste, and pour over the filling. Sprinkle with the remaining cheeses.

Bake for 5 minutes, lower the oven to 350° F., and bake for 25 minutes, or until a testing knife comes out clean.

Serves 8 to 10

. . . .

SMOKED SALMON QUICHE WITH YOGURT CRUST

CRUST
4 tablespoons (½ stick) butter, chilled and cut into pieces
1½ cups presifted all-purpose flour
½ teaspoon baking soda
    Pinch of salt
½ cup plain yogurt

SALMON FILLING
4 tablespoons (½ stick) butter
1 large onion, coarsely chopped
1 tablespoon all-purpose flour
¼ teaspoon dried summer savory
1 teaspoon chopped fresh chives, or
    ¼ teaspoon dried
3 eggs, lightly beaten
3 ounces smoked salmon, coarsely chopped
⅔ cup heavy cream
¼ cup grated Gruyère cheese
    Salt and white pepper
1 egg white, beaten

To make the crust, place the butter, flour, baking soda, and salt in the bowl of a food processor. Turn the machine on and off quickly several times until the contents resemble coarse meal. Pour in the yogurt and process just until blended. Wrap the dough in plastic and chill for at least 30 minutes.

Preheat the oven to 450° F.

Roll out the dough large enough to line a 9-inch pie pan. Prick the dough in several places with a fork, lay a piece of foil on it, and fill with dried beans. Bake for 10 to 12 minutes. Remove the beans and foil and let cool while you make the filling.

Heat the butter in a heavy skillet and sauté the onions for 10 minutes, until soft and lightly-browned. Add the flour, savory, and chives, and cook for 3 minutes. Set aside. Place the remaining ingredients except the egg white in a small bowl and mix well.

Brush the partially baked crust with the egg white, pour in the onion mixture, then pour over the egg-cream mixture. Bake for 25 to 30 minutes, or until a knife inserted in the center comes out clean.

Serves 6 to 8

. . . .

MEAT AND GAME

The Rocky Mountain West has always been a meat-eating region; game country supreme, where abundant venison, buffalo, elk, antelope, and bear provided sustenance to the native Americans and early settlers. These days buffalo, the traditional favorite, are raised commercially and the meat sold across the country. In big cities outside the Rockies, buffalo meat is usually carried by specialty meat markets that sell other game meats as well, but it is also available from mail-order firms (see page 187). Buffalo are the only game as apt to be served in a Rockies hamburger joint as in a gourmet restaurant. Game, in general, is frequently served in both restaurants and private homes. Popular with health-conscious cooks who have a taste for meat, game is far lower in fat and cholesterol than domestic meats.

Still, it is beef and lamb that make for major industries in the Rocky Mountains, and beef is, hands down, the most popular meat on restaurant menus. The recipes in this chapter for Grilled Sirloin with Homemade Ketchup, Tongue with Sauce Basquaise, and Meatloaf Supreme with Wild Mushrooms add a few fillips to traditional beef dishes, while the recipe for Barbecued Lamb Shanks provides an unusual method for cooking this meat.

Grilling, either over coals or wood fires (frequently built with special woods like mesquite), is a common way of cooking meat in the Rockies. The method is a natural here, a heritage of those years not long gone when cooking over an open fire was a necessity. Sauces and condiments such as homemade ketchup, chutneys, marinades, and relishes often accompany meats, especially game, which lacks the fat of domestic meat and tends to be dryer. The sauces suggested for game, such as the elegant Morel Sauce for buffalo, or the Huntsman's Mushroom Sauce described in the recipe for Grilled Venison Steaks, are just as tasty when used with domestic meats. The Ginger-Mint Relish served with the Fried Rabbit also goes well with most game. Stews, popular in the West, are marvelously transformed when made with venison instead of beef, as in the Venison Bourguignon.

Steak houses remain the most frequented restaurants in the Rockies. So prevalent are they that they occasionally vie with one another to see who can come up with the biggest steaks or lowest prices. One funky old bar in Butte, Montana, celebrates Derby Day with huge T-bones. For $3.95 you get steak, French fries, salad, bread, and coffee. The only question asked when you sit down on the counter stool is "How d'ya want 'em?"

GREEN CHILI WITH PORK

Whenever I see green chili on a Mexican menu I know the cuisine is authentic. Green chili can be quite hot, but it is as good as red chili, maybe better. Here is my version of the dish.

2 pounds boneless pork loin or shoulder,
**   trimmed and cubed**
1 teaspoon dried sage
2 garlic cloves, crushed
½ teaspoon salt
**   Freshly ground black pepper**
3 tablespoons lard or vegetable oil
1 large onion, chopped
3 tablespoons all-purpose flour
1 tablespoon chili powder
1 teaspoon ground cumin
2 (8-ounce) cans chopped green chiles,
**   drained (optional)**
1 teaspoon chopped jalapeño (optional)
½ cup fresh coriander (cilantro) leaves
**   Flour tortillas**

Put the meat in a 2-quart pot and cover with water to 1 inch above the meat. Add the sage, garlic, salt, and several grindings of pepper. Bring to a simmer and cook over low heat for about 20 minutes.

Drain the meat, saving the cooking liquid, and brown it quickly in the lard or oil in a deep heavy-bottom pot. Add the onion and cook gently for 10 minutes, until soft. Add the flour, chili powder, and cumin and cook for a few minutes more. Add the chopped chiles and jalapeños if using.

Bring the reserved cooking liquid to a boil, strain, and add to the pot. Cook at a simmer for about 30 minutes, until the liquid has thickened and the pork is very tender. Sprinkle with fresh coriander leaves and serve with warmed flour tortillas.

Serves 4

BAKED HAM WITH MUSTARD SAUCE AND PIQUANT ONION SALAD

Baked ham is a good standby in the Rocky Mountain West. It appears frequently on picnic tables and buffets and is often featured as a holiday entrée, sometimes coated with a shiny sweet glaze and served with pungent sauces and a variety of side dishes. For very fancy occasions it is wrapped in pastry. My own version has a crunchy bread-crumb crust.

1 precooked smoked ham (10 to 12 pounds),
**   pelvic and shank bones left in and skin**
**   left on**
2 cups apple cider, approximately
6 whole cloves
2 bay leaves
1 cup dark brown sugar, tightly packed
¼ cup Dijon mustard
2 egg whites, lightly beaten
1 cup dry bread crumbs
**   Mustard Sauce (recipe follows)**
**   Piquant Onion Salad (Page 122)**

Preheat the oven to 350° F. Line a large baking pan with foil.

Place the ham in baking pan. Mix the cider and cloves and bay leaves in a small bowl, and pour half over the ham. Cover with another large piece of foil, folding the edges of the 2 pieces together to form a sealed package (see Note).

Bake for 2 hours, open the foil, pour the rest of the cider mixture evenly over the ham, reseal, and bake for 1 more hour.

Remove ham from the oven and take off the foil cover, leaving the roast in the pan. When the ham has cooled slightly, pour off the cooking liquid and discard. Cut the rind off the ham, leaving a thin layer of fat and a collar of rind around the shank end.

Mix the brown sugar, mustard, and egg whites, adding a bit of water or apple cider, if necessary, to make a paste. Coat the top and sides of ham with the mixture, then pat the bread crumbs onto the top and sides. Return the ham to the oven and bake for 30 minutes more, or until nicely browned. Serve with Mustard Sauce and a side dish of Piquant Onion Salad.

Serves 15 to 20

Note: I sometimes use an oven roasting bag for this purpose, pouring all the cider and spices into the bag, securing it with a tie, then pricking about 10 holes in the top of the bag with a fork. This method steams the ham as effectively as the foil package and eliminates basting. Cooking time remains the same.

Mustard Sauce

    1 egg
 ¼ cup apple cider
 ¼ cup cider vinegar
    2 tablespoons honey
 1½ tablespoons dry mustard
    1 tablespoon butter, softened
 ¼ teaspoon salt
    Dash of white pepper
    Dash of grated nutmeg

Put all the ingredients in a blender and mix on medium speed for a few minutes until well combined. Pour the mixture into a small, heavy saucepan and stir constantly with a whisk over medium-high heat until the sauce has boiled steadily for a few minutes. Serve warm or at room temperature.

Makes 1 cup

BARBECUED LAMB SHANKS

Lamb shanks are a favorite in sheep country, where they are usually braised. The barbecue sauce and final grilling make this recipe unusual and especially good.

SAUCE
    2 tablespoons vegetable oil
    1 garlic clove, chopped
    1 medium onion, chopped
    1 medium green bell pepper, seeded and finely chopped
    1 teaspoon celery seed
 ⅓ cup ketchup
    2 tablespoons dark brown sugar
    1 teaspoon dry mustard
    2 cups chicken stock
    1 teaspoon salt
 ⅛ teaspoon cayenne (ground red) pepper
    1 teaspoon chili powder
    1 teaspoon Worcestershire sauce
    1 lemon, thinly sliced

    4 lamb shanks (about 6 pounds)

Preheat the oven to 350° F.

Heat the oil in a heavy-bottom pot. Add the garlic and onion, and cook over medium-low heat for 10 minutes, until the onion is transparent. Add the pepper and cook for 5 minutes, until softened. Stir in the remaining ingredients except shanks and bring to a boil. Add the shanks, stirring to coat them well with the sauce.

Place the pot, uncovered, in the oven and bake for approximately 3½ hours, or until the shanks are tender. (You can cook to this point from several hours to a day ahead, and refrigerate.)

Start a charcoal fire 30 minutes before serving time. Take the shanks from the sauce and pat off excess sauce with paper towels. When the coals have become almost completely white, grill the shanks, turning to brown on all sides and basting with the sauce, for 15 minutes.

Degrease and heat the remaining sauce to serve separately.

Serves 4

. . . .

OVEN-BARBECUED SHORTRIBS OF BEEF

These ribs are delicious and very simple to make if the barbecue sauce is prepared ahead of time. I like this sauce especially. It is the creation of Terry Capone, a talented Rocky Mountain cook.

- **2 tablespoons all-purpose flour**
- **1 tablespoon dried mint**
  Dash of cayenne (ground red) pepper
- **½ teaspoon salt**
- **6 pounds beef shortribs**
  Barbecue Sauce (recipe follows)
  Sprigs of fresh mint and parsley, for garnish

Preheat the oven to 300° F.

Combine the dry ingredients in a small bowl. Place the ribs on a piece of wax paper and sprinkle them with the mixture, turning to coat on all sides.

Place the ribs in an oven roasting bag and pour in 1 cup of the sauce. Put the bag in a roasting pan just large enough to hold it, secure the end with a twist-tie, and poke about a dozen holes in the top of the bag with a fork. Roast for 2½ hours.

Remove the ribs to a warmed serving platter, and pour all the sauce in the bag over the ribs. Garnish with sprigs of fresh mint and parsley.

Serves 6 to 8

. . . .

Barbecue Sauce

- **½ cup (1 stick) butter**
- **3 tablespoons onion, finely minced**
- **1 garlic clove, finely minced**
- **1 (14-ounce) bottle ketchup**
- **¼ cup Worcestershire sauce**
- **1 teaspoon cider vinegar**
- **1 teaspoon Dijon mustard**
- **¼ teaspoon dried red pepper flakes**
- **1 beef bouillon cube**
- **1 bay leaf**
  Juice of 1 lime
  Tabasco to taste
- **1 tablespoon finely minced fresh parsley**
  Large pinch each of dried thyme, celery seeds, ground cloves, ground cumin, sugar, and salt and pepper

Melt the butter in a heavy-bottom 2-quart pot. Add the onion and garlic and sauté for a few minutes over low heat until soft. Add the remaining ingredients and simmer over low heat for 15 minutes, stirring occasionally and adding a little water if the sauce gets too thick.

Leftover sauce will keep indefinitely in the refrigerator.

Makes 3 cups

. . . .

MEATLOAF SUPREME WITH WILD MUSHROOMS

In a good year, there are so many wild mushrooms in the mountains that we gather bagsful, dry them, and use them in almost everything. A meatloaf made with dried wild mushrooms is delicious, but with a wild mushroom sauce it is truly "meatloaf supreme." If you don't have dried wild mushrooms on hand, you can get satisfactory results with dried oriental mushrooms from the market.

This loaf can also be made with buffalo meat, which has no fat and is often more flavorful than beef. See page 187 for mail-order sources for buffalo meat.

- **½ ounce dried wild mushrooms, cepes, wood ears, or chanterelles**
- **1 cup warm water**
- **6 tablespoons (¾ stick) butter, 2 tablespoons softened and 4 tablespoons melted**
- **4 tablespoons finely minced onion (about ¼ medium onion)**
- **1 pound lean ground beef or buffalo meat**
- **½ pound ground pork**
- **½ pound ground veal**
- **¼ pound salt pork, blanched in boiling water, rinsed, and cut into small cubes (see Note)**

1 slice good-quality white bread, crust
   trimmed and soaked in a little milk
1 egg yolk
1 teaspoon lemon juice
½ teaspoon freshly ground black pepper
1 tablespoon tomato paste
2 tablespoons finely minced fresh parsley
   Pinch of dried thyme
½ cup dry white wine
½ teaspoon salt

Preheat the oven to 400° F.

Soak the mushrooms in warm water for
at least 1 hour. Heat 1 tablespoon of the
softened butter in a small frying pan, and
sauté the onion for 5 minutes, until soft. In
a large bowl, combine the meats, bread, remaining tablespoon of softened butter, egg
yolk, lemon juice, salt, pepper, tomato
paste, parsley, thyme, and sautéed onion
with the butter from the pan. Mix everything thoroughly with your hands. Drain
the mushrooms and combine with the
meat. Combine the melted butter with the
wine and set aside.

Shape the mixture into an oblong loaf
and place it in a Dutch oven. Bake uncovered for approximately 1 hour, or until the
juices run clear, occasionally pouring small
amounts of the butter and wine mixture
over the meat until it has all been used.
When done, remove the loaf to a warm
serving platter.

Serves 6

Note: You need the salt pork if using
buffalo, otherwise omit it.

....

GRILLED SIRLOIN WITH
HOMEMADE KETCHUP

This marinated sirloin can certainly stand
on its own as a delicious and satisfying entrée. Served with homemade ketchup, it
tastes even better. Homemade ketchup
bears only a faint resemblance to the familiar bottled kind found on the grocery shelf
and on the table of every cafe in the Rocky
Mountain West, where it is as indispens-
able as salt and pepper. The recipe here is

an old one for a really savory ketchup with
much more tang than its commercial coun-
terpart.

....

Marinade

1 tablespoon minced fresh marjoram
1 tablespoon minced fresh sage
2 teaspoons minced fresh rosemary
2 teaspoons minced fresh oregano
1 teaspoon minced fresh thyme
1 large garlic clove, minced
2 tablespoons olive oil
1 tablespoon soy sauce
2 tablespoons Worcestershire sauce
   Freshly ground black pepper
1 sirloin steak (3 to 4 pounds), 2 to 3
   inches thick
   Homemade Ketchup (recipe follows)
1 red onion, thinly sliced and separated
   into rings, for garnish

Combine the marinade ingredients in a
small bowl. Place the steak in a glass dish,
pour the marinade over, and refrigerate for
several hours. Bring to room temperature
before cooking.

Prepare a charcoal fire about 30 minutes
before cooking. The fire will be ready when
the coals have turned white. In the mean-
time, soak ½ cup mesquite or your preference of wood chips in water for 20 to 30
minutes, then throw them on the hot fire
when you put on the meat.

Grill the steak to desired doneness, testing with the point of a small sharp knife. It
is easy to overcook, so watch it carefully.
The steak is best served rare (grilled for
about 10 minutes per side). Brush the top
with some of the ketchup the last few minutes of cooking. When done, cut on the diagonal into ½-inch-thick slices, arrange on
a serving platter, and garnish with the red
onion rings. Serve a dish of the ketchup on
the side.

Serves 8 to 10

....

Homemade Ketchup

1 peck (12½ pounds) fresh, ripe tomatoes;
    or 10 (10¾-ounce) cans tomato purée
    combined with 1 quart tomato juice
1 large onion, chopped
2 tablespoons whole allspice
1 tablespoon whole cloves
2 cups cider vinegar
3 tablespoons salt
2 tablespoons dry mustard
1 teaspoon paprika
¼ teaspoon cayenne (ground red) pepper
1 teaspoon black pepper
    Olive oil

If using fresh tomatoes, wash and slice them, place them in a heavy pot, and simmer over low heat for about 15 minutes, until soft. Strain and put through a food mill, then return the pulp to the pot. (If using canned purée and juice, place in the pot, and proceed as follows.)

Tie the onion, allspice, and cloves in a cheesecloth bag. Combine the vinegar and the remaining seasonings and add them with the spice bag to the tomato pulp. Simmer slowly, stirring often, for about 1½ hours, until the mixture is the desired thickness, like commercial ketchup. Remove from the heat and let the mixture cool to room temperature. For use within a short period of time, pour the ketchup into clean glass jars and refrigerate. For long-term storage, pour into sterilized jars, add ¼ inch of olive oil to the top of each, and screw on lids.

Process in a boiling water bath for 15 minutes according to instructions on page 170.

Makes approximately 3½ quarts

ROAST SADDLE OF VENISON WITH TOMATO CHUTNEY

This makes an impressive offering for a very special occasion. Fresh venison can be ordered from specialty butcher shops or by mail order (see page 187). Frozen venison from New Zealand is available at some meat markets in fall and winter.

1 saddle of venison (6 to 8 pounds), bone in
½ pound salt pork, sliced
4 tablespoons (½ stick) butter, melted
2 garlic cloves, crushed
1½ cups dry red wine
2 tablespoons all-purpose flour
2 cups water
    Salt and freshly ground pepper
    Tomato Chutney (recipe follows)

Preheat the oven to 425° F.

Trim all fibrous sinew from the venison.

Boil the salt pork in water to cover for 10 minutes. Rinse, drain, and pat dry. Cut 2 or 3 slices of the salt pork into ¼ x 1-inch strips and lard the haunch with a larding needle, going into each fillet about ½ inch from the top. Or insert the salt pork into incisions made with the point of a knife. Lay the rest of the salt pork over the top of the meat.

Brush the bottom of a roasting pan with some of the melted butter. Set the roast in the pan, rib bones down. Combine the garlic, ½ cup of the wine, and remaining butter, and brush the meat with the mixture. Roast for 20 minutes, then reduce the heat to 375° F., and continue roasting for 30 to 40 minutes, basting several times, until a meat thermometer inserted in the thickest part of the meat registers 140° F. for rare. Put the saddle on a carving board, cover loosely with foil, and let rest for 10 minutes.

Meanwhile, make the gravy. Place the roasting pan on top of the stove over low heat, and stir the flour into the drippings, scraping up any brown bits and letting the flour brown lightly. Add the remaining wine and then the water, a little at a time, stirring after each addition until the gravy is smooth and about the consistency of heavy cream. Add salt and pepper to taste.

Remove the salt pork from the top of the meat and carve the saddle, cutting along both sides of the backbone down to the bone. Starting at the bottom, cut the meat away from the rib bones, working up to the backbone. Lift the loin from the bones and cut into 1-inch-thick slices. To serve, reassemble the meat on the saddle. Serve the gravy and Tomato Chutney on the side.

Serves 12 to 16

Note: Save any leftover roast and gravy to make Venison Pâté (page 172).

....

Tomato Chutney

3 to 4 firm, ripe tomatoes (1½ pounds), chopped
1 cup cider vinegar
1 medium onion, finely chopped
3 garlic cloves, minced
1 (4-inch) cinnamon stick, broken into small pieces
1 tablespoon salt
1 cup dark brown sugar, tightly packed
2 tablespoons finely chopped fresh ginger
6 whole cloves
    Seeds from 3 whole cardamom pods
2 fresh jalapeños, seeded and chopped (see Note)
2 tablespoons finely chopped fresh coriander leaves (cilantro)
3 tablespoons vegetable oil
2 tablespoons yellow mustard seeds

Combine the tomatoes, vinegar, onion, garlic, cinnamon, and salt in a heavy 3-quart steel or enamel pot. Bring to a boil, stirring constantly. Add the brown sugar, ginger, cloves, cardamom, jalapeños, and coriander. Reduce the heat and cook for 5 minutes, stirring constantly.

Heat the oil in a small skillet and fry the mustard seeds until lightly browned, about 1 minute. Remove with a slotted spoon and stir into the tomato mixture. Raise the heat and bring to a boil, watching closely and adjusting the heat so that the mixture just bubbles gently. Cook, stirring often, for about 10 minutes, or until the mixture is thick but still moist. For use within a short period of time, pour into clean glass jars and refrigerate.

Chutney not for immediate use should be canned according to instructions at right.

Makes 3 half-pints

Note: Wear rubber gloves to protect your hands when seeding peppers.

HOT-WATER BATH FOR JAMS AND CHUTNEYS

Processing jams or chutneys assures a good seal; the simmering water bath is adequate to sterilize the jars and their contents. Wash jars and lids in hot soapy water, rinse well in hot water, and place on a clean dish towel—the jars inverted—to drain. Fill the jars to within ½ inch of the top with the fruit mixture, cap the jars, and place on a rack in the bottom of a kettle filled with enough hot water to cover the tops of the jars by at least 2 inches. Be sure there is space between the jars; they must not be touching. Bring the water to a gentle simmer (180°–190° F.) and process for 10 minutes. Remove the jars with tongs, setting them on a towel to cool several hours, and test for seal by pressing the center of each lid. If the dome (center portion) is down or stays down when pressed, the seal is good. If a jar is not sealed, let it rest for 24 hours and test again. If it does not seal, refrigerate and use within a few days. Store sealed jars in a cool, dark place indefinitely. Refrigerate after opening.

....

VENISON BOURGUIGNON

This marriage of venison and good red wine is heavenly. Once you try it, you'll forget beef bourguignon. Serve with Baked Polenta Gratin (page 144) or with noodles, rice, or potatoes.

½ pound thick-cut lean bacon
4 pounds haunch or shoulder of venison, trimmed and cut into 1½-inch cubes
½ cup all-purpose flour
¼ cup vegetable oil
2 cups hot beef stock
2 cups Burgundy or Pinot Noir
2 garlic cloves, thinly sliced
½ teaspoon dried thyme
2 bay leaves
1 teaspoon salt
¼ teaspoon pepper
1 tablespoon crushed juniper berries
3 tablespoons butter
½ medium onion, chopped
½ pound large fresh mushrooms, quartered

Beurre manié (2 tablespoons butter blended with 2 tablespoons flour and formed into ½-inch balls)
Parsley sprigs, for garnish

Preheat the oven to 350° F.

Cook the bacon over low heat for 10 minutes, until browned. Drain on paper towels. Roll the venison in the flour to coat lightly, and shake off any excess flour. Heat the oil in a large, heavy pot and brown the meat, turning several times. Add the bacon, stock, wine, garlic, thyme, bay leaves, salt, pepper, and juniper berries. Cover and cook in the oven for 30 to 60 minutes, or until tender. (Cooking time depends on the tenderness of the venison.) Check often after 30 minutes, and remove as soon as the meat is easily pierced with a fork and tender to the bite, but with a good texture. Do not cook so long that the meat falls apart.

While the meat is cooking, put the butter in a heavy-bottom frying pan and sauté the onions for 10 minutes on low-medium heat, until browned. Add the mushrooms and cook for a few minutes more, until lightly browned. Reserve.

When the meat is done, stir in the onions and mushrooms, and bring to a simmer on top of the stove. Stir 1 *beurre manié* into the sauce. When thoroughly dissolved, add the remaining *beurre manié*, one at a time, until the sauce reaches the desired thickness.

To serve, place the meat on a large heated platter and garnish with parsley.

Serves 10 to 12

. . . .

GRILLED VENISON STEAKS WITH HUNTSMAN'S MUSHROOM SAUCE

In the fall, Rocky Mountain cooks prefer venison for barbecuing. The Huntsman's Sauce complements the meat, especially if made with freshly gathered mushrooms. Ginger-Mint Relish (page 174) provides a sour-sweet taste to stimulate the palate further, if desired.

4 venison steaks (about 1½ pounds)
1 teaspoon fresh or dried chopped chives
1 sprig of fresh thyme, or large pinch of dried
1 bay leaf
½ cup dry red wine
½ cup vegetable or peanut oil
Salt and pepper to taste
Huntsman's Mushroom Sauce (recipe follows)

Put the steaks in a shallow glass dish. Mix the remaining ingredients except sauce in a small bowl and pour over the steaks. Let marinate for several hours or overnight, turning the steaks at least once.

Place the steaks on a grill about 6 inches above a bed of hot charcoal. (For extra flavor, throw in a few mesquite or hickory chips that have been soaked in water for 30 minutes or more.) Turn the steaks only once, checking for doneness with the point of a knife. When cooked to your liking, about 5 minutes per side for rare, 10 minutes for well done, place the steaks on a warmed platter and serve with Huntsman's Mushroom Sauce.

Serves 4

. . . .

Huntsman's Mushroom Sauce

4 tablespoons (½ stick) butter
4 shallots, peeled and finely chopped; or 6 scallions, finely chopped with 2 to 3 inches of the green
¼ pound fresh mushrooms, wiped clean and quartered
2 tablespoons all-purpose flour
1 cup beef stock
2 tablespoons tomato sauce
1 tablespoon minced fresh parsley
Pinch of dried tarragon
Pinch of dried chervil
⅓ cup dry white wine
Salt and pepper to taste

Melt the butter in a heavy saucepan, add the shallots or scallions and the mushrooms, and cook for 2 minutes, until soft. Stir in the flour and cook for a few minutes more. Add the rest of the ingredients and simmer for 20 to 30 minutes.

Makes ¾ cup

VENISON PÂTÉ WITH SAUCE RÉMOULADE

This is an excellent way to use any leftover roast venison and gravy. The recipe was adapted by Hildegard Raeber from an 1879 German cookbook that belonged to her grandmother. Hildegard, who is of Swiss background, has lived most of her life in Ketchum, Idaho, where she has certainly contributed to the culinary scene just by cooking for her friends. You will find another of her recipes, Casserole of Venison and Partridge on page 157.

> 2 pounds cooked roast venison, cut into small chunks, fat and sinew removed
> 3 slices (4 ounces) white bread, soaked in milk and squeezed
> 1 (2-ounce) can flat anchovy fillets, rinsed, dried, and finely chopped
> 3 to 4 shallots, chopped
> 8 eggs, 5 lightly beaten, and 3 separated
> 6 slices bacon, finely chopped
> 1 cup grated Parmesan cheese
>   Salt and pepper to taste
>   Pinch of dried thyme
> ¼ cup leftover gravy
>   Sauce Rémoulade (recipe follows)

Preheat the oven to 350° F. Butter a 9 x 5 x 3-inch loaf pan.

In a large bowl, combine all the ingredients except the egg whites and egg yolks (save 2 yolks for the Sauce Rémoulade and the third yolk for another use). Divide the mixture into 4 portions, process each in a food processor until very smooth, then recombine in the mixing bowl. Beat the 3 egg whites until stiff but not dry, and fold into the meat.

Spoon the mixture into the loaf pan, and place in a shallow baking dish half-filled with boiling water. Bake for 1 hour, until pâté pulls away from the sides of the pan. Let cool in the pan, then refrigerate. Serve cold with Sauce Rémoulade.

Serves 4 to 6

Sauce Rémoulade

> 2 egg yolks
>   Yolks from 3 hard-cooked eggs, mashed
> 1 teaspoon dry mustard
> ¼ teaspoon salt
> ⅛ teaspoon black pepper
> ¾ cup olive oil
> 3 tablespoons fresh lemon juice
> ¼ cup heavy cream
> 1 tablespoon chopped drained capers
> 1 teaspoon chopped anchovy fillets
> 1 teaspoon minced fresh parsley
> 1 teaspoon minced fresh chives

With a wire whisk, mix the raw egg yolks with the cooked yolks. Mix in the mustard, salt, and pepper. Whisking constantly, add the oil in a very slow, steady stream. When half the oil has been incorporated, add the lemon juice and continue to whisk, adding the rest of the oil. When the sauce is thick, stir in the cream, capers, anchovies, parsley, and chives.

Makes 1½ cups

ROAST BUFFALO TENDERLOIN WITH MOREL SAUCE

The early explorers, mountain men, and native Americans of the Rocky Mountain West lived on buffalo meat, and all were said to be exceedingly strong and healthy. Today, buffalo meat is making a comeback in the area and becoming more widely used in other parts of the country as well. As the demand increases, more and more producers are making the meat available by mail order (see page 187). All cuts are rich and flavorful, but care must be taken to cook them at temperatures lower than for beef and not to overcook. For best results, use a meat thermometer.

> 1 4-pound tenderloin of buffalo
> 3 slices bacon, blanched and cut into 1 x ½-inch strips (optional for larding)
> 2 tablespoons olive oil
>   Salt and freshly ground pepper
> 10 (2-inch) sprigs fresh tarragon
> 2 tablespoons (¼ stick) butter, in pieces
>   Morel Sauce (recipe follows)

Preheat the oven to 325° F.

Trim any fat off the meat. Lard the meat, if you wish, by inserting the bacon strips with a larding needle. Rub the meat all over with the olive oil. Sprinkle with salt and pepper to taste.

Lay the tarragon down the middle of the tenderloin, reserving 4 sprigs for a garnish. Dot with the butter. Roll the tenderloin over the tarragon and tie it with heavy string. Place on a rack in a roasting pan and cook for 12 minutes per pound, or until a meat thermometer registers 140° F. for rare.

Let the roast rest for 10 to 15 minutes on a cutting board before carving into ½- to 1-inch slices. Lay overlapping slices on a warmed platter. Garnish the platter with the reserved tarragon sprigs. Serve with Morel Sauce, or with a horseradish sauce made with equal portions of horseradish and sour cream.

Serves 8 to 12

. . . .

Morel Sauce

1 quart rich beef stock, degreased
1 ounce dried morels or other dried wild mushrooms
1 teaspoon chopped shallots
½ cup Madeira
¼ cup heavy cream
4 tablespoons (½ stick) butter, in pieces
    Salt and freshly ground pepper

In a large saucepan, bring the stock just to a boil, lower the heat, add the morels, and simmer for 10 minutes. Remove the morels, drain, chop, and set aside. Continue to simmer the stock, skimming often, until reduced to 1 cup, about 1 to 1½ hours. Reserve.

In a small saucepan, cook the shallots in the Madeira until the liquid is reduced to 2 tablespoons. Strain the stock through several thicknesses of cheesecloth into the shallot glaze and boil until reduced to ¾ cup. Off the heat, add the morels and stir in the cream. Cover and let cool to room temperature. About 10 minutes before

serving, stir in the butter 1 tablespoon at a time over low heat. Add salt and pepper to taste.

Serves 8 to 12

. . . .

CHARCOAL-GRILLED ELK STEAK WITH HERB BUTTER

Most cooks who prepare game consider elk to be the most flavorful and tender of all. It does not have a gamey flavor or require marinating. I prefer to cook elk as simply as possible—just with an herb butter—and serve it with a side dish of sautéed onions.

4 tablespoons (½ stick) butter, softened
1 teaspoon dried marjoram
1 teaspoon dried tarragon
2 garlic cloves, unpeeled and smashed
1 teaspoon coarsely ground black pepper
½ teaspoon salt
    Pinch of dried cloves
1 elk steak (4 to 5 pounds), cut 2 inches thick

Start the fire at least 30 minutes before cooking time. It will be ready when the coals are covered with white ash.

Combine the butter with the herbs and seasonings. Make small cuts in one side of the steak with the point of a knife, and press some of the herb butter into each incision, reserving the rest for the other side. Grill the uncut side of the steak until it is nicely brown, about 7 minutes. Turn the steak and grill to desired doneness, spreading the remaining butter on top during the final few minutes of cooking. Slice the steak on the diagonal.

Serves 8 to 10

Note: The steaks can also be placed on a rack and broiled in the oven. Broil for about 7 minutes per side for rare, basting with any herb butter that has dripped into the pan.

. . . .

FRIED RABBIT WITH GINGER-MINT RELISH

Rabbit makes a delicious meal and can be prepared in many different ways. This is an easy recipe you can make with either wild or domestic rabbit.

2 young rabbits (2½ to 3½ pounds each), dressed
2 egg yolks, lightly beaten
3 cups milk
1¼ cups all-purpose flour
1 teaspoon salt
½ cup (1 stick) butter or good cooking oil
Salt and pepper to taste
1 tablespoon minced fresh parsley, for garnish
Ginger-Mint Relish (recipe follows)

Rinse the dressed rabbits thoroughly under cold running water. Pat dry with paper towels and cut into serving pieces.

Combine the egg yolks and 1 cup of the milk in a shallow bowl. Gradually stir in 1 cup of the flour, add the salt, and beat until smooth.

Heat the butter or oil in a large, deep skillet. Dip the rabbit pieces into the batter and pan-fry on all sides for about 15 minutes, until golden brown. Reduce the heat and continue cooking for 30 to 40 minutes, until tender, turning frequently. Transfer to a warmed dish, and cover with foil while you make the gravy.

Add the remaining flour to the fat in the pan, stirring well. Add the remaining milk gradually, stirring constantly, and heat just until the mixture comes to a boil. Remove from the heat and add salt and pepper to taste, then strain.

To serve, arrange the meat on a warmed serving platter, and garnish with parsley. Serve the gravy and the Ginger-Mint Relish on the side.

Serves 6 to 8

Ginger-Mint Relish

1½ cups finely minced fresh mint, loosely packed
1 cup finely minced fresh parsley, loosely packed
1 scant tablespoon grated fresh ginger
3 garlic cloves, minced or put through a garlic press
1 tablespoon fresh lime or lemon juice
¼ teaspoon salt
⅛ teaspoon cayenne (ground red) pepper (see Note)
¼ cup plain yogurt
2 tablespoons chopped golden raisins

Put all the ingredients in the bowl of a food processor and quickly turn the machine on and off several times, just until everything is blended. Serve at room temperature.

Makes 1 generous cup

Note: This relish is *hot;* use less cayenne to make a milder version.

TONGUE WITH SAUCE BASQUAISE

Basque menus have always included tongue and various organ meats. This traditional and very tasty recipe requires a fresh, not precooked, beef tongue.

1 fresh beef tongue (2½ to 3 pounds)
1 medium onion, stuck with 5 cloves
1 celery stalk
1 bunch parsley
1 medium carrot
1 teaspoon salt
Several black peppercorns
3 bay leaves
1 cup all-purpose flour
Salt and pepper
1 egg, lightly beaten
2 tablespoons vegetable oil
Sauce Basquaise (recipe follows)

Place the tongue in a large pot and add cold water to cover. Cover the pot and bring to a boil. Drain immediately. Add more cold water to cover, bring to a boil, and skim off the foam. Add all the vegetables, peppercorns, and bay leaves. Cover the pot, lower the heat, and simmer for 3 hours, or until the tongue is tender.

Drain and rinse the tongue quickly in cold water. When it is cold enough to handle, peel off the skin and trim off any fat or gristle. (The tongue can be prepared up to a day in advance to this point.) Cut the tongue into ¼-inch-thick slices.

Mix the flour with salt and pepper to taste. Dip the tongue slices in the beaten egg, then in the flour. Let stand at room temperature for about 30 minutes to allow the flour coating to dry.

Heat the oil to sizzling in a large skillet and brown the tongue well on both sides, adding more oil if necessary. Place the slices on a warmed platter and cover with Sauce Basquaise. Serve hot.

Serves 6 to 8

Sauce Basquaise

3 tablespoons olive oil
5 large ripe tomatoes (2½ pounds), seeded and chopped
1 medium onion, chopped
2 medium green bell peppers, seeded and chopped
1 large garlic clove, crushed
1 teaspoon salt
½ teaspoon cayenne (ground red) pepper
  Pinch of sugar
2 teaspoons tomato paste

Heat the olive oil in a heavy-bottom pot large enough to hold all the ingredients. Add the tomatoes and cook over medium heat for about 10 minutes, stirring often. Stir in the remaining ingredients and simmer for 30 minutes. Taste for seasoning. Put the mixture through a food mill, return it to the pot, and cook over low heat until thick. (This can be made in advance and stored in the refrigerator until ready to use.)

Makes about 2 cups

ROCKY MOUNTAIN OYSTERS

Here's the Basque recipe for this traditional Rocky Mountain dish.

4 pounds Rocky Mountain oysters (lamb testicles) (see Note)
1 medium onion, stuck with 5 cloves
  Salt and pepper

SAUCE
2 medium red bell peppers, or 1 (5-ounce) can pimientos, drained
3 tablespoons olive oil
3 garlic cloves, minced
2 medium onions, chopped
6 tablespoons cornstarch
1 cup cold water
3 cups dry white wine
  Salt and pepper

Wash the Rocky Mountain oysters in cold water and put them in a large pot with water to cover by 2 inches. Add the onion and salt and pepper to taste. Bring to a boil, skim the surface, and cook at a simmer for 30 to 35 minutes, or until the oysters are tender. Discard cooking liquid.

Preheat the oven to 400° F.

Roast the peppers in a small pan in the oven, for about 20 minutes, turning several times until the skin is blistered and charred on all sides. Place the peppers in a paper bag, close tightly, and let them steam for about 10 minutes. Peel and seed the peppers under cold running water. Cut into strips, and reserve.

Heat the oil in a large, deep skillet, and sauté the garlic and onions for 10 minutes, on medium-low heat, until soft. Add the pepper strips and simmer for 5 minutes.

Dissolve the cornstarch in the cup of cold water and add to the skillet. Add the wine and salt and pepper to taste; simmer for 5 minutes. Add the oysters to heat through. Serve steaming hot.

Serves 12

Note: There are also Rocky Mountain oysters from calves. Both the calf and lamb varieties can sometimes be purchased at specialty butchers.

CAKES, PIES, PUDDINGS, AND COBBLERS

· ·

Sweets are popular in the Rocky Mountains. Bakeries and restaurants present arrays of desserts that run the gamut from elegant to hearty. In small-town cafes, you can almost always find fresh-baked cinnamon rolls and sticky buns, ready for the ten o'clock coffee break. For home cooks, baking is a vital art, and baking contests are important events at state and local fairs, where carefully guarded family recipes garner prizes year after year.

Some of the best desserts are made with local fruits, including wild berries and wild rhubarb. Foragers reap the rewards of this bounty, while the less ambitious find commercially grown berries and rhubarb, as well as local peaches, cherries, and apples at farmers' markets, roadside stands, and greengrocers. Crabapple trees are not uncommon in Rocky Mountain backyards.

In the years when wild berries are especially abundant, home cooks freeze a good supply, enough to provide a taste of summer to the midwinter table, in, say, blueberry or boysenberry cobblers. Rhubarb, which also freezes well, brings its own special taste to the table—midwinter or summer. A quite wonderful use is in the Lemon-Rhubarb Lattice Pie. That tart little backyard crabapple, widely available in markets across the country come autumn, makes a delicious cake with a Ginger-Pear Topping.

Pine nuts, available to the forager in the southern parts of the Rockies but far easier to come by in supermarkets, combine with almonds in an irresistible Cream Cake with Pine Nuts.

The Mexican influence on Rocky Mountain cuisine also extends to desserts, where it is deliciously present in the combination of chocolate, coffee, and cinnamon in the Mexican Mocha Cake. For chocolate lovers, though, not much can beat the rich marvel of Allison's Chocolate Cheesecake. Cheesecake has, in fact, made a solid entry into the mountains, and there is hardly a restaurant where it is not on the menu.

Other favorite cakes in the region are those with a homey wholesomeness, like Hazelnut-Carrot Cake with Orange Icing. Carrot cake, in fact, is so popular that it is often used as a wedding cake.

But of all desserts, few are so wonderfully nostalgic, or so comforting on a cold winter evening, as the cobblers and puddings most people here prefer to elegant sweets. Indian pudding, made with cornmeal and molasses, is an old-fashioned dessert that fits nicely into today's healthful eating habits.

Whatever your dessert preference, you'll find a delectable variety to choose from.

· ·

CREAM CAKE WITH PINE NUTS

This recipe was brought to the Rocky Mountain West by the Scandinavians. The combination of pine nuts and almonds in the rich cake is irresistible.

> ¾ cup finely chopped blanched almonds
> 3 cups presifted all-purpose flour
> 1 tablespoon plus 1 teaspoon baking powder
> ½ teaspoon salt
> 2 cups heavy cream
> 2 teaspoons vanilla extract
> ½ teaspoon almond extract
> 2 cups sugar
> 4 eggs
> ¾ cup pine nuts

Preheat the oven to 350° F. Heavily butter two 9 x 5 x 3-inch loaf pans. Coat the sides and bottom of each pan with the chopped almonds.

Sift together the flour, baking powder, and salt. In the large bowl of an electric mixer, whip the cream until it is stiff. Add the vanilla, almond extract, and the sugar. Beat in the eggs one at a time. At the lowest speed, mix in the dry ingredients.

Pour about one-quarter of the batter into each pan. Sprinkle each with about 2 tablespoons of pine nuts. Cover evenly with the remaining batter. Smooth the tops and sprinkle each with the remaining nuts.

Bake for 1 hour, or until a cake tester comes out clean. Cool cakes in the pans for at least 30 minutes before unmolding.

Makes 2 large loaves

. . . .

COFFEE LAYER CAKE

An old-fashioned layer cake made in three easy steps, and they *are* easy.

BATTER
¾ cup (1½ sticks) butter
1½ cups light brown sugar, tightly packed
3 eggs
2½ cups pastry or all-purpose flour
1 tablespoon unsweetened cocoa powder
1 teaspoon salt
½ teaspoon baking soda
1 tablespoon baking powder
1 cup strong brewed coffee, cooled (not instant—I use French roast)

HAZELNUT FILLING
¼ cup (½ stick) butter
½ cup milk
½ cup light brown sugar, tightly packed
2 egg yolks
½ teaspoon vanilla extract
¾ cup finely chopped hazelnuts (reserve 2 tablespoons for garnish)

COFFEE MERINGUE FROSTING
1 cup (2 sticks) unsalted butter
2 cups confectioners' sugar
1 teaspoon vanilla extract
1 tablespoon instant coffee powder, preferably espresso, diluted in 1 tablespoon boiling water
2 egg whites
5 teaspoons granulated sugar mixed with 2 tablespoons confectioners' sugar

Preheat the oven to 350° F. Butter and flour two 9-inch layer pans.

For the batter, cream the butter in the large bowl of an electric mixer, adding the brown sugar gradually and continuing to beat until the mixture is light and fluffy. Add the eggs one at a time, beating well after each addition. In a separate bowl, mix the dry ingredients and add to the batter mixture in 2 batches, alternating with the coffee and stirring well to blend. Divide the batter evenly between the pans and bake in the center of the oven for about 35 minutes, or until a cake tester comes out clean. Let the cakes cool for 10 minutes in the pans, then turn out onto a wire rack to cool.

To make the filling, combine all the ingredients except the nuts in a saucepan. Cook over low heat, stirring for about 10 minutes, until the mixture thickens. Off the heat, stir in the hazelnuts. Beat the mixture with a wooden spoon until it is cool and of a good consistency to spread.

Place one of the cooled layers on a serving plate. Spread on the filling and place the second layer on top. Use toothpicks to secure the layers.

Make the frosting by beating the first 4 ingredients until they are creamy and completely blended. In a separate bowl, beat the egg whites until frothy. Continuing to beat, add the sugar mixture a little at a time. Beat until the mixture stands in soft peaks. Fold into the butter mixture. Frost the top and sides of the cake and sprinkle 2 tablespoons of hazelnuts on top. Chill until ready to serve. This cake freezes well.

Serves 10

. . . .

CRABAPPLE CAKE WITH GINGER-PEAR TOPPING

You can substitute any tart apple for the crabapples, in which case reduce the sugar by one-half cup.

BATTER
30 medium crabapples, cored, unpeeled, and grated, or 2 large cooking apples (Granny Smith), cored, peeled, and grated (3 cups)

1 firm, ripe pear (Bosc preferred), peeled,
    cored, and grated (1 cup)
1 cup sugar, plus ¼ cup if apples are very
    tart
1 cup honey
2 eggs, lightly beaten
1 cup vegetable oil
3 cups presifted all-purpose flour
½ teaspoon salt
2 teaspoons baking soda
1 tablespoon grated fresh ginger, or
    1 teaspoon powdered
1 teaspoon vanilla extract
1 cup chopped walnuts

GINGER-PEAR TOPPING
1 cup sugar
2 tablespoons water
1 tablespoon grated peeled fresh ginger, or
    1 teaspoon dried
1 fresh, ripe pear (Bartlett), peeled and
    sliced

Preheat the oven to 350° F. Butter and
flour a 10-inch tube pan.

Put the grated fruit in a large bowl and
mix in the sugar and honey. Stir in the
eggs and oil, add the remaining ingredients, and stir only until combined; don't
overmix.

Pour into the prepared pan and bake for
approximately 1 hour, or until a cake tester
comes out clean and the cake has slightly
drawn away from the sides of the pan. Let
the cake cool in the pan while you make
the topping.

Combine the sugar and water in a heavy
saucepan and boil for about 5 minutes,
until the mixture turns light brown. Add
the ginger and pear, lower the heat, and
simmer for about 5 minutes more, until
the pear turns slightly brown. Pour immediately over the cooled cake. Do not let the
topping sit or it will stiffen.

Serves 10

MEXICAN MOCHA CAKE

This rich almond torte, custard-filled and
chocolate-frosted, is an appropriate finale
for a fiesta-style meal. The chocolate-coffee
flavor combined with the cinnamon and almonds is typically Mexican.

COFFEE CUSTARD
1 cup milk
1 teaspoon instant espresso powder
2 tablespoons sugar
2 egg yolks
1 tablespoon cornstarch
½ teaspoon vanilla extract

BATTER
10 egg yolks
⅔ cup sugar
10 tablespoons (1¼ sticks) unsalted butter
8 ounces semisweet or German sweet
    chocolate
1 teaspoon instant espresso powder mixed
    with 1 tablespoon boiling water
1 cup very finely ground almonds (a light
    powder, not a paste)
¼ teaspoon ground cinnamon
8 egg whites
    Whole blanched almonds, for garnish

First make the custard.

Scald the milk in a heavy-bottom saucepan. Stir in the coffee powder, cover, and
keep warm. Beat the sugar and egg yolks on
medium speed with an electric mixer until
the mixture is light in color and forms a
ribbon. Gently stir in the cornstarch. Using
a hand whisk to blend, pour in the hot
milk. Pour the mixture back into the
saucepan and cook over low heat until it
comes to a boil, whisking constantly. Remove from the heat and stir in the vanilla.
Cool at room temperature. Cover and
chill in the refrigerator while you make the
cake.

Preheat the oven to 350° F. Butter and
flour a 9-inch springform pan.

In a large bowl, mix the egg yolks and
sugar with a fork just until blended; do not
beat. Let sit to give the sugar time to dissolve. Melt the butter with the chocolate in
the top of a double boiler over barely simmering water, and stir in the coffee. Stir
the egg yolk–sugar mixture again, and mix
in the chocolate-butter mixture, blending
well. Measure out 1 cup of this batter to use
as frosting, and chill in the refrigerator.
Fold the almonds and cinnamon into the
remaining batter.

In a separate bowl, beat the egg whites
until stiff but not dry. Stir one-third of the
egg whites into the batter, then gently fold

in the remaining whites. Pour the mixture into the prepared pan and bake for 50 to 60 minutes, or until a cake tester comes out clean. Set the pan on a rack to cool and gently use a knife around the edge so that the cake falls evenly as it cools. When cool, remove the sides of the pan.

Transfer the cake to a serving platter. Slice into 2 layers and spread the cooled coffee custard over the bottom layer. Replace the top layer and frost with the chilled icing (if too stiff, let the icing sit until it softens to spreading consistency). If desired, garnish the cake with whole blanched almonds arranged in a petal pattern. Refrigerate until ready to serve.

Serves 12 to 14

LEMON LOAF CAKE

This is a very nice cake to take to a potluck supper or give as a gift for Christmas, decorated with candied citron and glacéed cherries.

> ½ cup (1 stick) unsalted butter, softened
> 1 cup sugar
>   Grated rind of 1 lemon
> 2 eggs, separated
> 1 teaspoon baking soda
> 1 teaspoon baking powder
> 2 cups presifted all-purpose flour
> 1 cup sour cream
> ¼ cup coarsely ground toasted almonds
>   Pinch of cream of tartar
> ⅔ cup fresh lemon juice

Preheat the oven to 350° F. Butter and flour a 9 x 5 x 3-inch loaf pan.

Cream the butter and ½ cup sugar in a medium bowl using an electric mixer. Stir in the lemon rind. Add the egg yolks one at a time, mixing well after each addition.

Mix the baking soda, baking powder, and flour in a separate bowl. Add to the creamed mixture alternating with the sour cream. Stir in the almonds. In another medium bowl, beat the egg whites with the cream of tartar until stiff but not dry. Stir one-third into the batter, then fold in the rest with a spatula just until thoroughly in-

corporated. Pour the batter into the prepared pan and bake for 45 to 50 minutes, or until a cake tester comes out clean.

Let the cake cool in the pan for 10 minutes, then unmold and place top side up on a rack set over a platter. Mix the lemon juice and remaining ½ cup sugar, and pour over the still-warm cake. When this has been absorbed, wrap the cake in plastic wrap and refrigerate. It will keep well this way for several days.

Serves 8

HAZELNUT-CARROT CAKE WITH ORANGE ICING

Carrot cakes are an all-time favorite in the Rocky Mountains where they are often made as wedding cakes. I like to serve it on Halloween, decorated with marzipan carrots and pumpkins.

BATTER
> 4 eggs
> 1 cup light brown sugar, tightly packed
> 1½ cups vegetable oil
> 2 cups presifted all-purpose flour
> 2 teaspoons baking soda
> 1 teaspoon salt
> 1 teaspoon ground cinnamon
> ½ teaspoon ground mace
> 1 teaspoon ground allspice
> 1 tablespoon vanilla extract
> 4 cups finely grated carrots, dry and lightly packed
> 1 cup lightly toasted chopped hazelnuts
> 12 whole or ¼ cup lightly toasted chopped hazelnuts for garnish

ORANGE ICING
> 1½ pounds cream cheese, softened
> ½ cup (1 stick) unsalted butter, softened
> 4 cups sifted confectioners' sugar
> 1 teaspoon orange extract

Preheat the oven to 350° F. Butter and flour two 10-inch layer pans.

To make the batter, place the eggs in the large bowl of an electric mixer and beat at low speed. With the machine still on low, gradually add the brown sugar, then the oil. In a separate bowl, sift together the flour, baking soda, salt, and spices. Fold into the egg mixture, then stir in the vanilla, carrots, and nuts. Pour the batter into cake pans, and bake for 30 to 40 minutes, or until a cake tester comes out clean. Cool the cakes in the pans for 10 minutes. Run a thin knife around edges and invert onto racks to cool.

To make the icing, blend the cream cheese and the butter in a food processor or with an electric mixer. Mix in the confectioners' sugar and extract, and beat until thoroughly blended. Spread over the bottom layer, top, and sides of the cake. Garnish with whole or chopped hazelnuts.

Serves 12 to 14

. . . .

ALLISON'S CHOCOLATE CHEESECAKE

Long before cheesecake mania hit the Rocky Mountains, or anyone had even heard of a *chocolate* cheesecake, my friend Allison Evans would make this cake for special occasions. One bite was inevitably followed by overindulgence. The cake is worth every bit of the effort—and the cost in calories—of putting it together.

CHOCOLATE CRUMB CRUST
   1 teaspoon ground cinnamon
   4 tablespoons (½ stick) butter, melted
   3 cups chocolate-wafer crumbs

FILLING
   ¾ cup sugar
   3 eggs
  1½ pounds cream cheese, softened
   1 cup semisweet chocolate chips, melted
     and cooled
   2 tablespoons unsweetened cocoa powder
   2 teaspoons instant espresso powder,
     dissolved in 1 teaspoon boiling water
   1 teaspoon vanilla extract
   3 cups sour cream
   4 tablespoons (½ stick) butter, melted

   ½ cup heavy cream, whipped
   6 candied violets, for garnish (See Note)

Preheat the oven to 350° F.

To make the crust, mix all the ingredients with a fork until well blended. Pour into a 10-inch springform pan, and press the crumbs firmly against the sides with your hands, working them up the pan as far as possible. Press a thin layer of crumbs on the bottom of the pan. Chill while you make the filling.

Cream the sugar and eggs in a large mixing bowl. Stir in the cream cheese, 1 tablespoon at a time, mixing well after each addition. Stir in the melted chocolate and the rest of the ingredients in the order given, except the cream and violets. Mix well, and pour into the chilled crust.

Bake cake for 50 to 60 minutes. The cake will jiggle in the middle when moved and look underdone, but it will solidify as it cools. Let it sit for 30 minutes after taking it from the oven, then refrigerate for 3 to 4 hours or overnight before unmolding.

Decorate with small mounds of whipped cream dropped on top by the teaspoonful or piped on in rosettes, and add candied violets. Serve with a bowl of extra whipped cream, if desired.

Serves 12

Note: Candied violets are available at specialty food stores or you can make your own. Use only fresh, perfect blossoms. Rinse them well and pat dry. With a tiny brush, paint the petals on all sides with a lightly beaten egg white, then sprinkle with extrafine sugar. Lay the coated blossoms on a piece of wire mesh, such as a large strainer, placed over a piece of waxed paper. Let dry for several hours at room temperature before storing in an airtight container. These will keep indefinitely.

. . . .

JEWEL'S CHOCOLATE ZUCCHINI CAKE

Zucchini goes into just about everything in the Rocky Mountain cuisine, perhaps because it grows so abundantly here. Jewel Patterson, manager of a large ranch in Idaho, gave me her recipe for this wonderful concoction.

BATTER
½ cup (1 stick) unsalted butter, softened
½ cup oil
1¾ cups sugar
2 eggs
½ cup sour cream
1 teaspoon vanilla extract
2½ cups pastry or presifted all-purpose flour
½ cup unsweetened cocoa powder
½ teaspoon baking powder
1 teaspoon baking soda
½ teaspoon ground cinnamon
½ teaspoon ground cloves
1 teaspoon salt
2 cups finely grated zucchini, loosely packed
¼ cup semisweet chocolate chips
Confectioners' sugar (optional)

CHOCOLATE CREAM FROSTING (OPTIONAL)
3 ounces semisweet chocolate
½ cup heavy cream
1 teaspoon vanilla extract

Preheat the oven to 325° F. Butter and flour a 9 x 12-inch metal baking pan.

Cream the butter, oil, and sugar in a large mixing bowl. Add the eggs one at a time, mixing well after each addition. Add the sour cream and vanilla, and mix well. Mix the dry ingredients in a separate bowl. Add to the egg mixture alternating with the zucchini, ½ cup at a time, mixing well after each addition.

Pour batter into pans and sprinkle the chocolate chips evenly over the surface. Bake for 45 minutes, or until a tester comes out clean. Cool the cake in the pan, and top with a sprinkling of confectioners' sugar or frosting.

To make frosting, melt the chocolate in a double boiler. Add the cream and vanilla, beating with a whisk just until stiff enough to spread. Do not overbeat, or the mixture will stiffen too much and turn grainy. Frost cake. Cut into squares and serve right from the pan, Rocky Mountain style.

Serves 12

. . . .

ORANGE-RAISIN CAKE

My friend Beverly Morgan gave me this recipe from her mother's collection. In the Rocky Mountains, this kind of cake is usually baked in a square pan with a cover so it can be taken to someone as a gift, or to a potluck supper. It is somewhat like an English fruit cake, nice for afternoon tea.

BATTER
Rind of 1 orange, peeled thinly with a vegetable peeler
1 cup raisins
1 cup sugar
½ cup (1 stick) unsalted butter or vegetable shortening
2 eggs
2 cups presifted all-purpose flour
1 teaspoon baking soda
1 teaspoon baking powder
1 teaspoon salt
1 cup sour milk (See Note)

ORANGE GLAZE
½ cup sugar
Juice of 1 orange, unstrained

Preheat the oven to 350° F. Butter and flour a 9-inch square cake pan.

Put the orange rind and raisins in the bowl of a food processor and process just until finely chopped, but not mushy. Cream the sugar and butter or shortening in a large mixing bowl. Add the eggs one at a time, mixing well after each addition. Mix the flour with the baking soda, baking powder, and salt. Add to the egg batter, alternating with the sour milk and mixing well after each addition. Stir in the raisin-orange mixture.

Pour the batter into the pan and bake for 45 minutes, or until the cake starts to pull away from the sides of the pan and a tester comes out clean.

To make the glaze, combine the sugar and juice in a small saucepan, bring to a boil, and cook for 1 minute. Immediately pour the glaze on the cake while it is still in the baking pan. Cover when cooled. To serve, cut into squares and serve right from the pan.

Serves 8

Note: You can make sour milk quickly by stirring 1 tablespoon lemon juice or vinegar into 1 cup milk.

. . . .

LEMON-RHUBARB LATTICE PIE

This is one of my favorite rhubarb recipes. It never fails to satisfy rhubarb lovers and has even made converts of those who aren't. You might think that rhubarb is sour enough without adding lemon, but the lemon seems to bring out its flavor, making for a particularly delicious pie.

BUTTER CRUST
  2 cups pastry or presifted all-purpose flour
  2 tablespoons sugar
    Pinch of salt
  6 tablespoons (¾ stick) butter, chilled and cut into small cubes
  ¼ cup ice water

FILLING
1½ cups sugar
  3 tablespoons presifted all-purpose flour
    Grated rind of 1 large lemon
  1 large egg, lightly beaten
  3 tablespoons fresh lemon juice, diluted with enough water to make ¾ cup
1½ pounds fresh rhubarb, cut into 1-inch pieces

To make the crust, put the flour, sugar, salt, and butter in the bowl of a food processor. Turn the motor on and off quickly until the mixture resembles coarse meal. With the machine on, slowly add up to ¼ cup ice water until the dough starts to pull away from the sides of the bowl. Form the dough into 2 balls, one larger for the bottom crust. Wrap each in wax paper and chill for at least 30 minutes.

On a floured surface, roll out the larger portion of the dough into a round large enough to line a 9-inch pie pan. Fit into pan. Make a lattice crust by rolling out the rest of the dough and cutting it into strips 10 inches long and ¾ inch wide. Interweave the strips on a piece of foil. Refrigerate both crusts.

Preheat the oven to 350° F.

To make the filling, combine the sugar, flour, lemon rind, and eggs in a small, heavy saucepan. Add the lemon juice and bring to a boil, stirring constantly. Put the rhubarb into the pie shell and pour the hot mixture over it.

Invert the lattice crust over the pie, and seal the ends of the strips to the bottom crust with a little water. Bake for 40 minutes, or until browned.

Serves 8

APPLE BREAD PUDDING

  6 slices dry white bread, crusts removed and cubed
  3 tablespoons butter
  1 cup hot milk
  4 eggs, lightly beaten
    Pinch of salt
  ½ cup granulated sugar
  ¼ teaspoon ground cinnamon
  ½ cup golden raisins
  1 large apple, peeled and diced (1 cup)
  ¼ cup light brown sugar, tightly packed
  1 cup light cream

Preheat the oven to 300° F. Butter a shallow 2-quart casserole.

Brown the bread cubes in the butter. Off the heat, add the hot milk and let stand for 30 minutes.

In a mixing bowl, combine the eggs, salt, granulated sugar, cinnamon, raisins, and apple. Place the bread cubes in the casserole. Pour the egg mixture over and sprinkle the brown sugar on top.

Bake for 45 minutes, or until top is browned. Serve warm or at room temperature with cream.

Serves 6 to 8

NOODLE PUDDING WITH TOASTED ALMONDS

Noodle pudding is sometimes served as a side dish, but this one is sweetened, and makes a delicious dessert for a light dinner.

  ½ pound egg noodles
1½ cups sugar
  ½ cup (1 stick) butter, softened
  6 eggs, separated
    Grated rind and juice of 1 lemon
  ¼ cup slivered almonds
  ¼ cup golden raisins (optional)
    Pinch of salt

Cook the noodles in a large pot of boiling water until barely tender with a slight chewiness. Drain, rinse under cold water, and let dry in a strainer or colander.

Preheat the oven to 350° F. Butter a shallow 2-quart casserole.

Beat the sugar and butter in a large bowl until light in color. Add the egg yolks one at a time, beating after each addition. Stir in the lemon rind and juice, almonds, and raisins, if using. Carefully blend in the noodles.

Beat the egg whites with the salt until stiff but not dry, and fold into the noodle mixture. Pour into casserole and bake for about 1 hour, or until the top is browned.

Serves 6

. . . .

INDIAN PUDDING

Indian pudding was perhaps the most popular dessert in the early West. In mining towns it was a specialty on boardinghouse menus. I think it deserves a comeback.

   4 cups milk
   ½ cup yellow cornmeal
   ⅓ cup molasses
   2 eggs, lightly beaten
   ¼ cup sugar
   ½ teaspoon ground ginger
   ½ teaspoon ground cinnamon
   ½ teaspoon salt
   2 tablespoons (¼ stick) butter, melted
   ½ cup raisins

      Heavy cream or vanilla ice cream

Preheat the oven to 300° F. Butter a 2-quart casserole.

Pour 3 cups of the milk into a heavy-bottom saucepan. Refrigerate the remaining cup for later use. Scald the milk over high heat, lower the heat, and gradually stir in the cornmeal, using a whisk to prevent lumps from forming. Continue cooking over low heat for about 20 minutes, stirring often, until the mixture has slightly thickened.

Add the molasses and eggs to the corn-

meal. Combine the sugar, ginger, cinnamon, and salt, then stir into the cornmeal. Add the butter and raisins, and stir. Place in casserole, and pour the remaining cup of cold milk over the top; do not stir it in.

Bake for 2 hours or until lightly browned. Serve hot with either heavy cream or vanilla ice cream.

Serves 6

. . . .

OLD-FASHIONED RICE PUDDING WITH BROWN SUGAR SAUCE

This is the best of rice puddings and the easiest to make. It is very creamy and can be served with custard sauce, cream, or— one of my favorites—this brown sugar sauce.

   ½ cup plus 2 tablespoons long-grain rice (*not* precooked or instant)
   1 quart milk
   2 tablespoons sugar
   2 tablespoons (¼ stick) butter, melted
   1 (1-inch) piece vanilla bean, or 1 teaspoon vanilla extract
   Freshly grated nutmeg
   Brown Sugar Sauce (recipe follows)

Preheat the oven to 300° F.

Wash the rice under cold running water, drain, and place in a 6-cup casserole. Combine the milk, sugar, melted butter, and vanilla. Pour the mixture over the rice, and stir well. Grate some nutmeg on top.

Bake for 2 to 2½ hours, or until the rice has absorbed almost all the milk and is quite tender. Check often after 2 hours. The rice should be moist and creamy; if it is overcooked, it will be dry. If you used a vanilla bean, remove before serving. Serve with sauce.

Serves 6

. . . .

Brown Sugar Sauce

¾ cup dark brown sugar, loosely packed
2 tablespoons water
2 tablespoons (¼ stick) butter

Boil the brown sugar and water to the soft-ball stage (240° F., or when a small amount of the mixture forms a soft ball when dropped into cold water). Stir in the butter. Serve warm.

This sauce can also be made in advance, stored at room temperature, and warmed over low heat just before serving.

Makes about ½ cup

PARSONAGE PUDDING

The Finns who settled in the Rocky Mountains have contributed many wonderful desserts to our cuisine. This bread pudding traditionally is steamed, but it is also very good baked. Serve it as the Finns do, with lingonberry preserves, available in the fancy foods sections of most markets.

4 slices dry white bread, crusts removed and cubed
1½ cups buttermilk
1 teaspoon baking soda
½ cup sugar
½ teaspoon ground cinnamon
¼ teaspoon freshly grated nutmeg
1 egg, lightly beaten
½ cup raisins (optional)

Lingonberry preserves
Light cream

Preheat the oven to 350° F. Butter a 1½-quart casserole.

Combine the bread cubes and buttermilk in a mixing bowl. Let the mixture stand until the buttermilk is completely absorbed, about 15 minutes. Add the dry ingredients; mix thoroughly. Stir in the egg and raisins, if using.

Pour the mixture into the casserole and set it in a larger baking pan filled with enough boiling water to reach halfway up the sides of the dish.

Bake for 40 minutes, or until a knife comes out clean. Serve warm, accompanied by lingonberry preserves and cream.

Serves 4 to 6

BOYSENBERRY COBBLER

5 cups fresh boysenberries
½ cup sugar, depending on tartness of berries
1 teaspoon lemon juice
¾ cup presifted all-purpose flour
1 teaspoon baking powder
1 teaspoon sugar
1 egg, lightly beaten
⅓ cup milk
1 teaspoon grated lemon rind

Heavy cream or ice cream

Preheat the oven to 425° F. Butter a deep 2-quart casserole.

Wash the berries and toss them with the sugar and lemon juice. Pour into casserole.

Combine the rest of the ingredients in a small bowl, stirring well with a wooden spoon. Drop tablespoonfuls of the batter on top of the fruit.

Bake for 30 minutes, or until lightly browned. Serve warm with cream or ice cream.

Serves 8

PEAR COBBLER WITH CORNMEAL CRUST

I make this cobbler in early fall, when pears like Comice, Anjou, or Bosc are at their peak. The country-style cornmeal crust complements the pears.

¾ cup plus 2 tablespoons presifted all-purpose flour
Pinch of salt
¼ cup yellow cornmeal
⅓ cup sugar
3 tablespoons butter, chilled and cut into small dice
1 egg, lightly beaten
4 large, ripe pears
2 tablespoons raisins

3 whole cloves
1 tablespoon fresh lemon juice
¼ cup light brown sugar

Heavy cream

First prepare the crust by putting the flour, salt, cornmeal, sugar, and butter in the bowl of a food processor and blending just until the mixture forms small granular particles. With the machine running, add the egg and blend just until the dough begins to cling together; add a little cold water if needed. Form the dough into a ball. Cover and let stand for 30 minutes.

Preheat the oven to 375° F. Butter an 8-inch square baking dish.

Wash and slice the pears, leaving them unpeeled if the skins are unblemished. Toss the slices with the raisins, cloves, lemon juice, and brown sugar, and lay them in a single layer in the baking dish. Roll out the dough to a square large enough to cover the pears. Place on top and prick in several places. Bake for 35 to 40 minutes, or until the top is browned. Serve with heavy cream.

Serves 8

FRESH PEACH COBBLER

The old-fashioned biscuit crust is the kind my grandmother made when she served cobbler at her ranch table. Use tree-ripened peaches for a really pleasing country dessert.

RICH BISCUIT CRUST
1 cup presifted all-purpose flour
¼ cup sugar
1 teaspoon baking powder
⅛ teaspoon salt
1 tablespoon butter, chilled
¼ cup milk

FILLING
5 to 6 fresh medium peaches, peeled
(see Note) and sliced (5 cups)
½ cup sugar
⅛ teaspoon almond extract
⅛ teaspoon ground cinnamon

Heavy cream

To make the biscuit crust, combine the flour, sugar, baking powder, and salt in a mixing bowl. Cut in the butter with a pastry cutter or 2 knives. Add the milk, and mix well with a wooden spoon.

Turn the dough out onto a lightly floured board and knead a few times. Pat it into a ¼-inch-thick circle large enough to fit the top of a deep 1½-quart round baking dish. Set aside while you make the filling.

Preheat the oven to 450° F. Butter the baking dish.

Toss the sliced peaches with the sugar and almond extract. Place mixture in the baking dish and sprinkle with the cinnamon. Cover with the crust, and cut several slits in the top with the point of a sharp knife. Bake for 30 minutes, or until nicely browned. Serve warm with cream.

Serves 6 to 8

Note: Dip the peaches quickly into a pot of boiling water and the skins will slip off easily.

BLUEBERRY COBBLER

4 cups fresh blueberries
½ cup light brown sugar, tightly packed
½ teaspoon ground cinnamon
¾ cup presifted all-purpose flour
¾ cup whole wheat pastry flour
3 teaspoons baking powder
1 teaspoon granulated sugar
½ teaspoon salt
5 tablespoons butter
½ cup milk
1 egg, lightly beaten

Heavy cream

Preheat the oven to 400° F. Butter an 8-inch square baking dish.

Toss the berries with the brown sugar and cinnamon in a medium mixing bowl. Pour into baking dish.

Mix the flours, baking powder, granulated sugar, salt, and butter in a food processor just until the mixture forms small particles. Add the milk and egg, and process just until blended. Spread the dough with the back of a large spoon over the blueberries. Bake for 35 to 40 minutes, or until browned. Serve warm with heavy cream.

Serves 8

. . . .

MARBLE CAKE

Marble cakes always remind me of a church social, or perhaps a church bazaar. A marble cake stands out from other desserts, intriguing with its swirl pattern of two colors and its two flavors. And it's simple to make.

BATTER
¾ cup (1½ sticks) unsalted butter
2 cups sugar
4 eggs
3 cups cake flour, sifted
4 teaspoons baking powder
1 cup milk
¾ cup semisweet chocolate chips, melted
1 teaspoon grated orange rind
½ teaspoon vanilla extract

CHOCOLATE GLAZE
½ cup semisweet chocolate chips
1 tablespoon light corn syrup
1 tablespoon water

Preheat the oven to 350° F. Butter and flour a 10-inch tube pan.

Cream the butter and sugar in a large bowl, using an electric mixer. Add the eggs one at a time, beating well after each addition. Combine the flour and baking powder in a small bowl. Add to the creamed mixture, alternating with the milk and mixing well after each addition. When all the flour and milk have been added, beat the batter a few more minutes. Put one-third of the batter in a separate bowl and mix in the chocolate and orange rind.

Pour half of the light batter into the tube pan. Drop the chocolate batter by tablespoonfuls on top at intervals all around the brim of the pan. Pour in the rest of the light batter. With a knife, cut through in a zigzag design to create a marbleized effect.

Bake for 45 minutes, or until a cake

tester comes out clean. Let the cake cool for 15 minutes before unmolding.

To make the glaze, place the ingredients in the top of a double boiler over hot, not boiling water. When the chocolate chips have melted, remove from the heat, stir well, and immediately pour the glaze over the cake, letting it run down the sides in streams.

Serves 10

. . . .

COCONUT CHEWS

CRUST
½ cup light brown sugar, tightly packed
½ cup (1 stick) unsalted butter
1 cup presifted all-purpose flour

FILLING
2 eggs, lightly beaten
½ cup light brown sugar, tightly packed
½ cup honey
2 teaspoons vanilla extract
2 tablespoons presifted all-purpose flour
1 teaspoon baking powder
½ teaspoon salt
1 cup unsweetened grated coconut
1 cup chopped walnuts

Preheat the oven to 350° F.

To make the crust, blend the brown sugar and butter in a mixing bowl, using an electric beater. Stir in the flour, mixing well by hand. Pat the dough over the bottom of an unbuttered 9-inch square baking pan, pushing it up the sides about 1 inch. Partially bake for 10 minutes.

Blend the eggs and brown sugar in a small bowl. Stir in the honey and vanilla. Add the flour, baking powder, and salt, mixing well. Stir in the coconut and nuts. Spread evenly over the partially baked pastry, return to the oven, and bake for 25 minutes longer, or until brown. Cool in the pan before cutting into 1½ x 3-inch bars.

Makes 18 bars

. . . .

Source Directory

Meat, Game, and Fish

ALASKA

Cook Inlet Fisheries Products
P.O. Box 595
Kenai, AK 99611
(907) 262-9050 or
(907) 283-5019

Gourmet seafoods: Nova lox, smoked salmon, kippered salmon, salmon steaks, and salmon jerky, all produced from Alaskan wild salmon.

CALIFORNIA

California Sunshine Fine Foods, Inc.
144 King Street
San Francisco, CA 94107
(415) 543-3007

Fine Foods product line includes fresh and smoked meats and seafood, fine caviars, game birds, and specialty produce.

Mahogany Smoked Meats
P.O. Box 1387
Bishop, CA 93514
(619) 873-5311

Mountain mahogany from the Sierra Nevadas imparts a sweet, distinctive flavor to smoked ham, bacon, and pork chops, as well as sirloin-slab beef jerky.

COLORADO

Rocky Mountain Bison, Inc./ High Meadow Buffalo
7320 Country Road 53
Center, CO 81125
(303) 287-7100

A complete line of buffalo (bison) meats.

Rocky Mountain Natural Meats
6069 Weld Country Road 5
Erie, CO 80516
(303) 287-7100

High-meadow buffalo, rabbit, pheasant, wild boar, venison, and other exotic meats.

CONNECTICUT

Brae Beef
100 Greyrock Place
Stamford Town Center, Level 3
Stamford, CT 06901
(203) 323-4482 or
(800) 323-4484 (outside Connecticut)

All natural, organic beef, lamb, chicken, and turkey.

McArthur's Smokehouse, Inc.
P.O. Box 190
Route 202
Litchfield, CT 06759
(203) 677-0294

Country smoked meat and fish products, cheeses, and condiments.

IDAHO

Trapper Creek
400 South 147 West
Jerome, ID 83338
(208) 324-7211

Smoked trout pâté, smoked trout and salmon, smoked pheasant, quail, and chicken.

IOWA

Amana Meat Shop and Smokehouse
1854 Smokehouse Lane
Dept. R.M.C.
Amana, IA 52203
(319) 622-3113

Smoked meats and cheeses.

KANSAS

Butterfield Buffalo Ranch
R.R. 3
Beloit, KS 67420
(913) 738-2336

Buffalo meat and meat products.

MAINE

Ducktrap River Fish Farm, Inc.
R.F.D. 2, Box 378
Lincolnville, ME 04849
(207) 763-3960

A complete line of naturally smoked seafoods.

MICHIGAN

Wilderness Gourmet
P.O. Box 3257
Ann Arbor, MI 48106
(313) 663-6987

Venison, buffalo, wild boar, game birds, wild rice, and seasonings.

NEW JERSEY

D'Artagnan, Inc.
399 St. Paul Avenue
Jersey City, NJ 07306
(800) DARTAGNAN or
(201) 792-0748

Foie gras, fresh and smoked game and game birds, free-range chicken, pheasant, quail, rabbit, venison, wild boar, and buffalo.

Jugtown Mountain Smokehouse
77 Park Avenue
Flemington, NJ 08822
(201) 782-2421

A full line of smoked meats.

NEW YORK

Caviarteria, Inc.
29 East 60th Street
New York, NY 10022
(212) 759-7410

Direct importers and mail-order distributors of all varieties of fresh and preserved Caspian caviar, Scotch and Norwegian smoked salmon, and French *foie gras*.

Forst's Catskill Mountain Smoke House
CPO Box 1000 P
Kingston, NY 12401
(914) 331-3500 or
(800) 453-4010 (outside New York)

Smoked ham, turkey, bacon, and fresh and frozen game birds and steaks.

PENNSYLVANIA

Jamison Farm
R.D. 2 Box 402
Latrobe, PA 15650
(412) 834-7424 or
(800) 237-LAMB (outside Pennsylvania)

Jamison Farm lambs are raised naturally, without additives, hormones, or antibiotics. Meat is cut to order and shipped frozen nationwide.

SOUTH CAROLINA

Manchester Farms, Inc.
P.O. Box 97
Dalzell, SC 29040
(803) 469-2588

Quail, partially boned or whole, fresh or frozen.

SOUTH DAKOTA

National Buffalo Association
10 Main Street
Fort Pierre, SD 57532
(605) 223-2829

Inquiries can be made for information on sources of buffalo (bison) meat in a specific area.

Native Game Co., Inc.
1105 West Oliver
P.O. Box 1046
Spearfish, SD 57783
(605) 642-2601

Game birds, buffalo, elk, venison, boar, rabbit, bear, alligator, quick-frozen berries, and other exotic food items.

WASHINGTON

Specialty Seafoods
605 30th Street
Anacortes, WA 98221
(206) 293-4661

Smoked salmon and other specialty food items.

WISCONSIN

Nueske Hillcrest Farm Meats
R.R. 2
Wittenberg, WI 54499
(715) 253-2226 or
(800) 382-2226 (out of state); (800) 372-2226
(in Wisconsin)

Honey-glazed baked ham, bacon, turkey, and sausage, smoked over glowing embers of sweet applewood.

Usinger's Famous Sausage
1030 North Old World Third Street
Milwaukee, WI 53203
(414) 276-9100

Specialty sausages containing no nitrites or preservatives.

Herbs, Spices, and Condiments

CALIFORNIA

J & K Trading
10808 Garland Drive
Culver City, CA 90230
(213) 836-3334

An excellent source for hard-to-find foods and ingredients including Indian chutneys and rice, caviars, seafood, herbs and spices, specialty meats, fancy vegetables, jellies, preserves and marmalades, oils from France, and authentic Chinese ingredients.

Nature's Herb Company
281 Ellis Street
San Francisco, CA 04102
(415) 474-2756

Suppliers of dried herbs and spices.

S & H Organic Acres
P.O. Box 1531
Watsonville, CA 95077
(408) 761-0574
(7:00 A.M.–5:00 P.M.)

Producers of elephant, Suzannville, silverskin, Italian, and German red garlic as well as red, yellow, brown, and gray shallots.

Nick Sciabica & Sons
P.O. Box 1246
Modesto, CA 95353
(209) 577-5067

Manufacturers of high-quality extra-virgin California olive oil and barrel-cured red wine vinegar.

Tsang & Ma
P.O. Box 294 RM
425 Harbor Boulevard #6
Belmont, CA 94002
(415) 595-2270

Specially blended oriental
sauces, oils, and seasonings as
well as oriental cookware and
utensils.

Willacrik Farm
P.O. Box 599 RM
Templeton, CA 93465
(805) 238-2793 or
(805) 238-2776

French elephant garlic and
related gourmet items.

INDIANA

Indiana Botanic Gardens
P.O. Box 5
Hammond, IN 46325
(219) 931-2480

Herbs and spices for cooking.

NEW YORK

Mr. Spiceman
615 Palmer Road
Yonkers, NY 10701
(914) 961-7776

A full selection of herbs and
spices.

Paprikás Weiss
1546 Second Avenue
New York, NY 10028
(212) 288-6117

Herbs, spices, cooking
ingredients and equipment,
and specialty food items.

Select Origins, Inc.
Box N
Southampton, NY 11968
(516) 288-1382 or
(800) 822-2092 (outside
New York)

Premium-quality herbs,
spices, and other cooking
ingredients; rices; olive oils;
dried wild mushrooms, etc.

OHIO

Bickford Flavors
282 South Main Street
Akron, OH 44308
(216) 762-4666

A full line of flavors for use in
cooking or baking.

Jams and Syrups

MONTANA

Bear Creek Fishery
358 Bear Creek Road
Libby, MT 59923
(406) 293-6498

Wild rose petal, blackcap
raspberry, and huckleberry
jams; chokecherry, elderberry,
and Oregon grape jellies;
huckleberry syrup. (This is a
fishery and smokehouse
which has a sideline of berry
products. They do not mail
their fish products.)

**Eva Gates Homemade
Preserves**
P.O. Box 696
Bigfork, MT 59911
(406) 837-4356

Wild huckleberry, red cherry,
strawberry, raspberry,
blackcap raspberry, and spiced
apple preserves; wild
huckleberry, wild cherry, and
blackcap raspberry syrups.

NEW JERSEY

Berry Best Farm, Inc.
P.O. Box 189
Lambertville, NJ 08530
(609) 397-0748

Growers and producers of
fresh berries, fine jams and
marmalades, and other
specialty foods.

OREGON

Cascade Conserves, Inc.
P.O. Box 8306
Portland, OR 97207
(503) 224-2824

High fruit content, low-sugar
fruit conserves and fruit
syrups made from selected
berry varieties grown in the
Pacific Northwest.

WASHINGTON

Granger Berry Patch
Route 1, Box 1150
Granger, WA 98332
(800) 346-1417

Growers and producers of
fresh berries and fruit spreads
made with honey (no sugar or
pectin). Gooseberry,
marionberry, loganberry, and
blackcap raspberry spreads.

Wilds of Idaho
1308 West Boone
Spokane, WA 99201
(509) 376-0197

Huckleberry jam, syrup, and
dessert pie filling.

Miscellaneous Foods

CALIFORNIA

Timber Crest Farms
4791 Dry Creek Road
Healdsburg, CA 95448
(707) 433-8251

California's finest organically
grown dried fruits, nuts, and
tomatoes as well as apple,
pear, and plum butters.

IDAHO

Good Taste
P.O. Box 4569
Ketchum, ID 83340
(208) 726-8881

Ruby Rainbow Idaho smoked trout, Idaho grown rare legumes; French flageolets, cranberry beans, black turtle beans, French navy beans; dried mushrooms, morels, oyster and chanterelles; premium-quality Idaho baking potatoes (gift boxes).

St. Maries Wild Rice
P.O. Box 293
St. Maries, ID 83861
(208) 245-5835

St. Maries grows, harvests, processes, packages, and markets the finest long-grain, lake-variety wild rice.

Spring Creek Farms
P.O. Box 881
North Fork, ID 93466
(208) 756-4158

Sourdough starter and batter.

MICHIGAN

American Spoon Foods
411 East Lake Street
Petoskey, MI 49770
(616) 347-9030 or
(800) 222-5886 (out of state);
(800) 327-7984 (in Michigan)

Fruit preserves, ketchups, sauces, varietal honeys, dried fruits, nuts, wild rice, blue cornmeal, pancake and waffle mixes, dried mushrooms, and tomatoes.

NEW MEXICO

My Santa Fe Connection
517½ Central Avenue N.W.
Santa Fe, NM 87102
(505) 842-9564

A mail-order company featuring green chiles (in season), dried red chiles, posole, blue corn products, pine nuts, and other New Mexican products.

NEW YORK

Le Gourmand
Box 433, Route 22
Peru, NY 12972
(518) 643-2499

Ingredients and equipment for baking; vinegars, mustards, herbs and spices, and imported jams.

PENNSYLVANIA

Great Valley Mills
687 Mill Road
Telford, PA 18969
(215) 256-6648

Stone-ground flours and grains; pancake, waffle, and muffin mixes.

WISCONSIN

Chieftain Wild Rice Co.
P.O. Box 1080
Hayward, WI 54843
(800) 262-6368

Pure long-grain wild rice and top-quality rice blends.

Special Equipment

CALIFORNIA

Williams-Sonoma
P.O. Box 7456
San Francisco, CA 94120-7456
(415) 421-4242

The Smoke 'N Pit for smoking, roasting, steaming, or barbecuing foods. Available at all Williams-Sonoma stores nationwide or mail order from above address.

KANSAS

American Wood Products
9540 Riggs
Overland Park, KS 66212
(913) 648-7993 or (800) 223-9046 (outside of Kansas)

Mesquite lump charcoal; mesquite, hickory, apple, cherry, grapevine, and sassafras wood chips for use in charcoal, gas, or electric grills.

NEW YORK

The Sausage Maker, Inc.
177 Military Road
Buffalo, NY 14207
(716) 876-5521

Sausage casings and books on sausage making.

OREGON

Luhr Jensen
P.O. Box 297
Hood River, OR 97031
(503) 386-3811 (ask for customer service)

Electric Little Chief Smoker (a smoker for meats and fish, not a cooker). Recipe books on smoking; fishing, tackle and bait.

Index

....